The Strength of Our Commitments

Chicago Series on International and Domestic Institutions

Edited by William G. Howell and Jon Pevehouse

The Strength of
Our Commitments

National Human Rights Institutions
in Europe and Beyond

CORINA LACATUS

The University of Chicago Press
Chicago and London

The University of Chicago Press, Chicago 60637
The University of Chicago Press, Ltd., London
© 2024 by The University of Chicago
Published 2024
Printed in the United States of America

33 32 31 30 29 28 27 26 25 24   1 2 3 4 5

ISBN-13: 978-0-226-83139-8 (cloth)
ISBN-13: 978-0-226-83141-1 (paper)
ISBN-13: 978-0-226-83140-4 (e-book)
DOI: https://doi.org/10.7208/chicago/9780226831404.001.0001

Library of Congress Cataloging-in-Publication Data

Names: Lacatus, Corina, 1978– author.
Title: The strength of our commitments : national human rights institutions in
    Europe and beyond / Corina Lacatus.
Description: Chicago : The University of Chicago Press, 2024. | Series: Chicago
    series on international and domestic institutions | Includes bibliographical
    references and index.
Identifiers: LCCN 2023029769 | ISBN 9780226831398 (cloth) | ISBN 9780226831411
    (paperback) | ISBN 9780226831404 (ebook)
Subjects: LCSH: Human rights—Europe.
Classification: LCC JC599.E85 L34 2024 | DDC 323.094—dc23/eng/20230701
LC record available at https://lccn.loc.gov/2023029769

♾ This paper meets the requirements of ANSI/NISO Z39.48-1992 (Permanence of Paper).

To Floarea, Ion, and Alex

Contents

Introduction

On 9 October 2011, when Poland's Law and Justice Party failed to win in parliamentary elections, its leader, Jarosław Kaczyński, declared: "I am deeply convinced that the day of our success will come and we will have Budapest in Warsaw." It was not long before these words came true. Four years later, on 25 October 2015, Law and Justice won the election. Since then, democracy has faced unprecedented illiberal contestation in postcommunist Poland. Legal and institutional reforms led to the steady erosion of the rule of law and the weakening of institutions considered vital for human rights, particularly the judiciary and the Constitutional Court. Attacks on liberalism moved beyond the legal and institutional realms into the personal. Adam Bodnar, the commissioner for human rights at the time, became the target of virulent public attacks and character assassination campaigns. Practitioners in the field of human rights promotion and protection working for organizations around the country received personal threats related to their work. In other words, the exercise of political rights has grown increasingly difficult.

In this context, the Polish Commissioner for Human Rights (also called the Ombudsman) is the sole democratic institution still standing in the country, as fieldwork for this book has brought to the fore. Despite direct attacks and indirect threats, the Polish Ombudsman has remained a beacon of democracy in the country. It was a widely respected anticommunist institution in the aftermath of 1989 and, working in accord with national governments, it played a key role in the country's transition to liberal democracy. In the six years of the Law and Justice government, the Office of the Ombudsman has become a strong dissenting voice, using legal tools at its disposal (i.e., numerous motions) to push back against the government's legal reforms, and running communication campaigns to restore a more positive public image of its work. For some societal groups, like the LGBT community, the Commissioner for Human Rights is undoubtedly the main, if not the only, official institution still representing their rights. When Adam Bodnar's term as ombudsman came to an end in 2020, the appointment of the new institutional leader became a political battleground that lasted more than half a year. Six candidates from both the Law and Justice Party and the opposition were considered by the Senate and the Seim, but none of them received sufficient political support across the aisle. To put an end to the bitter political conflict, the Law and Justice Party surprised the public in July 2021 and decided to support the candidature of Professor Marcin Wiacek, which was also supported by many of the opposition parties.

The story of the Poland's Ombudsman body is not unique. In times of strong opposition to liberal democratic values, national human rights institutions come under great pressure even in established democracies. They often see their budgets cut and have to weather legal changes aimed at weakening them, and in some cases face open hostility directed at their work and their leadership. Nevertheless, if the institutional development of the recent decades is an indication of future developments, it might be fair to expect that national human rights institutions will continue to fare well. Whether or not they will be able to fully carry out their human rights mandate in increasingly hostile domestic and international contexts remains to be seen. But their institutional strength and their overall resilience in the past decades offer some proof that they will likely continue to be important players working toward closing the gap between international human rights law and domestic implementation.

This book contends that national human rights institutions' great potential for survival lies in the dual nature of their mandate: on the one hand, they are representatives of the international community and the values advanced by international organizations like the United Nations, the Council of Europe, and the European Union. At least in principle, they can benefit from international support when they face domestic opposition to their activity from governments less inclined to accept human rights accountability. On the other hand, in different national contexts some governments can see national human rights institutions as institutional instruments necessary for the advancement of some broader political goal, such as the further consolidation of national sovereignty (see, for instance, the analysis of the role of the Scottish Human Rights Commission below). Even domestic governments not normally supportive of international human rights law can end up treating their national human rights institutions as useful bodies that help them achieve other political and diplomatic goals. They can treat these bodies and their work as formal vehicles to reinforce national sovereignty and to assert a certain position in the international arena.

What Are National Human Rights Institutions?

On paper, national human rights institutions (NHRIs) are independent and formal regulatory bodies, such as human rights commissions, commissioners' offices or ombudsmen, mandated to facilitate the independent implementation of international human rights norms in domestic policymaking (de Beco 2007; Cardenas 2003). Since the mid-1990s, widespread international support from the United Nations and the Council of Europe has triggered a norm cascade on a global scale, with NHRIs increasing from 20 structures before 1992 to approximately 130 NHRIs in 2015 (Linos and Pegram 2016b). They have become key actors in the domestic implementation of international human rights law, enjoying support from regional and global organizations.

In 1993, the UN adopted a set of criteria—the Paris Principles—that specified the core functions and design features of NHRIs (OHCHR 2016). They lay emphasis on the necessity to observe a number of principles such as pluralism and independence, while maintaining a broad human rights mandate, providing advice to governments and monitoring of human rights violations. The General Assembly emphasized that a state establishing an NHRI has "the right to choose the framework that is best suited to its particular needs at the national level" (UN General Assembly 1993). This novel human rights norm, the Paris Principles, lays out the main criteria of design for NHRIs around the world, and forms the standard on which the Office of the UN High Commissioner of Human Rights (OHCHR) carries out an accreditation process for NHRIs that seek to become and remain members of the network of NHRIs, the Global Alliance of National Human Rights Institutions (GANHRI). Based on a voluntary process of application and demonstrated compliance with the Paris Principles, states can become accredited and become members of GANHRI. Every five years, countries undergo reaccreditation, to assess their performance and suggest improvements. The accreditation process grants NHRIs two possible grades (formerly three grades), with A-status certifying full compliance with the Paris Principles, a stronger voice inside the OHCHR, and full rights of participation in decision-making processes in GANHRI. GANHRI has also four regional counterpart networks: the European Network of National Human Rights Institutions (ENNHRI), the Asia Pacific Forum, the Network of National Institutions for the Promotion and Protection of Human Rights in the Americas, and the Network of African National Human Rights Institutions.

In Europe, the Council of Europe was the first to encourage the creation of NHRIs and their cooperation with European Union institutions in the 1990s (Council of Europe 1997). Over the years, the European Union Agency for Fundamental Rights, the Council of Europe, and the Organization for

Security and Cooperation in Europe have specifically targeted the development of NHRIs across the region by encouraging further integration of NHRIs in domestic and regional efforts to implement human rights by coordinating trainings and information sessions, and by facilitating the annual meetings of the regional network of NHRIs. Additionally, the European Union has coordinated the efforts directed at strengthening the capacity of NHRIs through including them in instruments that bind participating states to standards of human rights performance. The European Instrument for Democracy and Human Rights supports NHRIs to strengthen their role as key national actors mandated to promote and protect human rights in line with the Paris Principles. Importantly, the European Union has increased its reliance on NHRIs as key actors in the enlargement process. Assessments of institutional performance and recommendations for strengthening capacity and effectiveness are included in the annual country reports of states that have had candidate status to EU membership. The European Commission also includes NHRIs are its biannual monitoring reports on corruption control in Romania and Bulgaria, part of the Cooperation and Verification Mechanism.

NHRIs hold a unique position in the universe of formal domestic institutions working as regulatory intermediaries between national governments and international organizations, such as the United Nations (Pegram 2015; Lacatus 2018). In some national contexts, they can be seen as national representatives of international organizations that support national governments in their efforts to implement international human rights law. At the same time, they cannot exist without the support of national governments, as they require financial resources from state budgets. Regardless of national context, they cannot carry out their mandates effectively unless they can foster continued constructive partnerships with national governments. For NHRIs to make an impact on domestic human rights records, governments must be willing to work collaboratively with them and offer them continued financial support, while allowing them the freedom to work independently from political interference. In other words, governments must be willing to support and not suppress independent formal bodies that are formally mandated to monitor the rights-based relationships they foster with the very citizens they govern and, when they deem necessary, hold governments to account.

The Strength and Effectiveness of National
Human Rights Institutions

National human rights institutions are key actors in the domestic implementation of human rights. Their impact is important whether they work in increasingly hostile environments, as does the Polish Commissioner for Human Rights using their formal independence to fight for human rights and for liberal values more generally, or they work with more limited formal powers to move the needle on human rights promotion and protection. When they are endowed with adequate powers and can function independently from government intervention, NHRIs hold governments to account, report to international treaty bodies and monitor human rights violations, investigate individual complaints, and carry out impartial investigations in cases of human rights violations (Linos and Pegram 2016a; Lacatus 2019). In this respect, their role is to represent international organizations as well as oversee and assist states in the implementation of their human rights obligations.

At the same time, NHRIs require government support for their activities, in the form of a guaranteed budget and a general willingness on the part of public institutions to cooperate, but not intervene, in institutional activities. This dependence on government can be a point of structural weakness for NHRIs. In the right national context, however, this feature can also be a point of departure for the consolidation of their position relative to government. Success stories have at their center strong and effective NHRIs that owe their continued growth to their ability to gain the respect of government for their expertise in human rights, and their capacity to form partnerships with public institutions without jeopardizing their autonomy. Effective NHRIs often become a country's only independent voice for human rights promotion, education, and awareness.

In a sense, a state that is willing to endorse a strong NHRI makes an implicit commitment that it has nothing to hide from its citizens or from the international human rights community as far as its human rights practices are concerned. Thus, it is open to being held accountable for its actions, and willing to cooperate and change behavior when the NHRIs recommend redress on human rights violations it investigates. As such, a long-term commitment to supporting strong NHRIs on their territories can be seen as synonymous with a strong commitment to human rights protection as foundational for liberal democracy and liberal internationalism. As the analyses in this book will show, these promises are rarely kept with the same levels of consistency and dedication over the years. This is the case in newly democratized states and as well as old democracies. While the global trend of the past two decades has seen NHRIs grow stronger overall, they have not been immune to changes in political agenda and attempts to weaken their mandates and effectiveness.

Variation in institutional strength and its effectiveness in shaping human rights outcomes are worthy of systematic examination, particularly considering

recent political and social developments in Europe and beyond. As this book
will show, the study of institutional strength in the case of NHRIs is necessarily
articulated by the tension between institutional autonomy and dependence on
domestic support which manifests itself at the junction of international norms
and domestic actors. These very tensions lie at the center of this book, framing
its argument and analyses.

Human Rights Institutions under Threat

There is no better time to study these independent national bodies than today.
The rising success of far-right populist parties around the world signals disenchantment with the Western tradition of liberal democracy, grounded in the
promotion of human rights and democratic norms, and the institutions up-
holding these values for more than half a century. National human rights institutions play the dual role of promoting and protecting rights at the domestic
level. They assist governments in key efforts to address adequately a range of
rights-related challenges, such as the protection of fundamental rights and social and political rights. NHRIs represent an innovation in the field of human
rights. They occupy a unique place on the domestic stage, working between
government, civil society, and nongovernmental organizations (Smith 2006)
to promote and monitor the efforts of governments efforts to implement international human rights law. This position has allowed NHRIs to become
important players in processes of democratization and in the diffusion and
consolidation of liberal democratic norms around the world.

In Europe, the region where rights promotion has been at the center of
democratic governance since the end of World War II, far-right parties are
gaining momentum. Governments with Euroskeptic illiberal agendas, like
the ones in Hungary and Poland, have launched virulent attacks on liberal
institutions in their countries, threatening to weaken human rights commissions and ombudsmen, and to silence human rights activists. These are signs
that the commitment to human rights might be shrinking. At the same time,
parties with pro-immigration platforms and an awareness of climate change
have garnered more votes than ever in the 2019 election for the European
Parliament. In the face of such social pressures, how strong are domestic institutions charged with human rights promotions and protection? How well
equipped are human rights commissions or ombudsmen to weather political
changes and continue holding national governments accountable on rights
violations?

At the core of this book is a twofold argument about the incredible resilience of NHRIs. The first part of the argument contends that NHRIs are

dynamic bodies, and this is reflected in changes in their strength and effectiveness over the years. The formal, mandated strength of NHRIs is normally hard (albeit not impossible!) to change, as it often requires amendments to institutional legislation at the end of lengthy parliamentary processes. Having said this, even when they have been in existence for a long time and when national constitutions have safeguarded their existence, institutional designs can become stronger or weaker, and entire institutions can also be dismantled or replaced by new ones in response to changes in political support and priorities over the years. In other words, not all NHRIs are created equal, despite a global tendency toward isomorphism endorsed by the international community.

As scholars have shown, the diversity of institutional models and the associated choice of design features are the outcome of a complex interplay of international and domestic processes—institutional learning from peer bodies in other countries, governments' efforts to comply with the requirements of international organizations, and the existence of sufficient resources available at the time of institutional establishment (Reif 2004a; Pegram 2010; Goodman and Pegram 2012; Cardenas 2014). The inherent diversity of institutional models is even more visible when in studying NHRIs we focus on processes underlying institutional development after a human rights body has been established. Changes to institutional strength do take place, and recent decades have seen an overall constant increase in the formal strength of NHRIs in Europe and around the world. As our analysis will show, NHRIs have tended to become formally stronger in response to both international and domestic incentives. This increase in formal strength has not resulted in an equivalent increased institutional impact on the ground in all countries. However, as the second part of this book's argument will propose, the choice of institutional strength does matter for institutional effectiveness and impact.

Key players in the overall positive development of institutional strength over the years are in fact international institutions such as the United Nations, the Council of Europe, and the European Union. To that end, an analysis of institutional strength offers a valuable window into institutional dynamics of transformation, and its operationalization can allow us to capture changes in formal mandates and principal types of activities over time. Building on the scholarship on institutional strength, this book defines institutional strength in terms of two main dimensions of institutional safeguards embedded in formal design—durability and enforcement—thus capturing the ability of institutions to survive the passage of time and changes in contextual conditions, as well as the extent to which rules "on paper" are designed to make compliance possible in practice (Levitsky and Murillo 2009; Lacatus 2019).

This book expands on these conceptual and empirical insights with an original operationalization of strength in the case of NHRIs.

Can Human Rights Institutions Make a Difference?

The second part of the argument advanced in this book focuses on institutional effectiveness, proposing that strong NHRIs matter on the ground, and make a positive impact on human rights outcomes. In other words, formal strength is key to institutional effectiveness. Effectiveness is broadly understood as the capacity of NHRIs to carry out their mandated duties and make an impact on human rights outcomes on the ground. In most cases this impact is measured in human rights outcomes in the countries where NHRIs are mandated to operate. In a relatively small number of cases, such as that of the Danish Institute for Human Rights, this impact can also be observed in other parts of the world through the institutions' work to support capacity building in countries of the Global South. At the same time, formal strength is not the sole factor determining the effectiveness of NHRIs. As the analysis in the following sections will show, the effectiveness of such institutions depends on several different factors. One of the most important ones is a strong institutional figurehead who not only provides managerial and strategic direction, but often also enhances public credibility and the legitimacy of institutional activity, and plays a key role in maintaining the relationship between the human rights body and the government and political class in a country.

Governments and members of parliament wishing to limit the effectiveness of NHRIs can also do so without necessarily changing institutional mandates or country constitutions and legislation. Members of the political class can limit the impact of NHRIs on the ground in three main ways. First, they can maintain control of institutional budgets and use it to limit institutional budgets when they wish to create operational and financial challenges for the NHRIs. They can also interfere in the appointment of an institutional leader, such as an ombudsman or human rights commissioner. As we will see below, this is a strategy commonly used by antiliberal parties in Central and Eastern Europe. Finally, governments can limit the work of NHRIs by refusing to work collaboratively. This has occurred often in Poland in recent years, when the government has sought to undermine the work of the Human Rights Defender by refusing to implement the defender's recommendations, and even by missing consultation meetings and ignoring reports on government activity.

As the empirical chapters in this book will illustrate in more detail, NHRIs are under increasing pressure to demonstrate their impact and justify why national governments ought to continue supporting them. Although not all existing work is in agreement over the effectiveness of NHRIs, and though in fact some contest their powers (Carver 2000; Goodman and Pegram 2012; Simmons 2002), we have some evidence in support of the institutions' capacity to impact on human rights outcomes. Work by practitioners (Carver 2000, 2005; Burdekin and Naum 2007) and studies by international nongovernmental organizations (NGOs), as well as recent scholarly contributions (Agbakwa and Okafor 2002; Domingo 2006; Finkel 2012; Goodman and Pegram 2012; Harvey and Spencer 2012; Linos and Pegram 2017; Uggla 2004), suggest that some national human rights bodies are contributing significantly to the improvement of human rights in their countries. They have aided truth and reconciliation processes, supported torture victims in seeking redress, contributed to drafting legislation protecting vulnerable groups, and mobilized public opinion on environmental rights (Agbakwa and Okafor 2002; Finkel 2012). Two recent large-n studies conclude that adopting an NHRI reduces physical integrity violations (Cole and Ramirez 2013) and that institutions with formal design safeguards are more effective than those that lack these features, especially in democratic states (Linos and Pegram 2017). They find that bodies with strong investigatory capacity, starting with the ability to receive and process individual complaints, are more effective than those without these features (Linos and Pegram 2017). That said, we have much to learn about the extent to which NHRIs make a difference on the ground by changing human rights outcomes.

Scholarship to date has measured the effectiveness of NHRIs in binary terms, considering the effect of establishing three main types of institutions—human rights commissions, classical ombudsmen, and human rights ombudsmen (Cole and Ramirez 2013) on human rights outcomes. In addition, a recent study has assessed institutional safeguards for independence through measures of institutional compliance with the Paris Principles in accredited NHRIs (Linos and Pegram 2017). While these two studies reach the broader conclusion that these human rights bodies do matter for human rights outcomes, they offer divergent explanations for successful effectiveness. This book builds on existing scholarship, and contributes additional empirical and conceptual nuance to this debate by focusing on understanding the variation in institutional strength and its different dimensions as key to investigating institutional effectiveness.

The research in this book seeks, therefore, to further develop existing scholarship that has been primarily interested in explaining the international and domestic factors influencing states' decisions to adopt NHRIs on their territories, and the main determinants of design features of institutions at the time of their establishment.

International Organizations and Peer Networks

In a nutshell, this book contends that while the actions of domestic actors—governments and civil society—are arguably the most important determinants, the creation and design choices when NHRIs are first created, international organizations, and the actions of NHRIs themselves (working with civil society and participating in international peer networks) are more important when it comes to shaping institutional development over time, determining whether NHRIs become stronger or weaker. In theoretical terms, this lends stronger support to constructivist explanations regarding socialization and the important role of peer networks supported by international organizations. When it comes to institutional effectiveness, institutional and domestic factors become important, often more so than international actors, as governments can use different tactics to make the work of NHRIs less impactful. For instance, they have the power to withhold financial support for NHRIs, ignore recommendations made by the NHRIs, make political appointments to institutional leadership, and to question and oppose publicly the work of the NHRIs. In this context, institutional leaders can play key roles in shaping the broader direction of activity, setting goals for priorities of action and being the public voice of the institution and its interests in working with government and parliament.

The Scope and Structure of the Book

The empirical analysis in this book follows a mixed-method research design and unfolds at three levels: national, regional, and global. The use of both quantitative and qualitative methods allows a more comprehensive view of institutional strength and its effects on human rights outcomes in several European counties.

   To capture the complex nature of these institutional dimensions, the book begins with a set of analytical frameworks considering the mechanisms that help to explain changes in formal institutional strength and effectiveness. Chapter 1 of the book proposes a set of explanations for the cross-border patterns of strength and effectiveness in the case of NHRIs. The mechanisms underlying causal explanations for institutional strength build on ideal types that align with two major lines of debate in international relations theory, consisting of four different sets of factors accounting for cross-border variation in institutional design: domestic factors versus international factors and material versus ideational factors. Drawing from the literatures on the cross-border diffusion of liberalism, on social influence for human rights, and on the literature on Europeanization in candidate and new member states, two international causal mechanisms—network-based learning and incentive-setting—explain institutional change in response to international factors. In addition, chapter 1 includes a discussion of two domestic mechanisms of influence by domestic elites on institutional change: cost and benefit analysis, and the existence of a national democratic identity that embraces human rights. Chapter 1 also offers an overview of how existing scholarship has conceptualized institutional effectiveness, and discusses different factors that can limit the capacity of human rights institutions to carry out their mandated duties and make an impact domestically and internationally.

Chapter 2 is the first empirical section of the book, presenting country-level analyses of institutional strength and effectiveness in four NHRIs active in four Central and Eastern European states. The qualitative case analyses complement the discussion of broader regional and global trends in institutional strength and effectiveness. Case selection is motivated by the intention to capture variation in strength across institutions (ranging from strong bodies, like that of the Polish Ombudsman, to formally weaker and less effective institutions like that of the Macedonian Ombudsman) and variation in the main international actors explaining institutional diversity and change over time. Case studies are grouped in two larger parts. Central and Eastern European institutions are clustered in chapter 2 of this book, and Western European institutions are grouped in chapter 3—reflecting the different pathways to institutional development in the two parts of Europe, and the different incentives for institutional change, with democratic conditionality linked to membership in the European Union being the key incentive for institutional change in Europe's eastern states. Case studies build on qualitative data collected from interviews with more than ninety staff members working at human rights institutions in eight European countries, as well as staff at European Union institutions in Brussels and Vienna. Interviews inform detailed case studies of institutions in eight Western and Eastern European countries, assessing their strength and effectiveness.

The division of cases according to the two main subregions—Central and Eastern Europe and Western Europe—is informed by the intention to capture variation in institutional strength across borders, and also by the findings of the regional analysis, which shows that institutional development is motivated by learning from peers through membership in the Global Network of National Human Rights Institutions, as well as by democratic conditionality in the case of institutions in Central and Eastern Europe. This formal separation allows us to disentangle in more detail the effects that these two main explanatory factors have on institutional development.

Finally, chapter 4 captures the regional and global patterns of institutional strength in Europe and the world. This book expands the insights of the existing scholarship on institutional strength, proposing new types of measurements, adapted to human rights bodies, and an original index of institutional strength for NHRIs. The index captures different aspects of formal strength measured with the help of eleven different indicators. Along these different indicators, NHRIs are ranked as strong, medium, weak, or nonexistent. Chapter 4 offers a regional quantitative analysis that builds on a first original data set for fifty countries in Europe and its neighborhood during the period from 1994 to 2017. The second part of the quantitative analysis in chapter 4 opens the empirical discussion to an exploration of global trends. The second quantitative analysis consists of a second original data set at the global level, including data on the strength and of NHRIs in 180 states.

The three-stage analysis allows us to better understand the complex nature of institutional strength in the case of NHRIs. It provides much-needed clarity on the different factors that shape institutional development and effectiveness over time.

1

The Strength and Effectiveness of National Human Rights Institutions

In the past decades, national human rights institutions have spread around the world and have generally grown stronger. Nevertheless, they remain vulnerable to institutional change and to attempts at weakening their effectiveness, whether they are in old democratic states or transitional countries. As the main actors motivating institutional change are different in different countries and regions—for instance, the European Union's membership conditionality as an important mechanism of institutional development in Central and Eastern Europe, while the Global Alliance of National Human Rights Institutions is influential globally and regionally—NHRIs are always at risk of having their formal strength weakened. Changes in domestic political priorities can result in varying degrees of support for liberal democracy and human rights norms, and can become additional limiting factors for the effectiveness of NHRIs.

But the relationship between the domestic environment and the strength of NHRIs is not necessarily linear. For instance, NHRIs in Central and Eastern Europe are formally stronger than some of their counterparts in the older democracies of Western Europe. As case studies will show, institutional strength or weakness depends on different constellations of factors in each domestic context, encompassing everything from historical accident (as is the case of Poland) or the powerful influence of democratic conditionality linked to the promise of membership in the European Union (as is the case with the Czech Republic and Hungary). At the same time, despite their having stronger mandated powers, their formal strength does not necessarily translate into higher effectiveness. Whether an NHRI can fulfill its mandate (even just in part) and make an impact on human rights outcomes depends on the leadership steering the institution just as much as on the political and social context in which it operates. The leadership of a strong NHRI needs to walk the fine line between gaining financial support from the state and seeking to maintain independence from political intervention.

This chapter is composed of two main parts. The first part introduces a theorization of institutional strength for NHRIs, conceptualizing the main components of institutional strength and their operationalization strategies. The second part of the chapter proposes a two-part causal theory of institutional strength and of institutional effectiveness in the case of NHRIs.

Conceptualizing Institutional Strength

Compared to other regions, Europe has relatively strong national human rights institutions. Institutional development and change are also commonplace in advanced industrialized countries (Thelen 2004; Streeck and Thelen 2005), but generally take place more gradually (Levitsky and Murillo 2009). In these contexts, institutional development is often characterized by periods of radical shifts punctuating an otherwise relatively continuous process of institutional development (Pempel 1998). The region that experienced the most dramatic wave of institutional establishment and transformation was Central and Eastern Europe in the early 1990s, bringing with it the creation of NHRIs. The NHRIs have increased their formal strength ever since, albeit at a slower pace in comparison to their rapid diffusion in the decade following the fall of the Berlin Wall.

In countries where formal rules are often broken or challenged, domestic actors (usually governments) interested in institutional change have more options, including wholesale replacement of existing institutions. When institutions are not durable, the cost of institutional dismantling and replacement is lower (Grzymala-Busse 2006). Examples of dramatic changes in actors' expectations and behavior are rife in transitional societies around the world: for instance, the efforts to increase economic liberalization in postsocialist China and Vietnam (Tsai 2006; Malesky 2008), or the radical changes brought about by Peronism in Argentina (Levitsky 2003; Levitsky and Murillo 2009, 2013).

The strength of NHRIs is conceptualized as a set of formal characteristics—like country legislation and institutional mandates—which define the main functions, operations, and the powers of a formal institution. This definition draws on the conceptualization of institutional weakness in transitional countries (Levitsky and Murillo 2009) and expands on it to theorize institutional strength for NHRIs.

I propose that formal institutional strength can vary along two main dimensions: *durability* and *enforcement*. *Durability* can be understood as the institutions' ability to survive the passage of time and to weather changes in the social and political environments in which they operate (Levitsky and Murillo

2009). Most NHRIs have several features—or safeguards—guaranteeing their durability built into their formal designs. Such safeguards encompass, for instance, their legal status embedded into country constitutions or through statutory law, as opposed to a decree or some other document, or the degree of financial independence from political interference in the running of the institution. As the chapter in this book dedicated to NHRIs in Central and Eastern European countries will show, durability safeguards are particularly evident in transitional democratic states, often intended to ensure a certain "lock-in" of human rights institutions in the domestic context, and protection from future attempts to weaken them.

The second dimension of institutional strength is *enforcement*, which can be best thought of as the extent to which parchment rules, or the institution's de jure powers, are complied with in practice (Levitsky and Murillo 2009). Just like the formal measures that ensure the durability of a formal institution, enforcement powers are also embedded in the design safeguards of the institution, allowing it to carry out its mandate. In the case of NHRIs, a key design feature that makes up institutional enforcement powers is the degree of independence, financial and otherwise, that NHRIs have from political interference with their activities. As other scholars have shown, institutional independence is a central precondition to carrying out institutional mandates effectively (Linos and Pegram 2017).

OPERATIONALIZING INSTITUTIONAL STRENGTH FOR NATIONAL HUMAN RIGHTS INSTITUTIONS

Institutional strength is a multidimensional concept, best operationalized as a multidimensional index. The two main dimensions of institutional strength—*durability* and *enforcement*—are made up of three subdimensions each, corresponding to the main mandated characteristics of NHRIs (table 1.1). These subdimensions capture the main formal features identified in the mandates and annual reports of national human rights around the world (for the global analysis in chapter 4) and in Europe (for the regional analysis also in chapter 4).

TABLE 1.1. Two main dimensions and six subdimensions of NHRI strength

Durability	*Enforcement*
Legal embeddedness	Autonomy from government
Institutional mandate	Predominant promotion or protection activities
Powers of promotion and protection	Pluralism of representation

In their turn, the total of six subdimensions that make up the durability and enforcement dimensions capture formal institutional strength and predominant areas of activity along eleven different indicators of institutional strength (see table 4.2 and the appendix for more information on the operationalization of all indicators).

Legal Embeddedness in National Constitutions and Laws

Legal embeddedness, the first subdimension of institutional durability, captures the extent to which the existence and the mandate of an NHRI are safeguarded through the legal text that establishes it. The strongest legal safeguard for the durability of an NHRI is the inclusion in the country's constitution of provisions for the creation of the NHRI as well as for the appointment and dismissal of leadership, and the main elements of the institutional remit. The amount of detail specified in country constitutions varies from country to country. But the very insertion of institutional strength specifications and of main changes to formal strength after the institution's establishment can be an important deterrent to a government wishing to weaken or dismantle the institution. Often, constitutions only make provisions for institutional establishment and a few other elements of formal design, leaving the details of infrastructure, governance, and day-to-day operations to the text of statutory law and the mandates of NHRIs.

When working well and effectively, NHRIs rarely see any direct benefit from having constitutional legal status. When the institution faces external pressures, however, constitutional provisions for institutional existence and independence can prove auspicious, even if only in the short run. When faced with direct threats from a hostile government, as has been the case with the Polish Ombudsman in recent years (see chapter 2 of this book), an NHRI whose existence is guaranteed by the country constitution is much less likely to be dismantled or replaced with a different type of formal body. Constitutional change is much more difficult and time-consuming.

No doubt, constitutions can be amended, and such amendments can also affect the status of NHRIs. Given that constitutional changes are far more politically costly and require strong support in parliaments, they are less likely to take place than are modifications to other types of statutory law. One recent example is Hungary, where the formal strength of the national human rights institution—the Commissioner for Fundamental Rights—increased as a result of the new constitution that came into force in January 2012. However, Hungary's new fundamental law does not make provisions for the formal independence of the commissioner's appointment and dismissal processes, thus leaving the door open to political interference in the leadership of the NHRI (interviews 82, 86, 87). When not included in fundamental law, NHRIs are commonly established through statutory law, which often specifies both their formal mandate and their rules of operation and governance. Human rights commissions in Europe, such as the ones in the United Kingdom, and human rights institutes, like the German and Danish ones, are established through national law alone. While legal amendments often require political pressure and parliamentary majorities (though sometimes executive orders can suffice), they are procedurally easier to amend than are constitutional changes. At least in principle, NHRIs with formal status embedded in statutory law are more vulnerable to changes in political majority and fluctuations in political priorities. A smaller number of NHRIs in Europe and around the world have weaker legal safeguards, as they are established through presidential decree or governor's decree.

The Inclusion of Human Rights in Institutional Mandates

The subdimension *institutional mandate* (tables 1.1 and 4.2) measures the extent of human rights inclusion in the formal features of design and duties of an NHRI. The measure ranks as "strong" a human rights institution with a dedicated human rights mandate that is broad in terms of the scope of rights it encompasses. If the institutional remit also contains other duties, such as the promotion and protection of equality and diversity, the body is considered as having "medium strength," while a body with no explicit formal mandate in human rights promotion and protection is considered "weak." This measure is of particular interest when studying the strength of human rights institutions in Europe. More than half of existing NHRIs in the region began as equality and nondiscrimination bodies with different rights mandates that were expanded to include human rights duties and work. For instance, equality and diversity commissions, research institutes, and *defensores* ("defenders" in Spanish) in Western Europe became designated NHRIs as well. Some of these bodies were completely reinvented and given new specialized responsibilities, like the Danish Institute for Human Rights and the human rights commissions on British territories. Others, like the Belgian NHRI, have continued carrying out human rights-related work even without a dedicated formal human rights mandate.

De Jure Powers of Promotion and Protection

The subdimension *powers of promotion and protection* (tables 1.1 and 4.2) captures the main formal powers granted "on paper" to NHRIs to carry out their promotion and protection work. They are a key component of the durability dimension of institutional strength, as they frame the spectrum of activities NHRIs can perform. Assessing institutional strength along this subdimension, we encounter great variability across the region, as institutional mandates specify different types and degrees of promotional and protection responsibilities. The strongest powers of promotion usually include research and education in the field of human rights, confirming the human rights body as the sole institutional authority, or one of the few, with expertise in the field. In most cases, specialized research also includes human rights reporting to United Nations–based treaty bodies, and the provision of other public institutions with expert studies on the rights dimension of policymaking. Most institutional change has taken place along this dimension of institutional strength. While many institutions, like those of the classical ombudsmen, were primarily protection and investigation bodies, recent years have seen their mandates expand to also include a degree of research and specialized reporting. In fact, the United Nations' Office for the Commissioner of Human Rights and the regional networks of NHRIs have greatly emphasized the importance of broadening institutional remits to include promotional work in recent years.

Even when not endowed with the power to carry out research and educational work, all NHRIs are expected to issue annual reports on their activities to submit to national governments and parliaments and, in the case of accredited institutions, also to the Subcommittee on Accreditation for review during the reaccreditation process. Despite being common institutional practice today, annual reporting was not always included in the remit of NHRIs. In recent years, new initiatives have appeared proposing to streamline the design of annual reports across institutions and to create more standardization in their format. These suggestions consider annual reports important formal instruments that can showcase the activities that NHRIs perform, and their effectiveness in carrying out mandated duties.

The de jure powers to protect human rights can differ greatly across institutions. The institutions with the strongest protection powers usually can be involved in legal litigations, can represent victims of human rights violations in legal cases and in court, and can also impose fines when the recommendations they make to public bodies are not complied with. NHRIs with medium-level protection powers can handle individual complaints as well as initiate and perform independent investigations on human rights violations. NHRIs that have protection powers included in their mandates commonly have investigatory and complaint-handling powers, in Europe and beyond. A smaller number of NHRIs are primarily promotional bodies and have no protection powers. In Europe, some NHRIs are specialized research institutes with strong promotional powers but no protection powers, as can be found in Germany, Denmark and, until recently, Norway.

THE SECOND DIMENSION OF STRENGTH: INSTITUTIONAL ENFORCEMENT AS COMPLIANCE "IN PRACTICE"

The Extent of Autonomy from Government Interference

Autonomy from government is a dimension that captures the extent of independence an NHRI holds in its relationship with the executive and other public bodies. Independence from interference is a formal aspect of institutional design that has long been considered key to an NHRI's successful functioning and effectiveness in carrying out its mandate (Linos and Pegram 2016a, 2016b; A. Smith 2006). Independence from government can take different forms: financial autonomy, independence in the appointment of institutional leadership and in decision-making structures, or autonomy in reporting structures.

The first indicator captures the extent of *financial autonomy*, based on a ranking of main funding sources reported by NHRIs. The highest degree of funding independence is safeguarded by permanent inclusion of the institutional budget as a separate category in the national budget. Political preferences can influence budgetary decision making, based on the priorities of the party majority in a national parliament, but the inclusion of a guaranteed institutional budget in a separate line in the national budget makes it less likely for financial support to be denied and for major fluctuations in financial support to take place over the years. NHRIs that are subordinate to national ministries enjoy less financial autonomy from governments, as their budgets are up to the executive, and major spending decisions are often conditional upon the government's approval. They are more likely to see their budgets impacted by electoral cycles and changing political agendas. A small number of NHRIs in Europe and around the world are largely or partly dependent on money from external sources, such as project-based donations and capacity-building funding from international organizations like the European Union, the Organization for Security and Cooperation in Europe, and

United Nations–based agencies. Full dependency on external support is rare for NHRIs in Europe. NHRIs in former Yugoslavian states during the first years of their existence depended on external support, but now they tend to have budgets disbursed by the state and receive project-based funds for human rights promotion work, cross-border institutional partnerships, and capacity-building efforts.

The degree of government representation in institutional decision making is also key to institutional autonomy. Fully independent NHRIs have no government presence among their leadership. When government representatives are present in the governance of NHRIs but are not allowed to take part in decision making, political influence can be limited or at least controlled. Institutions who have representatives from government or political appointees in their executive boards or among human rights commissioners are often considered less independent in their decision making and their actions. Often, NHRIs report a loss of public credibility when they are perceived as being affiliated with political agendas through their leadership; and relatedly, they are seen as less trustworthy.

Institutional autonomy captures also a third dimension of institutional governance, made up of *the system of appointment for institutional leadership* and of *the dismissal processes of institutional leaders*, such as NHRIs' chairs, ombudsmen, or human rights commissioners. When the institution is allowed to elect and appoint its own executive board without political interference, it has the highest level of autonomy. A common model of leadership appointment around the world and in Europe is based on parliaments having the final word on the appointment and dismissal of the human rights commissioner or ombudsman, welcoming input from country presidents, civil society or even staff members of the human rights institution. Weaker institutions, often those with public agency status or those fully integrated in national ministries, have very limited say in the appointment of their own leadership. They enjoy much less autonomy in selecting their own leaders, as usually prime ministers and hosting ministries appoint the human rights commissioner or the ombudsman.

Finally, the autonomy of the human rights institution's *system of reporting* on its own operations, finances, and governance is also an important measure of independence. Institutions enjoying the highest level of reporting independence are the ones that are accountable to national parliaments, writing annual reports on their activities and submitting them to parliaments and to the public. More independent NHRIs often have the power to generate independent public reports on the human rights situation in their countries, to submit their separate reports to the Universal Periodic Review for their countries, and, in those reports, to hold governments accountable on their human rights violations. NHRIs that are part of ministries or are otherwise subordinate to government report directly to government bodies and tend to lack the independence necessary to carry out independent investigations on governments' human rights violations and to issue public reports on them.

De Facto Powers of Promotion and Protection

The second subdimension of enforcement captures the *predominant types of human rights promotion and protection activities* that institutions prioritize in their work. NHRIs prioritize certain activities in response to staff capacity in certain rights areas, because of project-based funding allocation or to capture policy interests and realities of human rights violations on the ground. Institutions with strong promotion powers emphasize research and educational programs, leading to better information and analysis of states' human rights performance and of the situation of rights enforcement on the ground.

In recent years, nearly all human rights institutions around the world have acquired some powers of human rights promotion. Historically, most ombudsmen were created primarily to carry out human rights protection work (i.e., investigations, legal cases, complaint handling), and promotional work was not as important for their mandates. In the past decade, however, most of them have begun to conduct some promotional activities, such as awareness raising, public communication, and sometimes even human rights research. Most of them issue reports on their activities in the form of standardized annual reports. Even in cases when NHRIs did not carry out promotional work at the start, as is the case of many classical ombudsmen in Central and Eastern Europe, they began to engage in more promotion work as a result of mandate expansion. NHRIs with mixed mandates including additional rights responsibilities in the areas of torture prevention, equality and diversity, or the rights of persons with disabilities are also required to issue regular reports on the rights situations in their countries, and to carry out promotional work.

Most institutions with complaint handling and investigation powers prioritize these duties over promotional work, channeling institutional resources in this direction of activity. Nevertheless, some variation exists in activities of *human rights protection*. Some institutions can face political backlash if they pursue independent investigations on politically contested cases. Additionally, NHRIs with fewer staff choose to prioritize certain human rights protection work over other such work; for instance, they can prioritize complaint handling over independent investigations. These structural and contextual limitations, which are often political in nature, can lead to weaker NHRIs overall.

Pluralism of Representation

Pluralism of representation in institutional decision making and activity is the
final dimension of institutional enforcement. In its broadest sense, it entails
concrete efforts by the NHRI to involve representatives of different societal
groups in decision making. Despite many institutions having formal mandates that address a broad spectrum of rights-related issues for all citizens
in a country, pluralism of representation is not a common feature included
in the formal strength of most institutions. An example of an NHRI with a
high degree of pluralism is the Northern Ireland Human Rights Commission.
It was set up with great support from specialized organizations and activist
communities, and continues to be led by human rights commissioners who
represent different ethnic and religious groups in Northern Ireland.

A pluralist and inclusive setup at the level of institutional leadership is
generally rare, with most NHRIs having very limited or no direct collaboration with civil society. The most common way to engage with civil society
members is through project-focused partnerships that target rights issues on
the ground and require civil society participation or consultation. In these
cases, a nonprofit organization does not have decision-making power inside
the NHRI, but can steer the direction of work in specific projects. However,
most NHRIs have limited openness overall to specialized nonprofit organizations and civil society more broadly being involved in their decision-making.

The formal strength of NHRIs can vary along any of the above dimensions,
in response to several domestic and international factors with direct impact on
their work. Changes in contextual determinants can shape the strength of an
institution, weakening or further consolidating it over time. What factors shape
formal institutional strength, including durability and enforcement safeguards?
Which factors explain changes in institutional strength over time? The next
section proposes a set of explanations for the causes of institutional strength,
which will be tested in the empirical chapters, broadening our understanding
of the causes of institutional change in Europe and beyond.

Toward an Explanation of Institutional Strength

Changes in international policy priorities and in domestic political agendas
have shaped the development of NHRIs over the years. This section presents
a set of four mechanisms that can explain patterns of institutional development over time. This analytical framework for institutional strength com-
bines four main logics of action, and expands on insights from three main

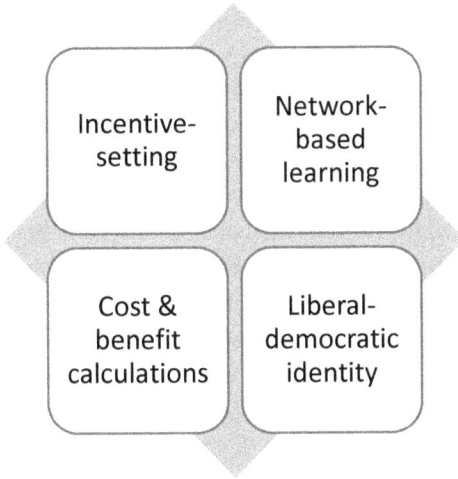

FIGURE 1.1. Explaining the strength of national human rights institutions: an analytical framework

traditions of scholarship on the cross-border diffusion of liberalism (Simmons 2002; Simmons, Dobbin, and Garrett 2006; Simmons and Elkins 2004), on social influence for human rights (Risse-Börzel 2012; Risse, Ropp, and Sikkink 1999; T. A. Börzel and Risse 2012; Goodman and Jinks 2013) and the literature on Europeanization and institutional change in candidate and new member states (Sedelmeier 2011).

In short, institutional strength can increase as a result of peer network-based learning, which can lead to either persuasion or acculturation effects. Specialized peer networks, such as the Global Alliance for National Human Rights Institutions and the European Networks of National Human Rights Institutions, as well as regional networks of states with human rights mandates, such as the Council of Europe, can offer opportunities for learning and knowledge exchange as well as specialized support aimed at strengthening individual NHRIs in the region. In other instances, states can respond to international incentives of material nature, and can support stronger NHRIs on their territories because of indirect coercion. In Europe, the European Union is the main actor that has exercised such influence, through political conditionality tied to the process of negotiation for accession to membership. Conditionality began with the 2004 wave of enlargement when ten Central and Eastern European states joined the European Union. But international factors are not the sole possible drivers of institutional change.

National human rights institutions can become stronger because of pressure from domestic environments, or thanks to strong support for institutional development from elites who promote liberal democratic norms and values. At least in principle, political elites in states with long-standing traditions of democratic rule are more likely to identify with liberal norms, and thus to support the establishment of stronger institutions to promote and protect the rights of their own citizens. In their turn, political elites in transitional and newly democratized states are likely to offer their support for the establishment of stronger NHRIs as they calculate the costs and benefits of creating a solid institutional foundation for the consolidation of democracy. By supporting strong liberal institutions, governments seek to secure as much as possible the democratic transition from potential intervention by future governments that may seek to undermine it. These main four mechanisms of institutional strength and development will be explored in greater detail below.

It is important to note that, while these factors and the corresponding causal mechanisms are presented as analytically distinct, in practice they often overlap and complement each other. In other words, no government is solely motivated by material incentives or by normative factors. In reality, states act in response to different combinations of factors at different points in time. Government preferences and priorities vary from one domestic context to another. Even when examining institutional strength within the same national domain, governments' policy priorities change, and also change the degree and nature of support they are willing to offer their NHRIs.

NETWORK-BASED LEARNING AS A PATHWAY TO ACCULTURATION OR PERSUASION

The most prevalent scholarly explanations for the spread of human rights institutions and also of compliance with human rights around the world stem from the broader tradition of constructivist thought, including processes of norm diffusion and behavioral change through socialization (Goodman and Jinks 2013). Often, socialization takes place in network settings, where communities of peers facilitate mutual learning. Sometimes international organizations can act as norm leaders, advancing normative agendas and supporting their adoption by member states and other countries in their area of influence (Greenhill 2015). Regionally, the European Union has long advanced a self-image of being a normative power advancing liberal democratic values in the region and beyond, and treating human rights as foundational to both its enlargement and its foreign policy.

Writ large, socialization-focused explanations tell a constructivist causal story about the diffusion of institutions as a process driven by normative and socially constructed institutional and policy properties (Checkel 2005;

Gilardi 2013). They follow the idealist or constructivist logic by which policy-makers decide in favor of institutional and policy adoption as they attempt to conform to what they perceive as a more widely accepted role or position in a global or regional context. Although there is little scholarly consensus regarding one unique definition or a set of manifestations of socialization (Alderson 2001), most constructivist scholars engaged in the study of social-ization acknowledge the significance of norms and values as principles to be shared among states, organized as a part of international networks and dif-fused within these networks through the coordination of international or-ganizations (Alderson 2001; Whitehead 2001; Bearce and Bondanella 2007). This normative context is subject to change over time; as internationally held norms and values change, they generate coordinated shifts in interests and be-havior across borders and institutions (Finnemore 1996). International orga-nizations can play an important role in creating environments that facilitate the socialization of states into accepting new political goals and new values that have a lasting impact on international political processes, such as the struc-ture of states themselves, the workings of the international political economy, and so on (Finnemore 1993).

When learning is complete and successful, it often results in persuasion by which actors "internalize" new norms and rules of appropriate behavior and reconfigure their interests and identities accordingly (Checkel 2005). Persuasion is a mechanism consisting of a set of complex processes linked to norm learning. Persuasion explains social influence as a result of learn-ing and information sharing among actors, be they individuals, institutions, or states (Finnemore and Sikkink 1998; Keck and Sikkink 1998; Risse 2000; Goodman and Jinks 2013). International organizations and transnational net-works provide the right environment in which members can learn through argumentation and deliberation (Johnston 2001). The members are social-ized into following the rules and norms that are considered appropriate in the community. In domestic settings where national elites consider human rights protection to be unfamiliar and thus cumbersome, or even a deterrent of their power to govern domestically, the establishment of strong NHRIs is unlikely. But these elites are more likely to change their human rights com-mitments when they are exposed to the choices of peers in other countries, through membership in cross-border networks.

In the case of NHRIs, persuasion can be considered successful when do-mestic actors show continued support for a robust and effective institution over time. When learning leads to persuasion and to a transformation of be-liefs and an internationalization of norms, we can expect that the strength of NHRIs will remain high or continue to improve over time if the institutions were weaker at the time of their establishment. This effect is reflected in both the durability and the enforcement safeguards of an NHRI, indicating support for strong mandates of human rights promotion and protection, matched by institutional power sufficient to enforce these mandates.

Nevertheless, socialization processes do not always result in successful learning. Actors can partially adopt norms because they might be under pressure or might be shamed into doing so, or because they seek to show that they belong in a certain community of peers. Acculturation is the process by which "actors adopt the beliefs and behavioral patterns of the surrounding culture, without actively assessing either the merits of those beliefs and behaviors or the material costs and benefits of conforming to them" (Goodman and Jinks 2013). Acculturation shows that learning can be incomplete, and that it can stop short of persuasion and full identification with the norms and practices of the reference group (Goodman and Jinks 2013; Hatch 1989; Johnston 2001). Following this logic, NHRIs can be created to conform to the expectations of good governance practice in a certain community of states. To the extent that acculturation depends on integration in a social or broader institutional context, the process at work is partly identical to the one of socialization, though the latter leads to attitude change as a result of the interactions with the group to which one belongs (J. R. Smith and Hogg 2008).

The pressure to conform to the acceptable behaviors and norms of a reference group (Meyer and Rowan 1977; Zucker 1977; Powell and DiMaggio 1991; Scott and Meyer 1994; Yzer 2012) is usually situated in their surrounding environments. Conformity to acceptable behavior can take place through the process of identification with a certain group with which an individual actor wishes to establish or maintain a satisfying self-defining relationship. Evidence of acculturation for NHRIs has been found in both qualitative (Pegram 2010) and quantitative studies (Kim 2013; Lacatus 2019). The former makes a case for such a causal mechanism being at work in the global diffusion of NHRIs, while the latter finds evidence for shaming in the relationship between international organizations and developing nations in the process of establishing NHRIs. Kim (2013) argues that, in the case of NHRIs in developing countries, "naming and shaming" strategies carried out by international NGOs determine that states will establish NHRIs. International NGOs can criticize some governments' human rights records in general, putting pressure on them to make structural changes to address their shortcomings, and also supporting the efforts of local activist organizations to persuade the political class to conform to international recommendations (Wiseberg 2003; Kim 2013). Some governments that become targets of sustained international criticism choose to establish NHRIs as a form of political concession, and as a demonstration of political will to seek longer-term institutional solutions that would redress their human rights records (Kim 2013).

For NHRIs, we expect that the effects of acculturation processes will be more visible through the creation of institutions with stronger safeguards for durability but weaker safeguards for enforcement. As the empirical analyses will show, NHRIs in some Central and Eastern European states, such as Hungary and North Macedonia (and others in the region that are not included in this book) follow this design. While their establishment is included in national constitutions and their formal independence from government intervention is high, their formal capacity to carry out human rights mandates effectively is weak, mostly due to political interference in the leadership appointment processes.

Globally, a key normative leader is the United Nations–based Office of the Head Commissioner for Human Rights, through the Global Alliance for National Human Rights Institutions, which has played an important role in the diffusion of NHRIs (Cardenas 2003; Kim 2013; Linos and Pegram 2016b). With the help of four regional counterpart networks, GANHRI coordinates information sharing and learning across member institutions in their respective regions, and offers assistance and technical advice to weaker national institutions in preparation for the accreditation process. The restrictive model of membership in the Global Alliance of National Human Rights Institutions, coupled with a system of monitoring based on peer-review, is particularly well suited for persuasion, though likely to be ineffective or counterproductive in mobilizing the social and cognitive pressures linked with acculturation (Goodman and Jinks 2013).

Through the accreditation and re-accreditation process, the Global Alliance provides NHRIs with an independent system of monitoring institutional design and performance. We know that this peer review process plays a key role in prompting countries to establish these national institutions for the promotion and protection of human rights and grant them certain formal design characteristics at the time of creation (2014; 2017). We expect that accreditation and re-accreditation have a similar effect on institutional development over time. Based on a peer review process, which assesses institutional design and performance and generates a report, the Subcommittee on Accreditation at the Global Alliance offers states feedback and recommendations on how to strengthen institutional capacity. For accredited institutions, performance monitoring takes place every five years, at the time of re-accreditation. GANHRI facilitates cross-institutional learning through peer interaction, knowledge sharing, and collaborative work as part of specialized committees and working groups. Over the years, the process of peer review assessing institutional design and effectiveness has become more structured and more detailed. As the criteria for assessment of compliance with the Paris Principles have become increasingly clear, they have also been more systematically applied to all institutions when they seek accreditation or re-accreditation. These clearer rules have facilitated institutional learning and have made it easier for NHRIs to strengthen their formal mandates and improve their performance in response to recommendations made to them through the peer review accreditation and re-accreditation processes.

The accreditation process leads to a degree of recognition as members of the community of NHRIs, which in turn can lead to complex learning. The recognition that NHRIs are in full compliance (A-status) with the Paris Principles grants them the right to speak at the UN Human Rights Council and before UN treaty bodies, as well as voting rights and the ability to hold governance positions in the global and regional networks of peer institutions. Failure to demonstrate compliance can lead to shaming and indirect peer pressure to strengthen the institution. The assessment and monitoring processes carried out by peer countries and institutions as members of the community of NHRIs can operate on the basis of peer shaming, with the potential to incite institutional change.

Regionally, Europe has had several regional bodies actively supporting the creation and continued development of NHRIs (in addition to regional networks of NHRIs). They offer support to member states that have NHRIs and seek to strengthen them, or to create new domestic bodies mandated to implement regional and global human rights laws. Over the years, the European Union Agency for Fundamental Rights, the Council of Europe, and the Organization for Security and Cooperation in Europe have specifically targeted the development of national human rights in their member states by encouraging further integration of national human rights in domestic and regional efforts. They have also coordinated trainings and information sessions, and have facilitated annual meetings of the regional network of NHRIs since its establishment in 1993.

The Council of Europe is particularly important in Europe's human rights architecture. With a long history of human rights promotion and protection as well as a membership that spans more widely than the European Union membership, it has played a key role in liberal norm diffusion in the region. Overseeing a dense network of human rights treaties and protocols, the Council of Europe ties its membership to the requirement to ratify and commit to enforce regional human rights instruments. It was the first to encourage the creation of NHRIs and their cooperation with European Union institutions as early as the 1990s (Council of Europe 1997). In 1999, it established the Commissioner for Human Rights as an independent and impartial non-judicial institution mandated to engage in permanent dialogue with member states. Through collaborative programs, country visits, awareness-raising campaigns, and advice tailored to domestic actors, the Commissioner has offered coordinated support for the implementation of regional human rights treaties, and facilitates the development of stronger national human rights bodies.

The European Union is arguably the most influential actor in changing norms and institutional practices on human rights in greater Europe. It has been considered a "teacher of norms" in its relationship with member states and accession candidates, as a large-scale socialization agency that actively seeks to promote rules, norms, practices and structures of meaning (Risee-Börzel 2012; Goodman and Jinks 2013). In past decades, the EU has increased its reliance on NHRIs as key actors in the enlargement process. Assessments of institutional performance and recommendations for strengthening capacity and effectiveness are included in the annual country reports of states with status as candidates for EU membership. The European Commission also includes NHRIs in its monitoring reports on efforts to curb corruption and facilitate integration in Romania and Bulgaria, part of the Cooperation and Verification Mechanism (European Commission 2019c). Additionally, the efforts directed specifically at strengthening the capacity of NHRIs have been coordinated by the EU through inclusion of these domestic bodies in instruments that bind participating states to certain standards of human rights performance. One recent example is the European Instrument for Democracy and Human Rights, which explicitly supports NHRIs mandated to promote and protect human rights in line with the Paris Principles. The following section details the effects of membership-linked democratic conditionality on the strength of NHRIs.

INCENTIVE-SETTING THROUGH MEMBERSHIP CONDITIONALITY

In Central and Eastern Europe, the prospect of membership in the European Union has been the most powerful incentive to establish and strengthen NHRIs over time. As the EU enlarged toward the east to incorporate Central and Eastern European countries, it used a system of external incentives to facilitate and encourage the transfer of rules, policies, and institutions across borders as part of the negotiations for membership. This approach to preparing postcommunist states for future membership also encompassed policies and institutions for human rights implementation, associated with

democratic conditionality intended to advance and consolidate liberal democracy in the newly democratized states.

The logic driving EU conditionality is a "bargaining strategy of reinforcement by reward, under which the European Union provides external incentives for a target government to comply with its conditions" (Schimmelfennig
and Sedelmeier 2004). Schimmelfennig and Sedelmeier speak of two major
contexts for this kind of external governance driven by the EU in Central
and Eastern Europe: democratic conditionality centering on "the fundamental political principles of the European Union, the norms of human rights
and democracy (669)." This first wave of conditionality began after the fall
of communism, when Central and Eastern European countries embarked
on the transitional path to democracy. At this stage, the EU aimed to establish institutional ties through an association process, followed by the official
opening of the accession process. Democratic conditionality becomes the
backdrop for accession negotiations when the EU sets in motion a second
type of conditionality, *acquis conditionality*, based on the specific rules of
the *acquis communautaire*. Membership is the key external incentive for rule
transfer. In the case of the Central and Eastern European countries, the EU
made extensive pre-accession alignment a condition even before the start of
accession negotiations.

Research on the integration of human rights in accession conditionality
is limited, though human rights have been part and parcel of the European
Union's requirements of countries from the Eastern bloc. The first such requirements for candidate states were enforced after the end of the Cold War,
once the Yugoslav War brought to light the deeply troubling effects of human
rights violations. In 1993, the EU formulated the "Copenhagen Criteria," to
prepare postcommunist transitional states for membership by setting political standards to be met prior to the start of formal accession negotiations:
stable institutions guaranteeing democracy, the rule of law, human rights,
and the protection of minorities (de Búrca 2003; Grabbe 2006; Sedelmeier
2011). In one extensive study of the role of human rights in EU conditionality,
Conant finds that transitional democracies have made progress in respecting
human rights, but their commitments have remained shallow. Moreover, the
process of transition to liberal democracy is at high risk of being reversed
(Conant 2014).

Membership conditionality has not been uniformly effective in advancing
democratization in all countries in which it has been implemented since it
was established in preparation for the 2004 wave of EU accession. The EU's
success in employing conditionality strategies has been inconsistent and dependent on the nature of the policy to be adopted and the domestic context.

Such is the case of minority rights in countries experiencing ethnic conflict, where the cost of compliance is too high (Schimmelfennig 2012). In addition to adoption costs and the credibility of conditionality, factors such as the clarity and formality of EU requirements and the size and speed of rewards inform national policy reform in response to EU conditionality (Schimmelfennig and Sedelmeier 2004). Some countries—Hungary, Poland, and the Czech Republic—were already on their way to democratic consolidation by the start of the negotiations. EU conditionality merely furthered compliance among parties that did not endorse liberal rules, such as minority protection, while autocracies generally did not respond to conditionality. Political conditionality has had the most significant impact in the Central and Eastern European countries that had credible EU membership perspective, where it contributed to the consolidation of liberal forces and motivated liberal parties in government to advance Western integration and thus raise the cost of potential future reversal (Schimmelfennig, Engert, and Knobel 2006b).

EU membership conditionality constitutes the coercive strategy associated with greater success at inducing better behavior than typical international human rights agreements (Hafner-Burton 2005, 2009). Though democratic conditionality is different for different candidate states, many observers agree that overall, EU conditionality has been successful in promoting political change in the region and has contributed to an increase in the quality of democracy and rights protection (Hafner-Burton 2005; Hafner-Burton and Ron 2009; Kelley 2004; Roberts 2010; Vachudová 2005). Scholars of the diffusion of NHRIs have found that EU membership conditionality has been an effective coercive tool for the creation of these bodies in Central and Eastern European countries (Carver 2011; Pegram 2010; Lacatus 2016, 2019). One study of institutional strength for human rights bodies in the region has confirmed that democratic conditionality plays a key role in the process of strengthening NHRIs in countries that have held candidate status to EU membership since the 2004 wave of accession (Lacatus 2019). As later chapters in this book will show, democratic conditionality has a positive impact on the strength of NHRIs and on their impact on human rights outcomes in their countries.

COST AND BENEFIT CALCULATIONS

For institutional change to take place, domestic environments must be favorable. Without a doubt, processes of cross-border learning or incentive setting can have an impact on the decisions of states to establish and support strong human rights institutions. Nevertheless, a favorable domestic political context is key to institutional existence and good functioning over time. Given their nature, human rights institutions need government support to function well. At the same time, they are accountability bodies, designed to advise and monitor government behavior in the field of human rights, holding public institutions accountable for violations against their own citizens (Cardenas 2014). This intermediary, dual status—that of being dependent on government support while working to hold public institutions to account—creates great variability in the extent of support that NHRIs receive over time. Not all governments will embrace their existence or will be equally open to supporting their continued development. In fact, as the empirical analyses will show, some governments do oppose the activity of these institutions and actively seek to limit the effectiveness of their work.

The interest that governments show toward strengthening or collaborating with their NHRIs is often a result of elites' calculations. Given that the distinct role of human rights regimes is to empower citizens to challenge the domestic activities of their own governments (Moravcsik 2000), we can expect that elites in countries that have strong human rights records and a tradition of support for citizens' rights ought to incur smaller political costs when they decide to have strong NHRIs. By implication, countries with a long-standing tradition of democracy might have established classical ombudsmen prior to the formation of the international human rights regime in the aftermath of World War II, as is the case with Sweden and Finland, among others. With some amendments and incurring relatively small material and political costs, countries have expanded the mandate of such institutions to include also some powers to promote and protect human rights. Although this has not necessarily resulted in more effective and impactful institutions, it has led to the existence of long-standing bodies that adapt well to changing political environments, have generally good relationships with governments, and enjoy a relatively high degree of de facto independence.

The higher the domestic cost of having a strong NHRI, the less likely states are to support institutional development and further strengthening. Depending on the type of political regime at the domestic level, such costs can potentially be very high—higher, even, than when states ratify international or regional human rights treaties that are generally seen as "lacking teeth." More specifically, binding international or regional obligations can be viewed as carrying an increased, if modest, risk of nullification of domestic laws without a corresponding increase in the expected stability of domestic democracy (Moravcsik 2000).

The trajectory of development for NHRIs' strength is not straightforward. Old democracies might have long-lasting human rights institutions, but they do not always show consistent support over time. This is the case in Western

Europe, as will be presented in chapter 3. In fact, some elites in new democracies might decide to support formally stronger NHRIs in their territories to create formal safeguards for the consolidation of liberal democracy. In other words, political transitions are closely tied to domestic elites' pursuit of democratic consolidation and commitment to international institutions to "lock-in" reforms, advance democratization, and diminish the opportunity of future backsliding (Moravcsik 1995; Moravcsik 2000a; Simmons 2009).

Newly democratized states are the most likely to seek to secure solid institutional foundations for their young democracies, for fear of destabilization and backsliding in the longer run (Moravcsik 2000). This potential of future benefits reflects variation in the nature of domestic pressures and representative institutions (Doyle 1986; Russett 1993; Snyder 1991; Bailey, Goldstein, and Weingast 1997; Moravcsik 1997; Van Evera 1999; Legro and Moravcsik 1999; Moravcsik 2000). In general, governing elites take into account the risk that opposing interests may gain traction in the future, and that other political actors could change the course of the relationship between citizens and authorities (Moe 1990). Democratic regimes endeavor to prevent political retrogression or "backsliding" into autocracy. It is important to note, however, that evidence of continued success in the post-accession period is mixed, with several scholars remaining positive (Levitz and Pop-Elechies 2010; Schimmelfennig and Sedelmeier 2004; Sedelmeier 2009) and others finding that, in the field of human rights in particular, commitments remain shallow, and transitions to rights-respecting democracies are reversible (Conant 2014).

It is also possible that states establish institutions for "window dressing" purposes (Levitsky and Murillo 2013). These bodies may be created and maintained if their existence generates some benefit for governments, but their enforcement powers are often very weak and their effectiveness low. Not as prevalent in Europe as they might be in other regions of the world (see, for instance, Latin America, as evidenced by Levitsky and Murillo 2013), such behavior was present in Poland prior to the fall of communism, where the Office of Human Rights Defender (currently referring to itself as the Commissioner for Human Rights) was created in 1987 to respond to public pressures toward democratization. As will be discussed in the dedicated case study, the institution survived the transition away from communism and became one of the strongest of its kind in the world. Formally very strong, the body was created with the intention to retain de jure powers but to be fully under political control and thus remain weak and ineffective. Moreover, this lack of support can be the result of limited political will and weak commitments to human rights implementation, as has been the case in Romania for years. The former Romanian NHRI, called the Human Rights Center, functioned for more than two decades without many formal powers and with virtually no activity except for participation in international networks for peer bodies. This can also be the case in nations where liberal democracies are eroding, such as contemporary Hungary, where the de jure powers of the Commissioner for Fundamental Rights have become stronger with the new Constitution of 2012. Nevertheless, the de facto strength of the institution of the Commissioner, reflected in enforcement powers and effectiveness, has weakened considerably and has been linked to political interference with the leadership of the NHRI.

To conclude, establishing an NHRI can be synonymous with a government surrendering some degree of national sovereignty and discretion, ultimately representing an agency cost at the domestic level. Some governments can find that the electoral or political cost of supporting the establishment or consolidation of a strong institution is too high to be worth undertaking. Countries with autocratic regimes offer clear examples of such opposition to establishing strong NHRIs. But examples of government resistance to supporting strong human rights bodies are common also in transitional and democratic states (see below, in the chapter on Poland and Hungary, for instance). Sometimes newly established human rights institutions can be seen as potentially threatening even in the long-standing democratic practices of countries with historically good human rights records (see, for instance, the cases of Belgium and the United Kingdom). Nevertheless, NHRIs in Europe have managed to weather political changes over the years, and have generally done so with the support of political elites who endorse liberal democratic norms.

THE "LIBERAL IDENTITIES" OF STATES AND
NATIONAL HUMAN RIGHTS INSTITUTIONS

To fully understand the choices that states make regarding the strength and effectiveness of their NHRIs, it is important to conceptualize the extent to which societies have accepted and internalized human rights as part of their identity. A country's demonstrated record of long-standing social and political commitment to liberal democracy can create a favorable environment for the establishment and further development of strong NHRIs. Indicators of commitment to liberal democratic institutions and norms are varied—for instance, in the ratification of international and regional human rights instruments, such as human rights treaties and membership in international organizations with a rights focus, like the Council of Europe. Such cases include some old democracies in Western Europe, particularly Scandinavian countries, which have some of the oldest ombudsman institutions in the world and have remained strong promoters of democracy and human rights across borders.

Yet commitment to liberal values can change over the years. Some governments might not agree with the international community that the establishment of a strong NHRI is a sign of commitment to human rights. This might happen due to limited awareness of the role that an NHRI plays for human rights promotion and protection in the country. It might also happen because human rights are a contentious issue in their domestic context. As country case analyses in later chapters of this book will show, even old democracies in Western Europe show varied levels of commitment to human rights promotion and protection, and the salience of their specialized institutions can vary depending on different governments and domestic contexts. Different support for human rights can occur even inside a country where regional governments might show relatively more support for their dedicated human rights institutions with subcountry mandates—as is the case of Scotland and Northern Ireland in the United Kingdom. Some other regions, like Flanders in Belgium, can see human rights as a much more politically contentious issue. Right-wing political leaders have been treating the establishment of strong NHRIs as counter to their political agendas and thus unworthy of political endorsement.

Some countries in Central Europe offer interesting examples of variation over time in levels of commitment to liberal democratic values. In fact, today they experience a clash between elites that support liberal democracy, including human rights promotion and protection, and far-right political elites that consider human rights to be at odds with national identity. As later chapters will discuss in more depth, current regimes in contemporary Poland and Hungary view NHRIs as a direct threat to national sovereignty and national values rooted in independence from international intervention, particularly by the European Union, and in the advancement of religious conservative values. From this perspective, the preservation of national sovereignty equates with the defense of national ideals, political culture, and even religious practices. By implication, NHRIs defend and promote values that are considered foreign to national values and ideals. As such, they come under direct attack and criticism by ruling party elites and by the newly formed civil society supporting far-right nationalist and conservative religious ideas.

Human rights and the institutions that defend them are deeply enmeshed in the political and cultural fabric of societies, informed by values and norms that constitute national identity. While some values are more deeply entrenched and more likely to withstand changes in government as well as transformations in national and international contexts, some aspects of national identity are inherently fluid and in constant transformation. This understanding of state behavior is in line with the constructivist approach. In broad strokes, identity can be understood as "a property of intentional actors that generate[s] motivational and behavioral dispositions" (Wendt 1999). Identity is fundamentally subjective and rooted in an actor's self-understanding, but it incorporates both internal and external structures. States are constituted of different actors with certain essential properties that constitute one such identity for each state (Campbell 1958). State identity is built on a material base—many bodies and a territory—plus a consciousness and memory of a collective *self* as a separate locus of thought and activity (Wendt 1999).

Social identity can be thought of in terms of two main types of constitutive characteristics: types and roles. By type, individual and the societies they form "share, or are thought to share, some characteristic or characteristics, in appearance, behavioral traits, attitudes, values, skills (e.g. language), knowledge, opinions, experience, historical commonalities (like region or place of birth), and so on" (Fearon 1997). This simultaneously self-organizing and social quality can be seen clearly in the states system where type identities correspond to "regime types" or "forms of state" (Cox 1987). Such a type is also represented by shared belief in the rights citizens have by virtue of being human, and the state's institutional responsibility to safeguard those rights through specific institutions and policies. Thus, a society's citizens can come together in their common views on a culture of rights, and with governmental and institutional support the society can be viewed by other states as having a strong human rights identity. In addition to types, societal identities can also be defined in terms of roles, which make possible the creation of a national self-image through comparison with individuals who are not members of the same society, or who are perceived as different in some defining respects. Such characteristics that account for the role-like nature of an identity are presocial and exist exclusively in relation to a social and political *other*. From this perspective, the intrinsic qualities that will make a country democratic are complemented by the position that the country occupies in the international order and by the behavioral norms toward other ones possessing relevant counter-identities (Crowe and Meade 2007; Burke 1980; Stryker 1980; Wendt 1999).

From this perspective, a strong liberal/rights identity can be reflected in the history of a state's behavior toward its own citizens, and by its formal structures of rights protection and promotion. The Universal Periodic Review process carried out by the UN Office of Human Rights Commissioner provides a framework of understanding an identity in which human rights are at center stage, mentioning in its reports some formal characteristics that can constitute a definition of a country's strong human rights identity (Universal Periodic Review, 2007). An additional indicator of a social identity centered on human rights is the existence of an active civil society that engages in the prevention of human rights violations, and the political will to cooperate with regional and international human rights mechanisms. Central to an active civil society is often a higher public awareness of human rights, complemented by continued and consistent government support for the promotion of those rights through information, education, integration of rights in policy-making, and so on. To the extent that a country has proven to be generally more inclined to promote and protect the rights of its own citizens, we can expect it also to support the establishment of a strong NHRI.

*

The first half of this chapter has introduced the analytic model of institutional strength for NHRIs, mapping the interplay of two sets of factors hypothesized to impact on countries' decisions to choose stronger institutional designs for their national bodies. Building on the literatures on institutional strength, cross-border diffusion, and Europeanization, four main ideal types of factors have been proposed as determining change in institutional strength over time and explaining countries' decisions to support strong mandates and effective institutions on their territories. These factors can be thought of as being aligned along two main dimensions regarding their source and their nature. More specifically, national elites can decide to offer their support for strong institutional designs as a result of material incentives or for ideational reasons. The support for stronger designs can be motivated by domestic factors, such as a preexistent strong support for human rights and liberal democracy more broadly. Institutions can be created and strengthened also as the result of the intervention of international actors, such as the United Nations or the European Union. When states make a commitment to establish and support strong NHRIs to promote and protect human rights on their territories, does that commitment result in more effective institutions and, ultimately, better human rights outcomes? The next section gives a definition of institutional effectiveness and a theoretical framework that can help us understand the factors enhancing or inhibiting the capacity of NHRIs to make an impact on the ground.

Why Do National Human Rights Institutions Matter?

The rapid advancement of national human rights institutions on the international stage has given rise to an interest in how, when, and why they make a difference on the ground. All NHRIs make an impact on the world in which they operate, and this impact is often indirect. A large proportion of the work carried out by human rights ombudsmen and commissions results in recommendations to government regarding the prevention of human rights violations, in advice on legislative amendments to align national policies with international human rights law and to improve compliance. Most of this work takes place in the backstage of policymaking, away from the public eye. Advisory work occurs over extended periods of time, during repeated consultations and because of long-term lobbying efforts. In general, NHRIs endowed with complaint handling powers can provide ample evidence of investigations of rights violations that results in resolved cases and subsequent retribution. Without a doubt, all strong NHRIs have shaped policy over the years. However, it is hard to disentangle institutional influence over the policymaking process from the actions of political, social, and economic actors with a vested interest in influencing policies.

Here, institutional effectiveness is understood as the capacity to successfully carry out the institutional mandates to improve human rights outcomes domestically and internationally. This section argues that five key determinants influence an NHRI's capacity to fulfill its mandate: the NHRI's formal strength, the sufficiency of its institutional funding, the strength of its apolitical leadership, its good working relationships with civil society and national and local courts, and its membership and participation in cross-border communities of peer networks. This section will first discuss the domestic and international impact of NHRIs, and will then examine the main factors determining their effectiveness.

The effect of NHRIs on human rights outcomes is difficult to observe and measure. Nevertheless, staff at NHRIs in Europe can provide rich anecdotal evidence of new policy agendas that they have spearheaded, and of numerous legislative amendments they have initiated. Perhaps nowhere is this influence more evident than in Eastern and Central Europe in the decades following the fall of communism, where legal and institutional reforms occurred at a rapid pace. NHRIs have also been influential in domestic environments with long-standing democratic traditions, even if major policy reforms have been rarer.

THE DOMESTIC IMPACT OF NATIONAL HUMAN RIGHTS INSTITUTIONS

Comparative scholarship on the domestic impact of NHRIs is in its infancy. Existing literature has shown that NHRIs can serve as a "prophylactic" against human rights abuses (Blau and Moncada 2007: 369), by fostering a human rights culture and monitoring government practices. The establishment and continued operation of NHRIs can also play a symbolic role in legitimizing and institutionalizing human rights norms (Cole and Ramirez 2013: 706). There is some evidence that, regardless of institutional model, the creation of NHRIs can improve long-term physical integrity outcomes, even if they require a longer period of time to manifest, but has no effect on civil and political rights practices (Cole and Ramirez 2013). Whether they monitor human rights implementation, advise governments on policy, or coordinate rights promotion, the influence that NHRIs have on human rights practices is often indirect and nonlinear.

Although not all existing research is in agreement over the effectiveness of NHRIs, and though in fact some contest their powers (Carver 2000; Goodman and Pegram 2012; Simmons 2002), there is evidence of the institutions' capacity to have an impact on human rights outcomes. Work by practitioners (Carver 2000, 2005; Burdekin and Naum 2007), studies by international NGOs, and recent scholarly contributions (Agbakwa and Okafor 2002; Domingo 2006; Finkel 2012; Goodman and Pegram 2012; Harvey and Spencer 2012; Linos and Pegram 2017; Uggla 2004) suggest that some NHRIs contribute significantly to the improvement of human rights in their countries. Moreover, NHRIs have stewarded truth and reconciliation processes, offered support to torture victims when they sought redress, mediated social conflicts, mobilized public opinion on environmental rights, and contributed to the improvement of legislation protecting vulnerable groups (Agbakwa and Okafor 2002; Finkel 2012). Two quantitative studies offer additional reason for hope. Cole and Ramirez find that, on average, adopting an NHRI reduces physical integrity violations (Cole and Ramirez 2013). Additionally, Linos and Pegram (Linos and Pegram 2017) focus on accredited NHRIs, offering an analysis of the role that formal design features established at the outset play in determining the institutions' effectiveness. They conclude that NHRIs with formal design safeguards are more effective than those that lack these features, especially in democratic states. Overall, more independent institutions with strong investigatory capacity, starting with the ability to receive and process individual complaints, are more effective than NHRIs without these features (Linos and Pegram 2017).

By facilitating the implementation of international law (Murray 2007a; Goodman and Jinks 2004, 2013), NHRIs can leave their mark on policymaking. In their advisory roles, they can advise governments and members of national parliaments on policy with relevance for human rights promotion and protection at the domestic level. They can also influence policy in other areas of practice by seeking to add a "human rights approach." Such work depends on raising awareness of human rights implications in a wide range of areas of public life not strictly in the domain of human rights. NHRIs can also influence foreign policymaking by advising and lobbying governments to join other states in signing and ratifying international human rights treaties.

NHRIs with investigative and complaint handling responsibilities can influence practices in public institutions with recommendations on how to redress and change institutional practices to prevent further violations. This type of work depends on the willingness of public bodies to collaborate with NHRIs, respond to their recommendations, and implement their suggestions for change and redress. While political support for NHRIs can come and go, depending on political agendas and the changing preferences of different political parties in governments, the public image that an NHRI cultivates can remain constant and highly influential in shaping public discourse on human rights. To that end, research interviews have all confirmed that the appointment of a human rights commissioner or ombudsman who is a respected public figure and is politically independent but maintains a good relationship with political elites is a key factor in advancing a positive image of the institution and ultimately increasing its domestic impact.

NHRIs can also influence public opinion on human rights issues through promotional work. Educational programs coordinated by NHRIs can raise awareness and spread knowledge about human rights in the population. This type of work has the potential to be particularly effective in transitional settings where civil society organizations can collaborate closely with NHRIs to monitor rights violations and raise awareness of human rights. Through project-based partnerships, NHRIs can collaborate with NGOs and empower them in their rights-related community work. Moreover, they can supply policymakers, civil society organizations, and the public with specialized and reliable research on human rights locally and nationally. In most domestic contexts in Europe, this research can inform government activity and can also motivate and inform public action. In the long run, this public influence has the potential to result in change in legislation and in the behavior of public institutions. Even though such efforts do not always result in immediate success, and though the direct involvement of an NHRI is sometimes contentious, such publicly visible work is key to fulfilling its institutional mandate of advancing the role of human rights.

THE INTERNATIONAL IMPACT OF NATIONAL HUMAN RIGHTS INSTITUTIONS

Cross-border networking has always been a key element in the development of national human rights institutions, ultimately stimulating the development of more effective institutions. Whether inside larger cross-border networks like the Global Alliance of National Human Rights Institutions and its regional counterparts, or in smaller networks made up of institutions in neighboring countries, NHRIs have interacted with peer institutions, learning from one another, sharing knowledge and information, and seeking common solutions to shared problems. As a result, all NHRIs have some degree of international activity and are involved in collaborative work with NHRIs in other countries. Importantly, these networks represent significant opportunities for institutional leadership in an international setting. Over the years, NHRIs choosing to play leadership roles in peer networks have actively contributed to an increase in institutional diffusion, strengthening, and overall effectiveness. They have spearheaded innovation within these networks, have shaped agenda setting by funding collaborative projects on rights-related issues, and have contributed to defining strategic priorities for NHRIs around the world.

A necessary condition for an NHRI to become effective in peer networks is the active involvement and influential leadership of a strong and credible human rights ombudsman or commissioner. Individual initiative to initiate change, advance innovation, and garner wider support to implement new ideas across NHRIs has been foundational for the development of these bodies. The formulation of the Paris Principles and the formalization of the accreditation system years later were both results of the coordinated efforts of a few active domestic human rights bodies in the 1990s. Among others, leaders of the Australian Human Rights Commission, the Danish Institute for Human Rights, and the Indian Human Rights Commission worked actively at the United Nations to promote NHRIs as a feasible and innovative solution to the problem of the domestic implementation of international human rights law. Historical research on the formation and consolidation of NHRIs will reveal that, among others, Chris Sidoti, Brian Burdekin, and Morten Kjaerum were instrumental in shaping the future direction and success of institutional diffusion, strengthening, and effectiveness.

Influential international leadership is not always a direct function of larger institutional resources. In fact, some European NHRIs have demonstrated that the size of an institution or its budget does not matter in motivating change regionally and globally. The Croatian Ombudsman, for instance, has played a significant role at the subregional level by encouraging cooperation with partner NHRIs in the Balkans to tackle shared challenges. In addition, the Croatian ombudsman, Lora Vidović, served as chair of the regional network of national human rights in Europe from 2016 to 2018 (ENNHRI 2018). Her appointment represented a strong signal that NHRIs from Eastern

Europe have become stronger over the years and can provide a vision for positive change across peer institutions in the region.

The importance of an influential individual human rights ombudsman or commissioner for effective change is perhaps nowhere as evident as in the case of smaller human rights institutions with subnational remits that become regional or global leaders and effect successful change for their peer human rights institutions with national remits. One such example is the Scottish Human Rights Commission. Despite being a human rights commission with a small staff and limited financial resources in comparison to those of the Equality and Human Rights Commission, members of the Scottish NHRI have been at the forefront of regional innovation in the field of human rights. For instance, the former chair of the Scottish Commission, Alan Miller, has been influential in liaising with the European Union and lobbying the UN High Commissioner for Human Rights and the Global Alliance of National Human Rights Institutions for support in establishing a formal secretariat for the regional network of peer bodies. Securing a start-up grant made possible the formalization and creation of the European Network of National Human Rights Institutions, through the consolidation of the smaller and much more informal European Group of National Human Rights Institutions. The creation of the secretariat in Brussels brought with it a structured system of coordination, communication, and governance across institutions in the region. Ultimately, the desired impact of the regional network is to offer support to member institutions and improve their effectiveness. Chapter 4 will discuss the key roles played by global and regional networks in the development and increased effectiveness of national human rights in Europe and beyond.

Without a doubt, leadership in regional and global forums is an indication of institutional strength and generally a good predictor of institutional impact abroad. At the same time, it is important to note that power hierarchies in regional and global networks of NHRIs are not without their challenges, and are often not a direct reflection of an institution's domestic impact or lack thereof. In other words, institutions that are strong by design and which carry out their mandates effectively might be reluctant to participate actively in regional and global networks and to take on leadership roles. The Czech Ombudsman offers a good example of an effective and impactful institution at the national level that has not applied for accreditation and thus has not been a member of regional or global NHRI networks (at the time of the research for this book). Although the Czech Ombudsman has engaged in collaborative projects with peer institutions in neighboring countries, it has not considered international impact and leadership a strategic priority in the past. In effect, as we will discuss in more detail in chapter 3 of this book, current staff members express frustration at the additional pressure the expanded mandate has created by including human rights duties. Nevertheless, in responding to this pressure, the institution has recently committed more resources to strengthening its involvement in specialized regional and global networks.

Regardless of the historic preferences of human rights bodies across Europe, the research in this book will show that there is growing interest among NHRIs for increased collaboration with fellow institutions in the region and beyond. In recent years, the expansion of institutional mandates to include duties linked to different areas of discrimination, monitoring, and reporting to the UN treaty bodies, and to human rights promotional work has offered more opportunity for peer collaborations and for intensified communication and learning across NHRIs. Against the background of increasing political pressure associated with the rise of far-right political parties, NHRIs have intensified their efforts to work collaboratively and increase participation in peer networks. Somewhat paradoxically, the very political threat to the existence and effectiveness of NHRIs might lead to an increase in their impact. When well-managed, the response to increased political and social hostility can become the catalyst for important cross-border partnerships and institutional leadership in search of ways to strengthen NHRIs and increase their effectiveness.

THE MAIN DETERMINANTS OF INSTITUTIONAL IMPACT

Five main factors can determine the domestic or international influence of an NHRI: its formal strength, as defined above; the sufficiency of its institutional budget; the appointment of a strong, apolitical human rights commissioner, ombudsman, or institutional president; its good working relationships with civil society and national and local courts; and its membership and active participation in cross-border networks of peer institutions.

Strong NHRIs are independent by design, and thus can carry out mandated duties more effectively and make an impact on the ground. An institutional system of budget allocation that is autonomous from national government is key to their institutional effectiveness. Financial resources can represent a prime tool of constraint in institutional practice that is commonly used by governments wanting to limit the activities of rights protection institutions working on their territories (Sedelmeier 2009a). In other words, an NHRI can be strong by design, with a mandate that clearly specifies that its funds allocation should be made independently from government and put on a dedicated state budget line. But financial resources and the consistency of budgetary allocation over the years are often up to negotiation in national parliaments and governments. The involvement of institutional leadership in this decision-making process is usually not specified in the official mandate, and in practice is often limited. Thus, the daily operations of NHRIs are often determined by the ideological preferences, as well as the political interests and priorities, of governing elites. Changes in political proclivities over the years can bring about fluctuations in the extent of financial support for NHRIs, negatively affecting their ability to carry out their mandates.

Financial limitations on NHRIs can take the form of budget cuts, as was the case from 2010 to 2013 for the three human rights commissions operating in the United Kingdom, when all public institutions suffered average budget cuts of 19 percent (Lacatus 2018). Financial obstruction can also be indirect and take the form of unwillingness to allocate sufficient additional resources when an NHRI is assigned a new set of mandated duties, or when it experiences an increase in the number of complaint cases it examines. In such a case it is also common for a government not to adjust the NHRI's annual budget for changes due to inflation. Research interviews revealed that in recent years this has been the case with the Office of the Polish Human Rights Commissioner, whose mandate has expanded to include new responsibilities on equal treatment and torture prevention, but whose budget has remained the same (interviews 52, 53, 56). An additional type of resource-focused limitation can take the form of lack of support for the infrastructure the NHRI has at its disposal. The Macedonian Ombudsman offers such an example, as interviews with its staff show that the institution has been relocated to the top floor of a building several stories tall with no elevator or means of access for disabled persons (interviews 42, 44, 45, 46, 48). These limitations can significantly disrupt the level of activity at an NHRI; they can exhaust staff resources and limit the public's access to the institution's services.

The appointment of institutional leadership—a human rights commissioner, ombudsman, or institutional president—is a key factor in explaining its impact. Regardless of national context, an institution's leadership can shape the trajectory of its development, its relationship with public bodies, and its effectiveness at promoting a positive public image for itself, fostering a constructive working relationship with government and civil society, and mitigating attempts at its own capture by domestic or international actors (Pegram 2017; Lacatus 2018).

The past or present political allegiances of a human rights commissioner or ombudsman represent a problem that has been particularly prevalent in Eastern and Central Europe. As the later chapters on the Hungarian and Macedonian ombudsmen will show, an ombudsman's past political career as a minister of justice can be perceived as a significant impediment to the credibility of an entire institution. By contrast, the Czech and Polish ombudsmen, who have legal expertise in the field of human rights and strong activist backgrounds, are widely respected, usually enjoy long-standing support from the public, and are successful in gaining the respect of public officials. The leadership of an NHRI is arguably the most important factor deciding the general direction of its development, as well as the public's perception and acceptance of its work.

The impact of an NHRI on the ground is highly dependent on the institutional domestic context in which it operates, and especially on the formal and informal relationships it fosters with specialized civil society organizations and the courts of justice. Although a close relationship with civil society organizations is recommended as part of the Paris Principles and the accreditation process, the reality of institutional practice shows a lot of variation across institutions. Arguably the most common type of collaborative work is at the project level, involving partnerships with NGOs in the field of human rights to address targeted rights-related issues. In some countries, civil society representatives are instrumental in the establishment of NHRIs. Such influence is particularly strong in regional environments that lack overarching regional mechanisms for the promotion and protection of human rights (Renshaw 2012; Murray 2007a). Although Europe has a developed human rights regime, a number of countries in Western Europe established their NHRIs as a result of activism and the efforts of civil society representatives. The creation of the Northern Ireland Human Rights Commission, for instance, offers a unique illustration of a closer type of relationship with civil society. Representatives of civil society organizations made up the main force behind the establishment of the commission, and continued to act as commissioners with the highest decision-making power inside NHRIs (Bell 2006; Lacatus 2018). The commissioners represent different societal and ethnic groups involved in the conflict prior to the Good Friday peace agreement. The diversity of backgrounds and the active participation of civil society activists in the commission guaranteed the institution's capacity to represent all aggrieved parties to the conflict and to carry out transitional justice work in a postconflict society. Given how rare is such full integration of civil society among NHRIs around the world, the commission in Northern Ireland is an important example of an institution that has continued to fully integrate civil society in fufilling its mandate.

Finally, the measure of an effective NHRI depends also on its capacity to rely on strong ties with an impartial and well-functioning system of courts. Domestic legal frameworks vary greatly, as do the reliability of a justice system and the political will not to interfere in the relationships between NHRIs and courts. By design, NHRIs can have multiple formal ties with courts (Wolman

2011), ranging from the ability to carry out independent investigations and make recommendations about cases of interest, to amicus curiae powers to represent victims of human rights violations in courts—and also, in rare cases, to impose fines when public bodies refuse to implement institutional recommendations for redress. We have evidence from the Asia-Pacific region that the relationships between NHRIs and courts can be very complex and can encompass a wide scope of actions such as collaboration, judicial training, participation in litigation, institutional defense of judicial independence, and interactions related to the adjudication of human rights petitions (Wolman 2011). It is important to note that not all types of cross-institutional links are formally included in institutional mandates. NHRIs often respond to complex legal realities in the domestic environments in which they operate. Effective bodies can adapt their work successfully to changes in their environment, while fostering good working relationships with the main institutions in the legal system.

In Europe, most NHRIs can carry out independent investigations, and some of the complaint cases they examine result in court cases. Courts generally have the legal obligation to try cases brought to their attention by NHRIs. Depending on the national context, however, significant delays in court proceedings and decisions can occur. Long waiting periods are more common in Eastern European countries such as Romania and Macedonia, and can have a detrimental effect on the institution's efforts to seek retribution for victims of human rights violations. Also important for an NHRI's effectiveness is the type of relationships it fosters with the highest legal institution in its country: the constitutional court. As we will discuss in detail below, Poland and Hungary offer recent examples of constitutional changes that limit the powers of the highest court and, therefore, significantly curb the effectiveness of the human rights ombudsman in cases brought to the court's attention.

Conclusion

In a world of rising discontent with liberal democracy, one of the greatest challenges NHRIs face is to make clear why they matter. Thus, it is essential to have a good understanding of the definitions and possible ways to measure how states establish these bodies and how NHRIs make a difference. To that end, this chapter has provided a comprehensive framework for the study of the strength and effectiveness of NHRIs.

This chapter began with a conceptualization of the strength of NHRIs in terms of two main dimensions of formal safeguards defined in their mandates and in the legislation defining their powers: durability and enforcement. A strong NHRI is necessarily independent of interference by government,

civil society, and other public agencies. Its establishment and powers are entrenched in the country's constitution, and its decision making is pluralist,
inviting input from different factions of civil society. When an NHRI is independent, it can carry out its mandated duties unencumbered. At least in principle, it can fulfill its mandate more effectively, making a positive domestic
(and in some cases international) impact on human rights records.

To further our understanding of the effectiveness of NHRIs, the analytical
framework proposed here systematizes institutional impact in terms of two
main dimensions of work. First, domestic impact can be defined as the ability
to influence policymaking, to raise awareness of human rights, and ultimately
to contribute to better human rights outcomes at the national level. Domestic
influence is often indirect and thus hard to observe and measure. It is also
dependent on the willingness of governments and public bodies to act on the
recommendations made by NHRIs and to put them into action. Importantly,
the appointment of a human rights commissioner or ombudsman who is a
respected public figure and is politically independent, but who maintains a
good relationship with political elites, is a key factor in advancing a positive
image of the institution and ultimately increasing its domestic impact.

NHRIs can also make an international impact. To that end, the active involvement and initiative of leaders in specialized institutional networks of
peer bodies is once again key. Without a doubt, only few NHRIs have successfully influenced the international direction of development for peer institutions around the world. Inside peer networks, strong institutional leaders
of NHRIs can coordinate cross-border learning and can work with international organizations to facilitate the continued development and increased
effectiveness of NHRIs around the world. Even when institutional capacity to
exert international influence is limited, most NHRIs do make an impact on
counterpart institutions in neighboring countries. Smaller subregional networks offer an environment in which institutions can collaborate, facilitate
learning on areas of common interest, and design innovative local solutions
to shared problems.

To capture as much of the complexity of the work that NHRIs do, as well
as the important yet often subtle ways in which they change the world around
them, the following chapters propose a multimethod investigation of institutional strength and effectiveness. Combining data from research interviews,
surveys, and quantitative data collected and coded from institutional reports
and national legislation, the empirical analyses in chapters 2, 3, and 4 will explore how the theoretical frameworks for institutional strength and effectiveness proposed above play in the work of NHRIs in Europe and beyond.

2

The Strength and Effectiveness of National Human Rights Institutions in Central and Eastern Europe

The collapse of the Soviet Union and the wave of liberal democratic transitions after 1990 brought with them increased political interest in the formal institutionalization of human rights protection. Newly independent Central and Eastern European states began to establish national human rights institutions as part of constitutional reform processes and post-independence efforts to build a solid institutional foundation for democracy building (Cardenas 2014; Moravcsik 2000). The institutional model that appealed the most to leaders in the region was the classical ombudsman, following the long-standing Swedish tradition of an independent parliamentary body charged with handling complaints and holding public institutions accountable. At the time of the ombudsmen's establishment in Central and Eastern Europe, the initial political interest was less to ensure human rights protection per se, and more to safeguard democratic governance by putting in place accountability institutions that could monitor government behavior. These institutions represented another formal effort to move away from authoritarian regimes and the concentration of state power in the hands of a few political leaders. They were also intended as signals to other states that the formerly communist region was committed to moving on from its authoritarian past and joining other liberal democracies in Europe. Over the years, the durability of these institutions has increased.

Since then, the mandates of many institutions in the region have expanded to include powers of human rights protection and promotion among their responsibilities through subsequent mandate amendments, or through processing complaints regarding rights violations. To this day, however, some institutions in the area have a partial human rights mandate, which does not include all rights or does not formally grant them protection and promotion powers. Nevertheless, some institutions with partial rights mandates do carry out human rights work, whether through cases of complaints and independent investigation or through promotional work.

As recent years have shown to be the case in Hungary, Poland, and even the Czech Republic, democratic backsliding and the rise of illiberal politics have tested the resilience of liberal democratic institutions. A host of newly established civil society organizations are supporting parties on the extreme far right of the political spectrum that advance anti–human rights, antiliberal, and broadly Euroskeptic agendas. As Poland's human rights commissioner, Adam Bodnar, stated in his address at International IDEA's twenty-fifth anniversary event: "One of the reasons for democratic backsliding is the low level of legal culture. In most Central and Eastern European countries, 'checks and balances' institutions are legal transplants. These institutions were modelled after bodies existing for years in other European legal systems. They appear not to have had enough time to become firmly rooted in CEE countries (Bodnar 2020)."

Broad Patterns of Institutional Development in the Subregion

Drawing inspiration from more established democracies in Europe, governments in the Central and Eastern European subregion opted for similar institutional models when they created their ombudsmen. They created and later strengthened their NHRIs in response to a small number of international and domestic factors, leading to the existence of a diverse body of specialized human rights bodies with different degrees of institutional strength. Without a doubt, the main international actor shaping institutional development has been the European Union, with the democratic conditionality tied to the prospect of membership for postcommunist states transitioning to democracy. As a result of the pressure due to conditionality, and after accession to further integrate in the norms and rules of the EU community, governments sought to expand and strengthen the mandates of their NHRIs. Most of these changes have resulted in strengthening the durability of institutions in the region by broadening their mandates to include powers of promotion and protection. To a lesser extent, these changes have also affected enforcement safeguards. Changes in formal mandate that included a wider spectrum of rights and powers did not necessarily result in an equivalent increase in activity in those new areas. Lack of sufficient financial and staff resources has usually been the main cause for this mismatch. Against the background of efforts to comply with EU conditionality, the peer networks of NHRIs supported in the region by the Council of Europe, GANHRI, and more recently also ENNHRI have performed the "softer" role of helping to build institutional capacity and facilitate cross-border learning for staff members actively involved in running these human rights bodies.

As will be discussed later in this book, the forerunners of democratic transformation in the region (Schimmelfennig, Engert, and Knobel 2006b), Hungary and Poland, began to establish their parliamentary ombudsmen in the late 1980s, including amendments to their national constitutions regarding the creation of these positions. Poland established its ombudsman institution as early as 1987, largely because of a political accident. To respond to social pressures for opening the country toward liberalism, the authoritarian government at the time created a new body, the Public Defender of Rights, and granted it a very strong institutional mandate, including most safeguards for durability and enforcement (except for pluralism). The continued support for the Defender was closely tied to the country's plans to join the EU and further integrate promotion and protection into its system of rights. In 1990, Hungary had its first Law of the Ombudsman, although the institutional mandate has undergone some amendments over the years, resulting in an increasingly stronger and formally more independent body. At the same time, compliance with EU conditionality does not appear to have led to complete learning or norm internalization in Hungary, where the institution is currently formally strong but has limited effectiveness. The Czech Republic established its Defender of Rights in 1999, after a decade of parliamentary discussion about the need to create such a position and the details of its design and mandate.

Despite an overall decline in government support for human rights, the three NHRIs mentioned here have largely maintained their strength. However, their effectiveness has declined over the years, in response to decreased political support for human rights more generally and for independent bodies with the power to provide checks and balances on government. In this sense, the overall performance of NHRIs in Central and Eastern European states confirms scholarly findings about the decline in human rights records in the subregion after accession to the EU (Conant 2014).

Other institutions in the region have developed more slowly. Bulgaria's Ombudsman was created in 2004, largely in preparation for the country's accession to the EU. Despite having strong investigative powers and a mandate that also encompasses the powers of a national preventative mechanism, the Bulgarian body is not regarded as particularly effective in carrying out its mandate. Weaker enforcement powers have led to a less effective institution overall. Lack of sufficient financial resources and limited transparency in the processes of selection and appointment of the ombudsman have not favored the successful growth of the institution over the years. Romania's People's Advocate has followed a similar path. Although the institution began its operations in the early 1990s, it has been the object of political controversy on numerous occasions since. During the same early stages of democratization, Romania also created the Romanian Institute for Human Rights complementing the ombudsman, and the institute was granted C-status by the Subcommittee on Accreditation in 2007 and again in 2011. Since its creation, the institute has had very limited safeguards of durability or enforcement. Although its representatives continued to participate in international forums, such as the European Group of National Human Rights Institutions (ENNHRI), its activity was limited to a couple of specialized human rights reports in more than twenty years of existence. Civil society organizations issued repeated public warnings of political capture regarding both bodies, linked to the ombudsman's alleged allegiances to political parties and their interests.

In the Balkan region, the story of NHRIs is mired in the challenges of democratic transition after armed conflict. Most ombudsmen were created as part of the early effort to transition to democracy in the 1990s, and in the aftermath of independence from the former Yugoslavia. While defining their territorial and political sovereignty, the newly formed states experienced what came to be known as the Yugoslav Wars, as a series of separate but related ethnic conflicts, wars of independence, and insurgencies fought from 1991 to 2001. In this context, the creation of ombudsmen represented a formal commitment to curbing human rights violations and supporting transitional justice efforts. A shared feat of all institutions in the region is their significant internationalization, as they were created with international assistance, and operated during the first decade of their existence with significant international participation and support (Wetzel 2007; Lacatus and Nash 2019). Conflict slowed down their consolidation. Thus, their formal strength took longer to develop, with durability and enforcement features becoming better defined and entrenched into mandates and institutional activities years and sometimes decades after the institutions' establishment.

The Croatian Ombudsman is arguably the strongest and most effective NHRI in the Balkans (interviews 12, 68, 69, 71). Created in 1992, the Croatian body is a "hybrid ombudsman" office with the investigative and complaint handling powers of a classical ombudsman, and a mandate to promote and protect human rights and equality as well as act as a national preventative mechanism. In 2013 it received A-status from the Subcommittee on Accreditation and, two years later, the ombudswoman Lora Vidović was also elected chair of the European Network of National Human Rights Institutions.

Another example is Bosnia and Herzegovina's Human Rights Ombudsman, who was included in the 1995 Dayton Peace Agreement and was part of the postconflict state building and democratic institutionalization in the aftermath of the Bosnian war. In a country where NATO troops and the Office of the High Commissioner for Human Rights were on the ground overseeing key aspects of governance during the transition, international institutions were actively involved in creating and strengthening the ombudsman over time. In 1995, the Organization for Security and Cooperation in Europe appointed the first human rights ombudsman months after the formal conclusion of the Dayton Accords. In 2006, the Law of the Ombudsman was amended in response to recommendations from the Council of Europe's Venice Commission, aligning the institution with international regulations and the Paris Principles. In 2010, the Subcommittee for Accreditation granted it A-status at its fifth attempt to seek accreditation in one decade of existence. As we will discuss in more detail below, the Macedonian Ombudsman was also formed at the time of newly acquired state independence, and has required significant international support to function over the years. However, the institution is not regarded as particularly effective, due to insufficient financial resources, political interference, and a dependence on international funding and operational support.

Four case studies of NHRIs in Central and Eastern Europe will qualitatively illustrate the main explanations for institutional change in the subregion. With the help of interview-based data, case studies bring to light the country-specific stories of institutional creation and of change in formal institutional strength and effectiveness. The remainder of this chapter will offer a discussion of the broader trends in institutional strength and effectiveness in the sub-region, followed by a more in-depth view of four NHRIs: the Czech Public Defender of Rights, Poland's Office of the Commissioner for Human Rights, the Hungarian Commissioner for Fundamental Rights, and the Macedonian Ombudsman.

Reinforcement of Institutional Strength against the Background of European Mobilization

National human rights institutions in Central and Eastern Europe emerged from the momentum toward democratic change, signaling commitment to democratic reform, to meeting the criteria for membership in the Council of Europe, to guaranteeing the rights of ethnic and national minorities, and to addressing international security concerns (Cardenas 2014: 260). Over the years, institutions have become stronger largely as the result of governments implementing measures tied to treaty ratification, as is the case with the Optional Protocol to the Convention against Torture, and the European Union's directives on discrimination and equality. Another important factor shaping institutional strength was the membership of countries in specialized regional and global networks with strict membership rules and human rights conditionality, such as the Council of Europe, the European Union, and specialized peer networks like European Network of National Human Rights Institutions and the Global Alliance of National Human Rights Institutions. In most cases, institutional strength was developed by including new (or strengthening existing) safeguards for durability, such as the formalization of human rights powers of promotion and protection through inclusion in national law or constitutions, or the changing of institutional mandates to include new powers of investigation or promotion. Institutional development continued with the expansion of enforcement powers, which increased independence from political intervention and put the new powers into practice by setting up new institutional departments and teams.

The creation of institutions and the subsequent reinforcement of their strength has taken place against the background of broader regional changes and momentum for transnational mobilization. For instance, the first meeting of the European NHRIs took place in 1994 and was followed by a second meeting in 1997, establishing a new peer institutional network known as the European Group of National Human Rights Institutions (later the European Network of National Human Rights Institutions). The role of the regional network was to aid in the diffusion and strengthening of NHRIs in the region by offering specialized advice and support to existing ombudsmen and, importantly, by providing technical assistance to governments that sought to establish new national human rights bodies and to seek accreditation for their independent human rights bodies. In addition, the Council of Europe formally supported the creation of NHRIs through two resolutions in 1997: Resolution 14, which encouraged institutional establishment; and Resolution 11, which highlighted cooperation among existing NHRIs operating in EU member states and member countries of the Council of Europe (Council of Europe 1997). In the years to come, the Council of Europe continued to provide learning opportunities for NHRIs, through its Office of the Human Rights Commissioner, by organizing regular conferences, training sessions, and workshops geared toward knowledge sharing among peer institutions in member states.

In the decades since their establishment, all ombudsmen in Central and Eastern Europe have consolidated their formal strength and have sought to increase their effectiveness. In practice, most institutional strengthening efforts have occurred as a consequence of NHRIs being included in institutional checklists of requirements for statehood and/or regional membership in European institutions (Cardenas 2014). Arguably the regional actor with the strongest consolidating effect has been the European Union, particularly through the system of negotiations and conditionality linked to states becoming members. During three main waves of enlargement in 2004, 2007, and 2013, the EU developed an increasingly complex system of assessment of compliance and alignment with its regulations as a set of preconditions for granting states candidate status and, usually three to four years later, membership. Independent institutional progress toward democratic consolidation included an assessment of ombudsmen bodies as the main and often sole domestic bodies charged with anticorruption efforts, human rights protection and promotion, and the advancement of the rule of law. The European Commission's regular country reports offer yearly assessments of state performance on predefined indicators, measuring progress toward EU demands (European Commission 2015a). As part of the broader compliance assessment, the European Commission assesses the design and effectiveness of NHRIs, and often also relies on reports from these national bodies as evidence to measure developments in the human rights situation in each state with membership candidate status.

Institutional Effectiveness in the Subregion

Few subregions have such diversity of institutional performance as do Central and Eastern Europe. Despite some degree of formal isomorphism across borders and access to the same sources of regional support, the effectiveness of NHRIs in this part of Europe varies significantly from country to country. Without a doubt, formal strength of all NHRIs has increased over time in the entire region, through constitutional and regulatory changes resulting in the enlargement of mandates to encompass growing human rights protection and promotion power. Yet formal mandate changes have not always resulted in a consistent increase in institutional effectiveness or a continued positive impact on countries' human rights records. While Poland, the Czech Republic, and Croatia have had largely effective institutions, the effectiveness of human rights ombudsmen in Hungary, Macedonia, and other countries in the Balkans has not improved significantly over the years.

One of the most important factors limiting the effectiveness of NHRIs in the subregion is the lack of a consistently good working relationship with national governments, which in some cases show limited responsiveness to ombudsmen's recommendations and decisions (interviews 22, 23, 51, 52, 53, 55,

56, 57, 58, 59, 61, 66, 67, 77). While human rights institutions carry out investigations in cases of complaints about violations by public bodies and issue
decisions and proposals for redress, their recommendations are not usually
legally binding. Thus, their implementation is dependent on the willingness
of public bodies to consider them and take action. Without a doubt, resistance to ombudsmen's recommendations for redress varies a lot, depending
on the nature of the rights violation and on the preferences and priorities
of governing elites. In Central and Eastern Europe, some governments' lack
of openness toward human rights ombudsmen can also be a symptom of a
broader lack of awareness about the activity of the ombudsmen and the social
value of human rights. As a recent response to increased opposition in Poland, the Czech Republic, and some Balkan countries, individual NHRIs and
regional networks have begun to increase human rights promotion and communication activities to raise awareness about the merit of understanding
and respecting human rights as well as the importance of having institutional
mechanisms like the ones provided by NHRIs to oversee and monitor rights
implementation (interviews 38, 39, 51, 52, 53, 54, 60, 61, 63, 66).

Moreover, institutional capacity to carry out mandated duties depends on
the availability of sufficient financial resources. Without exception, all ombudsmen in Central and Eastern Europe included in the study indicate that
they could benefit from budget increases to be able to carry out their mandates more effectively. The effects of the 2008 economic recession have had
an overall negative impact on NHRIs across the whole region. Budget cuts to
public institutions have often also affected the financial resources that policymakers could allocate to NHRIs. Even in cases such as the Czech Republic or
Macedonia, where annual budget cuts did not take place, national legislatures
have not ensured an adequate increase in financial resources when expansion
of institutional mandates has taken place (interviews 47, 48, 49, 60, 61, 62).
In other words, NHRIs have seen their formal strength increase so that the
scope of rights they protect includes equality and antidiscrimination measures and torture prevention, but their allocated financial resources have not
been sufficient to cover the additional cost of new responsibilities.

An additional factor restricting to the effectiveness and impact of human
rights institutions in the subregion is linked to the transparency of institutional leadership appointments (interviews 51, 52, 53, 54, 58, 69, 70, 71, 77, 83,
84, 85). Against the background of recent democratic backsliding and the
erosion of liberal institutions in some countries in the region—such as the
cases of Hungary and Poland we will discuss below—the risk of institutional
capture and the loss of institutional independence from political interference
is greater. One of the structural weaknesses of human rights ombudsmen in

the region is the system of appointment and dismissal for the institutional leadership. Although most ombudsmen are named by national parliaments, thus ensuring a degree of independence from government, processes are not always transparent or pluralist by design. The legal rules for nomination and hiring often do not specify clear criteria for an open process that invites input from civil society members and ensures the consideration of a diverse pool of candidates. This structural weakness leaves room for political preferences among the legislative to influence the consideration of suitable candidates, and ultimately also to influence their decisions to offer support to certain favorite applicants. Such decisions are crucial and directly consequential to the activity, sustainability, and long-term effectiveness of human rights ombudsmen.

Despite financial challenges and contextual limitations, the broader trend in institutional impact in the subregion over time is positive. However small and issue-specific, NHRIs in Central and Eastern Europe do contribute to addressing rights violations and improving overall human rights performance. In the past two decades, most institutions in the subregion have operated in transitional political contexts where the broader societal, legal, and institutional frameworks have also been undergoing change and seeking to consolidate. In fact, this is still the case in states in the Balkan region, and even more so in the states belonging to the European Neighbourhood Policy area. Despite operating in young democracies with developing legal and institutional infrastructures, NHRIs have made visible efforts to address rights violations, handle individual complaints, report on the rights situation on the ground, and support governments. It is fair to say that they have often been the main domestic presence on the ground in cases of crisis. As the case discussions will show more in detail, at the time this book is being written, NHRIs in the Balkans are continuing to coordinate transborder responses to rights violations in the ongoing refugee and migration crisis even when they have enjoyed only limited support from national governments (interviews 48, 49, 50).

Overall, the international impact of human rights institutions in this subregion has been very limited. Possibly due to limited access to international forums, insufficient funding, or a lack of domestic and international incentives to participate in transborder peer networks, national human rights bodies in the subregion have not been very active in leadership positions at regional and global networks of peer NHRIs (interviews 68, 69, 70, 74). The exception is the Croatian ombudswoman, who in 2019 ended her three-year term as chair of the European Network of National Human Rights Institutions. NHRIs in Central and Eastern Europe are generally active members of peer networks, and are often at the receiving end of capacity-building and

training opportunities funded and coordinated by some of the more experienced NHRIs in Western Europe (the Danish Institute for Human Rights, for
instance) as bilateral partnerships or in the activities organized by the European Network of National Human Rights Institutions (interviews 24, 27, 28,
30, 31, 69, 70). At the same time, all NHRIs in the subregion are more active
in collaborative work with fellow peer institutions in neighboring countries,
which is often motivated by the need to respond to shared rights-related cri-
ses or by the interest to learn concrete responses to similar social and political
challenges.

Case Selection

Four case studies are included below, to illustrate the dynamics of institutional change in the subregion with respect to both institutional strength and
institutional effectiveness and impact: Poland's Office of the Commissioner
for Human Rights, the Czech Public Defender of Rights, the Hungarian Commissioner for Fundamental Rights, and the Macedonian Ombudsman. While
all these NHRIs have seen their strength increase over time, they vary mark-
edly in terms of their levels of institutional strength and the pace of institutional change over the years, ranging from strong and effective in Poland, to
effective but with a partial human rights mandate in the Czech Republic, and
to medium strength in Hungary and low strength in Macedonia.

In addition, these cases illustrate how the main factors we identified above
explain changes in institutional strength over time, such as the role of membership in the global peer network of NHRIs and its accreditation process,
the impact of democratic conditionality imposed by the European Union as
part of its requirements for membership, and the significance of national political and social contexts in shaping institutional strength and effectiveness.
Case analyses draw from a wealth of interview data (more than ninety elite
interviews) to offer an in-depth investigation of institutional effectiveness
and impact. Given our generally limited understanding of institutional effectiveness as well as the current lack of quantitative data allowing us to assess
barriers to effective performance, these illustrative cases provide a unique
closer look at the domestic and international drivers for different degrees of
effectiveness and impact of NHRIs in the subregion.

The Polish Office of the Commissioner for Human Rights

The institutional development of the Polish Office of the Commissioner
for Human Rights stems from a combination of a strong domestic drive to

transition away from communism toward liberal democracy, as well as the pressure to comply with European Union conditionality requirements and continue institutional integration after accession. These national and international pressures made possible the creation of one of the strongest NHRIs in Europe, which enjoyed public respect and widespread recognition for its effectiveness. The Commissioner has had the advantage of strong durability and enforcement safeguards, and has maintained its formal strength throughout three decades of existence. Successive governments were supportive of the growth of the institution and its activity, partly motivated by the material benefits of complying with democratic conditionality and of becoming a successful candidate to EU membership. The most notable change taking place in the case of the Polish Office of the Commissioner is linked to its effectiveness in carrying out its mandated duties. While the institution enjoyed great government and public support in the first two decades of its existence, this support began to change visibly in the recent decade.

The early 2000s also saw the formation of a new centrist and Christian democratic party, the Solidarity Electoral Action, later called Law and Justice. Led by Lech Kaczyński and his brother, Jarosław Kaczyński, Law and Justice grew in popularity and came to power as part of a coalition with far-right parties after the 2005 election, and again in 2015 when it formed a majority government. Kaczyński's conservative law-and-order agenda embraces economic interventionism while maintaining a socially conservative stance and moving closer to the Catholic Church. Its position is strongly nationalist and mildly Euroskeptic and, infused with religious and conservative values, it has openly become increasingly hostile to human rights promotion and protection. The growing opposition to liberal rights agendas has led to a visible decline in the relationship between government and the Polish Commissioner body. In recent years it has led also to direct public attacks directed at both the institution and the integrity of its leader, commissioner Adam Bodnar. While the Polish NHRI has succeeded in maintaining formal strength, the commissioner's capacity to maintain a positive public image or make an impact on government's behavior has declined.

At the time of fieldwork, in 2018, public attacks on the the institution and its leadership were common, and the government had actively been obstructing collaboration with the NHRI on issues included on the official institutional remit, such as legislation and policy work and human rights reporting, as well as correcting behavior and offering redress for human rights violations. In the couple of years since fieldwork, direct attacks on the commissioner and obstruction of the institutions' work only intensified, all against the broader political background of antiliberal policy agendas and weakening of liberal institutions. In a public statement of support, several organizations and institutional networks—ENNHRI, EQUINET, GANHRI, IOI, and OHCHR Europe—issued a statement of support for Adam Bodnar and the institution he led, and pushed against the fierce public criticisms he faced from the government and the political parties in the majority: "The Polish Commissioner Adam Bodnar was exposed to a hateful campaign and hate speech of some politicians and media, including the attacks on his personal life, for publicly defending the right to a fair trial and the right not to be a subject to inhumane and degrading treatment of a murder suspect. This is to be considered as an attack on the independence of the Ombudsman in Poland and as a denial of his legal and constitutional obligation to defend human rights and fundamental freedoms of every person." A strong formal design of the Polish human rights institution, as well as a determined commissioner at the helm of the institution and significant international support, have helped to keep the human rights body active and to mitigate some of the marked efforts far-right politicians have made to weaken the NHRI. It remains to be seen whether the Polish Office of the Commissioner will remain independent and effective once Adam Bodnar's leadership comes to an end and a new ombudsman is appointed by Parliament.

The following sections discuss the creation of the institution and the main factors making possible its continued development in the past decades, followed by an analysis of the main determinants for effectiveness and impact.

INSTITUTIONAL STRENGTH: POLITICAL COST-BENEFIT CALCULATIONS AND PERSUASION

The establishment of the national human rights institution in Poland was a direct result of national elites' political cost-benefit calculations in response to domestic pressures to democratize. Over time, however, further strengthening of the institution's durability safeguards through mandate enlargement has been largely the outcome of norm learning and persuasion. In 1987, Poland became the first country in Central and Eastern Europe to establish an ombudsman (Letowska 1990). Paradoxically, the authoritarian government in Poland at the end of the 1980s vested its ombudsman body with a much broader mandate than counterpart institutions in other countries, granting it unusually high powers around the constitutional control of legal norms and acts, as well as oversight over the administration of justice. At the time, the ideological homogeneity of parliament appointing the ombudsman and deciding on institutional budget was seen as a guarantee of full future control of the institution, regardless of the office's mandated durability powers, rendering the human rights body ineffective from the very start, despite strong mandated powers (Arcimowicz 2002). Despite concerns that the office of the ombudsman would not survive the transition from communism to democracy, it continued to function successfully and has consistently been considered one of the strongest and most effective offices of its kind in the region. In effect, its durability increased through inclusion in the country's constitution, which consolidated and confirmed its mandated powers. The ombudsman body was included in the 1989 Constitution and was strengthened further in the 1997 Constitution (Reif 2004b). In the regular reports assessing the progress Poland made toward accession to the European Union, the European Commission recognized the Polish Ombudsman (currently called the Office of the Commissioner for Human Rights) as the main national institution charged with the protection of human rights, civil and political rights, and the rights of minorities (Commission of the European Communities 2002a).

The Polish human rights institution has largely enjoyed formal independence from government intervention throughout its existence. Enforcement safeguards ensured that by design, the Commissioner for Human Rights is an independent authority for legal control and protection of human and civic freedom and rights, acting pursuant to the Constitution of the Republic of Poland and the Commissioner for Human Rights Act of 15 July 1987 (Poland's Commissioner for Human Rights 2019). The Sejm appoints the commissioner for a five-year term, with the prior approval of the Senate. The institutional leader—the human rights commissioner—is assisted by the Office of the Commissioner for Human Rights, based in Warsaw, and the Offices of Local Representatives in Wrocław, Gdańsk, and Katowice. The main responsibility of the Commissioner office is to investigate whether actions undertaken by public institutions and other organizations violate human or citizens' rights, and to take appropriate measures in cases where the investigation finds infringements. Complaint handling and case work have been the primary area of activity since the institution's inception. In accordance with Article 80, everyone has the right to apply for assistance with the protection of their rights, and the number of applications and new cases has increased in the institution's three decades of existence. For instance, in 1990 the office received 22,764 applications and opened 18,114 new cases; and in 2000 it considered 49,602 applications and 31,532 new cases. The number of complaints peaked in 2013, when the commission processed a total of 70,002 applications and 35,310 new cases, and decreased to 52,836 applications and 22,800 new cases in 2017 (Poland's Commissioner for Human Rights 2018). The Office of the Commissioner has the right to initiate action before the Constitutional Tribunal or the Supreme Court, and can use provisions of international human rights instruments ratified by Poland in its cases (Poland's General Sejm 1997; Reif 2004b).

The formal strength of Poland's NHRI has increased over the years. Socialization through peer network-based learning has played an important role in strengthening the Polish NHRIs. Key in this process has been the institution's participation in the United Nations–coordinated accreditation system for NHRIs and membership in the Global Alliance for National Human Rights Institutions has motivated further strengthening of institutional powers, particularly relative to promotional activities and plurality of representation. The Office of the Commissioner for Human Rights received A-status as NHRI for the first time in 1999 and has maintained this status in two rounds of accreditation in 2007 and 2012, despite several shortcomings regarding institutional mandate, financing, and the appointment system. The NHRI has carried out promotional activities in human rights promotion, such as seminars with civil society members, research, and educational activities, though its mandate does not stipulate promotional work among institutional duties.

Persuasion motivated the pace of norm adoption in the realm of human rights in Poland and led also to a further increase in institutional strength. The formal strength of the NHRI grew further in the direction of mandate widening, to include additional rights. In January 2008 the Ministry of Justice expanded the mandate by entrusting the commissioner with the function of national preventive mechanism (NPM), enlarging the institution's mandate with duties related to overseeing the Polish state's compliance with the Optional Protocol to the UN Convention against Torture and Other Cruel, Inhuman, or Degrading Treatment or Punishment (OPCAT). Poland ratified the OPCAT in 2005. In October 2010, the National Preventive Mechanism Department separated operationally from the rest of the Polish commissioner's office. However, the small number of dedicated staff working on the NPM mandate (seven staff in 2019) cannot carry out the large volume of work it is mandated to do (interviews 52, 54, 55, 56). Thus, the department continues to receive significant support from staff members working in other specialized departments at the Office of the Commissioner for Human Rights. The National Preventive Mechanism Department has the power to examine the treatment of persons deprived of their liberty in places of detention, making recommendations to strengthen their protection against torture and other cruel, inhuman, or degrading treatment. In addition, the dedicated institutional department has the power to submit proposals and observations concerning existing or draft legislation, to ensure compliance with OPCAT.

Institutional strength grew further in December 2010, when the NHRI's mandate expanded once again to include duties related to the promotion

of equality and protection against discrimination on the grounds of gender, race, ethnic origin, nationality, religion, belief, age, sexual orientation,
or disability (Parliament of Poland 2010). Arguably the main dimension of
institutional strength added to the Commissioner's activities due to the expanded mandate was promotional work on different aspects related to equal
treatment. The main monitoring and protection tasks include that of examining motions addressed to the institution, including complaints about the
infringement of the principle of equal treatment, and responding appropriately, according to the Commissioner for Human Rights Act (Commissioner
for Human Rights 2019b). In addition, the deputy commissioner in charge
of equality and discrimination seeks to work with lawmakers and relevant
public bodies to amend legislation and policies in view of the European Directives and the Polish Act on Equal Treatment, and to ensure that policies are
implemented lawfully.

Though the Office of the Polish Human Rights Commissioner has A-
status accreditation and is generally considered a strong and effective NHRI,
its formal mandate could benefit from further strengthening. As the Subcommittee for Accreditation noted in its reports (Subcommittee on Accreditation
2007, 2012) and as research interviews confirmed, the Polish NHRI's mandate
law does not include strong enforcement safeguards. It does not require a
pluralistic composition of the institutional staff, and makes no provisions for
a transparent selection process or consultation with civil society prior to the
Sejm's appointment of the commissioner. In addition, the institutional mandate does not specify the importance of the institution's engagement with the
international human rights system, in particular the Human Rights Council,
the Treaty Bodies, and the global and regional networks of NHRIs. It is important to note that, in contrast to previous institutional leaders and despite
not having such powers included in the formal mandate, the current human
rights commissioner has tried to enhance the institution's active participation
in more actively in international forums (interviews 51, 52, 56, 57).

An area of activity that is a particular strength of the current commission
is its close collaboration with civil society, making it a priority to cooperate with associations, citizens' movements, and associations and foundations
acting for the promotion of freedom and of human and civil rights (interviews 51, 52, 55, 57, 58). The Office of the Commissioner for Human Rights
has historically maintained a good relationship with civil society, relying on
its reports of rights violation cases as well as on its firsthand knowledge of and
access to local communities. However, research interviews confirmed that
the strength of the link between civil society and the current commissioner,
Adam Bodnar, is unprecedented (interviews 51, 52, 55, 57, 58). Unlike other

commissioners in the past, Bodnar was appointed by the Sejm in 2015, with great support from sixty-seven civil society organizations including the Democratic Left Alliance Parliamentary Club, from independent members of the parliament, and from the Civic Platform Parliamentary Club (Commissioner for Human Rights 2019a). Prior to joining Poland's NHRI, Adam Bodnar had a long-standing record of leadership positions at NGOs and international institutions, such as the Helsinki Foundation of Human Rights (2004–15) and the board of directors at the UN Fund for Victims of Torture (2013–14); he has since continued to give lectures in law at the University of Warsaw.

Adam Bodnar's close connection with civil society organizations has continued since his appointment as commissioner, and has made the NHRI a unique organization in Poland. In fact, several civil society members consider the NHRI "the only remaining democratic institution in Poland today" (interviews 54, 55, 56, 57, 58), indicating that the institution has successfully remained outside of government influence despite encountering hostility and resistance to its work. Since 2015, government bodies and parliament stopped engaging in direct dialogue with NGOs specializing in human rights. For the first time in recent Polish history, the dialogue between governing politicians and rights activists ended. To the right-wing political majority, human rights are contentious norms, representing liberal values that are fundamentally irreconcilable with traditional nationalist values. In this challenging domestic environment, the Office of the Commissioner is perceived as the sole public institution that has maintained an open dialogue with civil society, organizing regular meetings and consultations to identify challenges it encounters in their work (interviews 51, 53, 54, 55, 57 58). The NHRI has sought to support and advance civil society interests even when they have not been in line with the ideological and social agenda of the far-right illiberal political majority. The challenges the Polish NHRI has faced to carry out its activity effectively in recent years will be discussed in more detail below.

INSTITUTIONAL EFFECTIVENESS,
BETWEEN DOMESTIC IMPACT AND THE
MITIGATION OF POLITICAL INTERFERENCE

During three decades of existence, the Polish Office of the Commissioner for Human Rights has been widely considered one of the most effective in the region. But in recent years, the Polish NHRI has faced unprecedented challenges to its activity and effectiveness. Since 2015, the national-conservative Law and Justice Party has been the largest in the Polish Parliament and has passed laws limiting the powers of the Constitutional Court, extending control over television and radio, and merging the functions of the formerly independent prosecutor general (Human Rights House 2016). The NHRI has been faced with challenges in carrying out its mandate (51, 54, 55, 57, 58), even if at the time of this writing the mandate of the Polish Commissioner has not been formally amended. Arguably the most important challenge is what has come to be known as the Polish Constitutional Court crisis of 2015, which resulted in a weaker legal and institutional framework for rights protection in Poland, including the Constitutional Court's decision-making powers, and a set of controversial political appointments to the Constitutional Tribunal (European Commission 2017). This domestic political situation has been the cause for concern in international forums in which the Polish NHRI is a member (interviews 52, 53, 68, 69). In October 2016, the European Network of National Human Rights Institutions and the International Ombudsman Institute issued a joint statement expressing their concern regarding the human rights situation in Poland and potential threats to the NHRI's independence (ENNHRI 2016). They confirmed the continued strength of the institution, the efforts to continue carrying out mandate duties with independence and effectiveness despite direct attacks and threats to the activity of the institution, and the integrity of the ombudsman himself. Therefore, they recommended maintaining the A-level accreditation level for the Polish ombudsman.

One of the main factors determining changes in the effectiveness of an institution in carrying out its mandated duties is the change of institutional support from governments. Although the formal mandate and main activities of the human rights institution have not changed, government support for the institution has decreased since 2015 (interviews 51, 52, 57). For instance, the government has not adjusted the institutional budget to changes in inflation, and has not supported the increase in financial and staff resources in response to the broadening of the institutional mandate in 2010 (interviews 52, 54). This leaves the institution vulnerable to decreased future staff attrition, and can lead to more limited effectiveness in carrying out its mandate. Inadequate financing is not a new challenge for the ombudsman's office, as over the years governments have not increased financial and human resources sufficiently in response to additional mandated powers (Poland's Commissioner for Human Rights 2011). However, recent open criticism of the activity of the Office of the Commissioner for Human Rights and of the commissioner himself make the possibility of future budget cuts a direct political threat to the effective operation of the institution (interviews 52, 53, 55).

Research interviews with members of staff and civil society representatives revealed that Parliament is increasingly obstructive of the NHRI's work, ignoring institutional recommendations for legislative change and the annual report of activities the defender submitted in 2017 and 2018 (51, 52, 54, 56, 58). A weakened legal framework for rights protection and a less powerful Constitutional Tribunal create real barriers to the casework and investigative work of the Commission for Human Rights. Although the Ombudsman can take cases to the Constitutional Tribunal, the support for its actions and the trust in the court's fair process of decision making have decreased significantly (interviews 52, 54, 55, 56, 57). The rise of a new civil society whose members tend to support illiberal nationalist political agendas more in line with right-wing political platforms has fueled personal attacks against the commissioner and campaigns against other members of civil society organizations charged with rights advocacy, such as Amnesty International or the Helsinki Committee (interviews 51, 53, 54, 55, 57).

Despite rising hostility and inadequate funding, the NHRI has been effective in carrying out its institutional remit and, to some observers, that effectiveness has increased over the years (interviews 51, 55, 56). When the equality mandate was instituted in 2011, the lack of resources and the politically and socially contentious nature of diversity issues were concrete challenges to institutional activity. However, the commissioner's office reduced expenditure for other statutory purposes and supported the activity of the Equal Treatment Department, to make possible the monitoring and assessment of compliance with the equal treatment principle in public institutions (interviews 52, 56). By 2012, the Polish Parliament allocated more funds toward the fulfilment of the new institutional mandate, so the NHRI was able to expand its areas of work to carry out research and create a new series of specialist reports titled *The Equal Treatment Principle: Law and Practice* (Poland's Commissioner for Human Rights 2012). Insufficient funds for the institution to carry out its mandate as a national preventative mechanism continued to be a problem over the years. Nonetheless, the number of monitoring visits has remained constant, from 83 in 2011 and 121 in 2012 to 85 in 2016 (Poland's Commissioner for Human Rights 2012, 2016).

To counteract public efforts by the far right to portray the institution negatively, the Office of the Commissioner for Human Rights used a new strategy to reach out to a wider public, as evidenced by its annual report of activities in 2017 (interviews 52, 56, 57, 58). Motivated by public support in the popular demonstrations in the summer of 2017, the commissioner reframed the presentation of the activities carried out by the NHRI in terms of constitutional duties to fulfill specific provisions made in the Polish Constitution to ensure the promotion and protection of human rights. Instead of a generic report listing institutional activities carried out in the previous year, the 2017 annual report of the Polish Commissioner was more comprehensive in scope, also including an assessment of the rights situation in Poland and an evaluation of the constitutionality of the activities carried out by the NHRI (Poland's Commissioner for Human Rights 2017). In a style reminiscent of manifestoes, the report highlights the importance of focusing on the country constitution to counteract some of the confusion and uncertainty caused by significant social and political changes in Polish society. Against the background of institutional erosion and significant changes to national legislation, the NHRI emphasizes in the annual report the significance of safeguarding constitutional order and the protection of rights. To that end, the Polish NHRI aims to use all means of communication at its disposal to combat misinformation and keep citizens informed of its activities and its interpretation of societal and political events during 2017 (Poland's Commissioner for Human Rights 2018).

The Polish Office of the Commissioner has also increased its institutional presence at specialized regional and global rights forums in recent years. Research interviews have indicated that the most active involvement of the ombudsman has been with the International Ombudsman Institute (interviews 51, 52). While the defender's office has been a long-standing member of the Global Alliance of National Human Rights Institutions and a member of EQUINET since the inclusion of equality and diversity in the institutional mandate, its presence in the activities of networks has been relatively limited (interviews 52, 56). Some observers indicate a certain reluctance on the part of previous ombudsmen to have their role and the image of the institution be associated with promotional rights and equality platforms both domestically and abroad—an attitude attributed to the highly contested position that rights agendas carry in a socially conservative and predominantly religious society (interviews 54, 55, 56, 57). Historically, the institution has maintained collaborative relationships with ombudsmen in other Visegrad countries, and has participated in occasional EU-funded capacity building projects targeting countries in Central and Eastern Europe, such as the EU Eastern Partnership project Partnership for Human Rights: Poland, Armenia, Azerbaijan (interviews 52, 56). The current leadership, both the commissioner and the deputy commissioner in charge of the equality and diversity mandate, have been more active and involved in international networks. They have sought to increase their participation in the working groups coordinated by the European Network of National Human Rights Institutions, as well as in EQUINET's activities (interviews 52, 57, 71, 73). However, a number of institutional staff fail to see any direct benefit to this international engagement, and mention the risk of overstretching institutional staff with added responsibilities (interview 52).

Arguably the greatest risk to the effectiveness of the institution today is national context and the far-right parties' open hostility to rights promotion and protection (interviews 51, 52, 53, 54, 55, 56, 57, 58). From the point of view of the governing party's members and sympathizers, the NHRI and its liberal mandate to enforce human rights represent a direct threat to national values in Poland that are grounded in religious and social conservatism. Thus, the Commissioner for Human Rights is not seen as worthy of continued public and political support. The current commissioner, Adam Bodnar, has been the object of increased public attacks in right-wing mass media outlets, which have sought to diminish the public credibility of the institution. In a largely hostile environment, Bodnar's strong collaboration with civil society organizations in the field of human rights is perceived as a clear bias in favor of the protection of the rights of minorities and in direct opposition to Polish nationalist and religious values. An underlying Euroskepticism fuels the debate, as human rights and the promotion of the rights of minorities and the LGBTQ are seen as fundamentally foreign to the core of the national values in Poland (51, 54, 56, 57).

If, as interviews indicate, the Office of the Commissioner for Human Rights is indeed the "last remaining democratic institution in Poland," as several civil society members have indicated, the risk of a decrease in the institution's effectiveness is heightened in the future. The institution's legal establishment through inclusion in the country's constitution makes it likely to withstand the current attacks and continue to exist, but it does not make it immune to political attempts at influencing the appointment of the next institutional leader once Adam Bodnar's term comes to an end. The lack of transparency in the procedures of appointment for the commissioner and the deputy commissioners is compounded by the predominantly illiberal agendas of the political parties that hold the majority in the current Polish Parliament and whose representatives would be appointing the new human rights commissioner. History shows that, while institutions can weather occasional budgetary constraints and temporary unsupportive political contexts, they struggle to remain effective once direct political interference results in changes in institutional leadership and a political appointment. If these factors remain unmitigated, they could further constrain institutional effectiveness and ultimately render the Polish Office of the Commissioner for Human Rights a body that is strong on paper but has very limited domestic or international impact.

The Czech Republic's Public Defender of Rights

One of the strongest and most effective ombudsman institutions in the region, the Czech Public Defender of Rights (known also as the Czech Ombudsman) was created in the late 1990s, at a time of great institutional and legal reforms. The main impetus for these changes was the promise of the membership in the European Union and democratic conditionality linked to the Czech Republic's candidacy. In preparation for joining in 2007, the Czech Republic had to meet a set of policy and institutional benchmarks which encompassed different domains, including human rights and other rights protection, rule of law, and good governance. When it was first created, the Public Defender of Rights was modeled after the classical ombudsman institutions first established in the Scandinavian countries. Although it had a broad rights mandate, it did not have explicit human rights defense duties. To this day, the defender's office does not have durability safeguards that include an explicit mandate for human rights promotion and protection, although it has handled cases of rights violations over the years. In this respect, the durability of the Public Defender as a human rights body is weaker than that of its counterparts in the Visegrad countries. Nevertheless, the rights mandate has grown to encompass new rights protection and promotion duties, even though not specifically focused on human rights. In 2006, the NHRI took on the role of National Preventive Mechanism, and since 2017 it has also established an internal office intended to strengthen the international ties with peer bodies charged with human rights promotion and protection in other countries.

Two main factors have led to the weaker durability of the Defender's formal mandate around human rights. Over the years, institutional staff have expressed concern about broadening the mandate to include human rights work, and have openly opposed it as well, for fear of moving away from the tradition of complaint-based case work and of lacking sufficient resources to establish a new and separate set of mandated duties. In addition, the ombudsman's legal status is not embedded in the country constitution, which is unusual for an accountability body of this kind in Europe. Changes to the mandate might bring with them further weakening of the institutional powers. Although the Public Defender has not experienced any direct threats to its existence, research interviews show that opening the public debate about a change in formal mandate might expose the institution to an unexpected change in formal duties and a significant weakening of formal strength. This risk has been particularly high in recent years, as the country's majority party, ANO 2011, has had a generally inconsistent and sometimes hostile position on human rights and on questions of discrimination.

Recent institutional changes might indeed be an indication of what the future holds for the Czech Public Defender of Rights. In February 2020, the six-year term of Defender Anna Šabatová came to an end and the appointment of a new ombudsman was mired in public controversy (Amnesty International

2021). In December 2019, President Milos Zeman nominated Helena Valkova, a former ANO justice minister who is now the Czech government's independent commissioner on human rights. Valkova's nomination came under fire due to her previous membership of the prerevolutionary Communist Party, her open support for the surveillance of political dissidents prior to 1989, and the fact that she was a sitting parliamentarian (Stephens 2020). Three months later, Zeman proposed a new nominee, Stanislav Krecek, a former politician and member of parliament for the Czech Social Democratic Party until 2013, when he was appointed deputy defender of rights. Krecek's appointment gained 91 (out of 175) cast votes in Parliament, including ANO and Krecek's own Social Democrats, as well as the Communist Party and the far-right SPD (Stephens 2020). In a letter signed by more than three hundred academics and public intellectuals, Krecek's appointment was criticized and seen as a threat to the independence and future work of the Czech Public Defender of Rights.

The next section will discuss more in depth the national and international context at the time the Public Defender was created, the main factors shaping its development, as well as the determinants of institutional effectiveness and the implications of the change in defender for the future of the Czech human rights institution.

INSTITUTIONAL STRENGTH THROUGH EUROPEAN UNION MEMBERSHIP CONDITIONALITY AND THROUGH PERSUASION

The creation and further strengthening of the Czech human rights institution has been largely the outcome of two main mechanisms explaining institutional creation and strength. On the one hand, the country made great efforts to comply with European Union membership conditionality prior to its accession in 2007. On the other hand, persuasion can explain post-accession developments, evident in further institutional strengthening and the continued integration of national legislation in the expanding system of rights protection laws in the community of European states. The Czech Public Defender of Rights was established in November 1999 by an act of Parliament (Parliament of Czechia 1999), after several years of debate over draft legislation to establish an ombudsman. Early discussions also considered including the creation of the new body through inclusion in the country constitution, but they did not materialize. The Public Defender's main mandated responsibilities relate to good governance principles, seeking to provide protection and redress in cases of rights violations by public employees. In this sense, the institution falls into the institutional design model of a classical ombudsman, which would be modified to include further durability safeguards such as the protection and promotion of equality and discrimination and, more recently, explicit human rights functions.

The position of public defender was created at a time of greater institutional reform and consolidation of democracy in the country, significantly motivated by the start of the negotiations for accession to the European Union. In the Regular Reports assessing the country's progress toward accession, the European Commission commended the work of the Public Defender of Rights as part of the state's efforts to consolidate the institutional framework in the field of human rights and minority protection (Commission of the European Communities 2002b, 2003). Signaling additional interest in guaranteeing rights promotion and protection, the government also established its internal Commissioner for Human Rights, who serves also as chair of the Council for Human Rights, and named one of the deputy prime ministers as chair of the Council for Roma Affairs and the Council for National Minorities.

Institutional strength increased over the years as a result of cross-border processes of persuasion, evident in the successful efforts to integrate the country further into the regional normative human rights regime. The Public Defender's office had its institutional mandate expanded several times during the 2000s, increasing its formal strength through new durability and enforcement safeguards broadening the spectrum of rights in its remit (interviews 59, 60, 62, 63, 64). In 2006, the Defender became also a national preventive mechanism, implementing the state's commitment to the Optional Protocol of the Convention against Torture and other Cruel, Inhuman or Degrading Treatment. In 2009, the Czech rights institution saw its formal strength increase by becoming the designated national equality body, in line with European directives on equality bodies, expanding its remit to include also a broad range of equality and discrimination responsibilities: "The Defender shall contribute to promotion of the right to equal treatment of all persons regardless of their race or ethnic origin, nationality, sex, sexual orientation, age, disability, religion, belief or opinions" (Parliament of Czechia 1999). To adequately carry out the increased mandated duties, institutional leadership has prioritized working with the executive to secure sufficient budgetary and human resources and has been successful. To comply with statutory requirements for protection from discrimination and the promotion of the right to equal treatment, the Public Defender established the Department of Equal Treatment, which has grown over time and currently has eleven employees (interviews 59, 60, 61). Also, in 2009 the Czech Republic ratified the Convention on the Rights of People with Disabilities. and amended the founding Law on the Public Defender of Rights to expand the institutional mandate with the obligation to monitor the rights of persons with disabilities. A new dedicated advisory body inside the institution coordinates research, issues recommendations, and has proposed measures to ensure the protection of people with disabilities (interviews 59, 60, 61).

One of the main areas of formal institutional strength for the Czech Public Defender is its case work. The principal preventative responsibility of the public defender's office is complaint handling, in response to individual grievances against all authorities in the state administration system. In recent years, the office has processed an average of eight thousand cases each year, out of which approximately four hundred have a discriminatory component (Public Defender of Rights 2018). Relatedly, the number of independent institutional inquiries has increased every year, from 176 in 2010 to 379 in 2015 (Public Defender of Rights 2010, 2015), though not all the inquiries have resulted in formal complaints. In inquiries the Czech rights body has the power to inspect official or court documents, request authorities to provide explanations, and investigate situations directly without prior notification. Although not binding, the defender's decisions and recommendations have historically been respected and have generally led to successful resolution in favor of the victims and the remedy of errors by public authorities (interviews 59, 61, 62, 63).

As a result of learning and norm internationalization, stronger formal strength through institutional mandate expansion brought with it more promotional powers. Thus, the Public Defender has strengthened its capacity to carry out research on questions of public interest related to discrimination (interviews 59, 61, 62, 63, 64). It also makes public recommendations about the prevention and redress of specific manifestations of discrimination in society. Moreover, it can issue statements on topics related to equal treatment that target a specialist audience and often include more complex legal argumentation and references to judicial decisions (Public Defender of Rights 2019b). Educational activities include thematic workshops and training seminars with civil society organizations and state administration employees.

Until recently, the impact of the regional and global networks of peer institutions on the strength or the performance of the Public Defender has been very limited. The Czech Ombudsman institution has not sought accreditation with the United Nations and, until recently, did not seek international recognition as an NHRI. Various international actors—the Council of Europe's Commissioner for Human Rights, the UN Human Rights Council, member states of the Universal Period Review, and more recently the UN Committee Against Torture,—have criticized the Czech Republic's failure to establish an NHRI that is fully compliant with the Paris Principles (United Nations Committee against Torture 2018). These international human rights actors view the Public Defender as an institution that is prepared to fulfill the role of NHRI, contingent on an expansion of mandate to include human rights (interviews 68, 69, 70, 71, 72). However, this expansion is politically and socially contentious, due to the increasingly contested status of human rights in contemporary Czech society and among political elites (interviews 61, 62, 63, 64, 67). In addition, institutional staff fear that a wider rights mandate would expose the institution to growing political and social criticism, as result of deeper involvement with contentious discrimination and rights issues. Additionally, some voices from within the institution view a possible further expansion to include duties specific to human rights and to acquire NHRI status as undesirable, fundamentally clashing with the more classical ombudsman duties of casework and complaint handling.

Interviews have showed that since 2016, the Public Defender has begun sporadic efforts to gain recognition for the promotion and protection work it carries out, which is normally associated with a NHRI (interviews 60, 61, 64). Although it did not have a human rights component to its mandate, the human rights body has employed staff with legal expertise in human rights, to dedicate specialized attention to the human rights issues and to integrate the institution further in regional institutional networks. Despite not having accreditation and thus not being able to become a full member of the European Network of National Human Rights Institutions, the Czech Defender recently acquired observer status with the regional network (interviews 60, 61). Staff members who have worked at the public defender's office for more than a decade mention that the institution has undergone significant change in its nearly twenty years of existence and find that these changes have generally been managed well (interviews 59, 60, 61, 63, 64, 65). However, not all staff members welcomed the expansion of mandate to include discrimination and equality duties when new responsibilities were introduced. The process of combining the existing case-based work with the promotional mandate of the equality body proved challenging at the start. In addition, the growth in personnel to nearly one hundred in 2017, because of the broader mandate, has created more bureaucratic institutional processes (interviews 60, 61, 62).

INSTITUTIONAL EFFECTIVENESS THROUGH CASEWORK, STRONG LEADERSHIP, AND TIES WITH CIVIL SOCIETY

Overall, the Czech Defender of Rights has been regarded as an effective institution with a particularly strong domestic impact. Arguably the main factor in the effectiveness and high domestic impact of the Czech institution is the traditionally good relationship it has fostered with different democratic governments and, more recently, also the partnerships it has fostered with civil society organizations specialized in rule of law, democratization, and rights-related work. Throughout most of its existence, the Defender's office has enjoyed great support from government and parliament. According to past and current staff, the institution has never experienced a direct threat to its existence or operations, nor has it faced budget cuts (interviews 60, 62, 63, 65, 66). Consistently during its existence, the institution has enjoyed recognition for its work, mostly manifest through a constructive partnership with government and through being widely considered effective in carrying out its mandate.

For the first time since its inception, the Public Defender of Rights faced the risk of budget cuts in 2017 and 2018, largely as a result of requests from far-right parties to curb the strength and effectiveness of institutions promoting and advancing liberal values. Tomio Okamura and other representatives of the far-right Freedom and Direct Democracy (SPD) party and the Civic Democratic Party (ODS) put pressure on the government to lower the budget for several different antidiscrimination and equality programs. For instance, they suggested that the budget for the programs for Romani community integration and projects aimed at multicultural education be cut. Despite the threats to reduce financial resources for the NHRI as well, the approved annual budgets for those years did not allocate a lower budget to the Public Defender (interviews 60, 61). Nevertheless, these pressures were early signs of what has since intensified and will likely continue for as long as parties with antiliberal agendas remain in power. In general, the growing numbers of far-right politicians in Parliament since 2015 have led to a stronger voice against liberalism and rights promotion and protection (interviews 62, 65, 66, 67). This has also generated increased direct criticism of the Public Defender's activity, and public accusations of the institution being biased in case selection and prioritizing cases pertaining to minority groups (interviews 62, 65, 66).

Civil society members and staff at the Public Defender's office have mentioned that in recent years they have noticed a change in the public perception of the institution's activity (interviews 60, 61, 62, 63, 65). Some media outlets supporting right-wing politics and antiliberal ideas have tended to focus their attention selectively on only a few of the many cases and reports on which the institution has worked in the past years, to present a generally negative view of the institution's work. The public rise in illiberal ideas fuels condemnatory discourse of an institution that stands for what the far-right derides as "leftist" values. These values and ideas are portrayed as fundamentally unpatriotic and too concerned with the advancement of a rights approach promoted by the European Union and other liberal institutions. This antiliberal nationalist stance bears similarity to the far-right political discourse in neighboring Poland and Hungary. As an institution with a rights-focused mandate, the Defender faced criticism in the media and far-right politicians for the position it took on a 2013 case regarding school-level regulation banning all Muslim headdress, resulting in the very early withdrawal from studies of a Muslim Somali immigrant who had enrolled in a nursing school. Assessing the former student's complaint, the Public Defender ruled in favor of the complainant, and in line with the Anti-Discrimination Act (Public Defender of Rights 2014). In the mass media, right-wing politicians offered scathing criticism of the institution's decision in this case, as one explicitly favoring minorities and ultimately ignoring Czech traditional cultural values. This was also the first incident to trigger political talk of budget cuts and imposing limitations on the human rights body's activity (interviews 61, 62, 63, 66, 67). In response to this criticism and to counterbalance misinformation about institutional activity and priorities, the institutional leader until 2020, Anna Šabatova increased her presence in the media, and highlighted other case work and promotional activities. Today, the Czech NHRI has arguably one of the most active social media profiles of public bodies in the country.

The popularity of the ombudsman institution over time is synonymous with the reputation of its leadership, and is generally considered impartial, apolitical, expert in law, and an all-around cultural and social model of integrity and rights activism. Often in the public sphere, the figure of the defender and the identity of the institution are equivalent (interviews 60, 63, 64). The recent deterioration of the institution's public image through the appointment of Stanislav Křeček stands in contrast to the long-standing positive perception associated with the activity of the institution since its inception. Although deputy ombudsmen have generally been more contested figures due to previous political activity, the two defenders of rights who served after the founding of the institution fit this profile (interviews 60, 63, 64). Otakar Motejl was the first Czech defender and was in office for two terms, until his death in 2010. A renowned Supreme Court judge in the late 1960s and again in the 1990s, Motejl participated in the defense of a number of dissidents and activists opposing the authoritarian Communist regime. A number of national and international awards, such as the Gold Cross of the Republic of Poland in 2006 and France's Ordre national de la Legion d'honneur in 2000, recognized his contributions to the protection of human and civil rights, and to the advance of law, justice, and democracy (Public Defender of Rights 2019a).

The key role of the institutional leadership in shaping both a constructive partnership with governments and the public impact and credibility of the Public Defender's work remains equally relevant today. The defender in office at the time of the research interviews for this book, Anna Šabatová, is a case in point. She is widely recognized for her work in rights promotion and protection, holds a doctorate in law, and has extensive legal experience working in the public sector (though she did not have political affiliation). From 2008 to 2011 she represented the Czech Republic as a member of the European Committee for the Prevention of Torture at the Council of Europe, and she has since maintained an academic career as an expert and lecturer in human rights in the context of social work. Prior to the fall of communism, she was an activist promoting democratic elections and became the victim of prosecution, serving a three-year prison sentence for subversion. In recognition of her rights-related work, she also holds several awards—such as the UN Prize in the Field of Human Rights, the Czech presidential Medal of Merit, the Alice Garrigue Masaryk Prize (awarded by the US ambassador in Prague) and the Order of Merit of the Republic of Poland—which recognize her work in the field of human rights. Compared to other NHRIs around the world, one of the unique, strong feats of Šabatová's tenure was that the institution developed a good working relationship with civil society, particularly with NGOs that specialized in rights advocacy and transparency. The ombudsman body relies on these organizations for reporting violations, which it often investigates and seeks to resolve (interviews 59, 60, 61). Although they are not the sole source of information about complaints for the defender, specialized civil society organizations have continued to be reliable collaborators for many years. With the expansion of the institutional mandate, especially around human rights promotion, collaborative work with civil society organizations has increased as well, incorporating project-based work for education and research campaigns.

As is the case with most NHRIs, the role of the institutional leader is key to maintaining autonomy in relation to national government and other domestic and international actors, for ensuring institutional integrity and maintaining the image of a reliable institution for rights protection in the public sphere, and for guaranteeing the effectiveness of mandate implementation. Although the institution of the Public Defender has enjoyed broad recognition for its effectiveness over the years, in the past years it has faced an increasing number of challenges to its activity, and pushback against formal mandate expansion to include human rights. At the time of the interviews for this book, several members of civil society and staff at the Public

Defender's office expressed concern about what the future could bring once Anna Šabatová's tenure came to an end (interviews 59, 60, 61, 63, 65, 66). Although Parliament has the final word in the defender's appointment, a political majority with right-wing illiberal sympathies could lead to increased support for a new defender with an institutional agenda fundamentally different from the ones advanced by the institution so far in its two decades of existence. Although the actual direction of development remains to be seen, concern about real challenges and fundamental changes was tangible among several staff members.

The appointment of the new defender of rights, Stanislav Krecek, in February 2020 is likely to confirm these concerns, as it will bring with it changes to the institution's broader direction of work, and possibly also to its formal strength. Soon after his election was confirmed, Krecek made public his intention to change the course of institutional activity. He remarked, "I would take a different, more non-NGO approach. I would regard it more as a state office, whose duty is to re-examine decisions of other institutions. I wouldn't bring in my own ideologies, for instance, about discrimination and so on. That doesn't suit my approach (Stephens 2020)." In other words, the new defender of rights does not prioritize the independence of the NHRI in relation to the government and, in fact, intends to transform the institution it leads into a public body. If carried out, this institutional transformation will change the nature of the Public Defender's position from an independent body mandated to hold government and public bodies to account on human rights violations into a state agency subordinated to government.

At the time of this writing, it is too soon to assess the impact of this change in leadership on institutional strength or effectiveness. However, there is wide consensus across different members of civil society, including academics and staff at specialized NGOs who opposed his appointment (Amnesty International 2021), that Krecek's appointment is yet another nail in the coffin of the Czech liberal democracy. The former defender, Šabatová, was among those criticizing Zeman's choice of Krecek as her replacement. The two had faced several disagreements while Krecek was deputy ombudsman, particularly as Krecek had supported the far-right parties in their criticism of Šabatová's support for the right of a Muslim schoolgirl to wear a religious headscarf (Stephens 2020). Okamura and other far-right politicians—including Vaclav Klaus Jr. of the extraparliamentary Tricolor party, and Tomas Vandas, leader of the neo-Nazi Workers' Party of Social Justice—welcomed Krecek's election. Shortly after the confirmation of Krecek's appointment, Vandas tweeted that he hoped the new defender would "take the office from a nest of activism in support of migrants, parasites, and the socially maladjusted, back to its original goal (Stephens 2020)." In the past, both Vandas and Klaus repeatedly criticized the Public Defender for carrying out unnecessary work and called for the institution's abolition.

In general, the international impact of the Czech human rights institution on the international community of peer institutions has not been strong, as the defender has not held leadership positions in institutional networks. The involvement in human rights institutional networks is limited, though likely to increase in the coming years (interviews 61, 62). At the same time, the Public Defender has been active in specialized international forums, predominantly in networks dedicated to cooperation among ombudsmen, such as the European Ombudsman Institute and, to a lesser degree, the International Ombudsman Institute (interviews 59, 60, 61). Moreover, mandate expansion to include discrimination issues has opened the door for specialized equality and diversity offices inside the ombudsman's office to become very active in their respective regional and global communities. The office in charge of preventing discrimination and promoting equality is one of the most active members of the regional European Network of Equality Bodies, and the staff overseeing the activities of the Defender as National Preventive Mechanism are involved in the network of fellow institutions around the world (interviews 59, 60, 61, 62, 69, 70, 71).

The Hungarian Commissioner for Fundamental Rights

Overall, the development of the Commissioner for Fundamental Rights in Hungary is an example of the creation of a formally strong institution as a sign of compliance with democratic conditionality linked to the promise of EU membership, which in turn leads to acculturation (incomplete normative learning). Consequently, Hungary currently has a formally strong body with low de facto independence from political interference, and with a significantly lower impact on the ground than that of its Polish or Czech counterparts. The Office of the Commissioner for Fundamental Rights has lost credibility in global and regional human rights forums in recent years, being considered fully captured by political interests and operating mostly as an extension of the institutional structure of the Orbán government. Declining institutional activity and the decreased domestic and international impact of the Hungarian Commissioner in the past decade is yet another symptom of post-accession backsliding in Hungary's support for liberal democracy.

In the early years of existence, the institution lacked a dedicated and broad human rights mandate but was nevertheless largely regarded as a well-functioning body. The election of Viktor Orbán's cabinet in 2010 brought

with it a series of constitutional reforms, including a merger of the existing
Rights Commissions in 2012 and a broadening of the institutional mandate
to include safeguards for durability covering human rights promotion and
protection, as well as the power to promote and protect several other rights:
since 2011, the protection of all fundamental rights and all vulnerable groups,
of the rights of national minorities, and of the interests of future generations.
In 2014 the Hungarian NHRI became a whistleblower's protection body, and
in 2015 it became a national preventive mechanism pursuant to Article 3 of
the Optional Protocol of the Convention against Torture and other Inhuman
or Degrading Treatment or Punishment. It also received the mandate to examine the ordering and conduct of the review procedure of national security
vetting. In February 2020 the Independent Police Complaints Board merged
into the institution; thus the Commissioner for Fundamental Rights has an
additional mandate for the independent investigation of complaints against
the police. In 2021 the Equal Treatment Authority was also merged into the
Office of the Commissioner for Fundamental Rights, with the institution taking over all its previous responsibilities and functions, including its authority
competences. Despite overall stronger safeguards for durability, recognized
in 2014 through awarding of A-status and membership in the Global Alliance
of National Human Rights Institutions, the Commission has lower enforcement safeguards due to its reduced activity, and is now regarded as ineffective. In effect, the Orbán administration used the broadening of the NHRI's
mandate as a strategy to weaken and even obliterate other rights-focused
bodies by subsuming them into a politically captured NHRI.

THE PARADOX OF INSTITUTIONAL DEVELOPMENT THROUGH CONDITIONALITY AND ACCULTURATION

The establishment of the Hungarian NHRI stemmed from the post-1989 government's efforts to consolidate the country's transition to liberal democracy.
In the aftermath of the fall of communism in 1990, amendments to the existing Hungarian Constitution made possible the establishment of the Parliamentary Commissioner for Civil Rights (Reif 2004b). It took three years before the first Ombudsman Act was presented before Parliament in 1993 with
the recommendation that "its adoption may create an important guarantee in
Hungary for respecting human rights and citizens' rights." (OBH 2008). Three
different independent parliamentary commissioners' offices were set up in
1995, and a fourth was created in 2007, with specialized remits in different
areas of rights promotion and protection: the Parliamentary Commissioner
for Fundamental Rights, the General Deputy Parliamentary Commissioner,

the Parliamentary Commissioner for Data Protection, and the Parliamentary Commissioner for the Rights of National and Ethnic Minorities. In 2007, the Hungarian General Assembly created a new ombudsman, the Parliamentary Commissioner, dealing with issues of environmental protection, replacing the Commissioner for Civil Rights in 2007. The resulting institutional setup was unique to Hungary, and was generally regarded as successful both domestically and internationally (OBH 2008).

From the start, the remit of the Parliamentary Commissioner for Civil Rights was broad, encompassing many areas of government administration, including aspects of the armed and security forces, police, prisons, organs of justice (aside from the courts), public utilities, public educational institutions, and local government (Reif 2004b). Among other monitoring and legal advisory powers, the institution could initiate investigations and make recommendations on complaint cases and legislative amendments, could interpret constitutional provisions, and could institute criminal and other proceedings against administrative officials. Although the Commissioner's first mandate made no explicit provisions concerning human rights, most of the constitutional rights included in its remit were in fact human rights, and many of the complaints the ombudsman receives relate to violations of human rights (Reif 2004b). As of 2012, the newly redesigned Office of the Commissioner for Fundamental Rights may initiate review of laws at the Constitutional Court and the Curia, in terms of their conformity with the Fundamental Law (Commissioner for Fundamental Rights 2019).

Changes in formal institutional durability during the first decade of the institution's existence were largely a result of processes of acculturation. Showing compliance with European Union democratic conditionality norms, Hungarian governments sought to increase the state's compliance with international norms concerning the domestic institutionalization of human rights protection. Despite efforts to signal commitment to liberal democracy and to institutionalize rights promotion and protection through the creation of dedicated bodies, normative learning was incomplete, stopping short of internalization and resulting in acculturation. This has been particularly evident in the nature of institutional change in the decade since Orbán came to power, and has become an indicator of liberal democratic backsliding. Somewhat surprisingly, the rapid expansion of the Hungarian NHRI's remit has no longer represented the consolidation of an ever-stronger human rights body, but rather has led to a weakening of the NHRI's enforcement powers and overall effectiveness.

Reflecting changes in the domestic political environment, the most significant changes to the formal strength of Hungary's NHRI have taken place in the past decade. Orbán's government took office in 2010 on a populist campaign against liberal values, and began a comprehensive process of constitutional reform that also impacted on the work of the Office of the Commissioner for Fundamental Rights. A new constitution in 2012 promised to meet international requirements and called for major institutional changes through the establishment of a single ombudsman office with continued quasijudicial powers and a complaint-handling mandate, while strengthening the promotional powers of the NHRI that included research, education activities, and specialized reporting (Ministry of Justice 2011). These changes to the formal design of Hungary's NHRI made possible the creation of a formally stronger body which was also more closely aligned with the institutional guidelines included in the Paris Principles. As research interviews have shown, however, greater formal strength has not necessarily led to increased institutional activity. Rather, it has coincided with a change of institutional leadership and the beginning of a new direction of institutional activity (interviews 86, 88, 90, 91, 92).

In addition, the formal powers of the NHRI were extended to encompass the role of National Preventive Mechanism in 2015 after Hungary ratified the OPCAT in 2012. In 2011 the Hungarian Parliament adopted Act 143, aimed at implementing the ban on torture and other cruel, inhuman, or degrading treatment or punishment (Commissioner for Fundamental Rights 2019). Until 2015, however, Hungary did not have a designated institution operating as a national preventive mechanism. Research interviews evidenced that this delay was due to a lack of political will on the part of government to make possible the implementation of the Optional Protocol to the Convention against Torture (interviews 86, 91, 93). As of January 2015, the Commission for Fundamental Rights performs also the task of National Preventive Mechanism, pursuant to Article 3 of the OPCAT (Commissioner for Fundamental Rights 2016). A minimum of eleven members of staff work toward implementing the OPCAT, carrying out inspections at places of detention or imprisonment and monitoring the extent to which the rights of people deprived of their liberty are respected. In addition, the Office of the Commission for Fundamental Rights may rely on the UN Convention on the Rights of Persons with Disabilities in its activities. Three years after its accession to the European Union, Hungary ratified the Convention on the Rights of Persons with Disabilities (CRPD) and its optional protocol on 20 July 2007. However, the areas of activity for the ombudsman did not include enforcement responsibilities linked to the CRPD until several years later. By 2016, the Office of the Commissioner for Fundamental Rights had dedicated programs focused on redefining the image of persons with disabilities in Hungarian society and on improving respect for their rights (Commissioner for Fundamental Rights 2016). The significant delay in the implementation of the CRDP was attributed to a lack of political will and to the lack of a dedicated institutional mandate or sufficient resources to carry out new duties (interviews 86, 87, 89, 90, 91).

The enlarged mandate spurred only a slow increase in promotional activity, focusing mainly on writing specialized reports. Nevertheless, promotional work and research have remained low areas of institutional activity, as the NHRI's main areas of operation have remained complaint handling and case-related investigations. Over the years, the number of complaints has varied, with high numbers in the mid-1990s—8,526 in 1996 and 8,358 in 1997—to lower numbers in the following decade—for instance, 6,416 in 2001 and 4,917 in 2002 (Commissioner for Fundamental Rights 2010). After the changes to the institutional structure and mandate, the institution processed a larger number of cases, linked to a higher number of rights violations in general, and in the context of the refugee crisis. In 2012 the commission received 7,049 complaints, and in 2016 it received 8,399, before registering a decrease in 2017, with 6,058 complaints (Commissioner for Fundamental Rights 2010, 2012, 2017).

The expansion of the institutional mandate continued in the years after 2015, too, with a similar effect of weakening the NHRI's powers. Furthermore, the Orbán administration used mandate expansion as an indirect means to weaken and even dissolve other institutions with rights-focused mandates. In February 2020 the Independent Police Complaints Board merged into the institution; thus, the Commissioner has an additional mandate for the independent investigation of complaints against the police. And in 2021, the Equal Treatment Authority was also merged into the Commissioner for Fundamental Rights, with the NHRI taking over all equality-related responsibilities, functions, and authority competences (EQUINET 2021). The European Commissioner for Human Rights, Dunja Mijatović, expressed serious concern about the Hungarian Parliament's decision to merge the two bodies: "I fear that several proposals contained in the complex legislative package, submitted without prior consultation and relating to matters including the functioning of the judiciary, election law, national human rights structures, scrutiny over public funds, and the human rights of lesbian, gay, bisexual, transgender, and intersex (LGBTI) people, could serve to undermine democracy, the rule of law and human rights in Hungary" (Mijatović 2020). The Equal Treatment Authority was established in 2005 as part to the efforts of the Hungarian government to align with European Union standards to combat inequality of sex, race, ethnicity, religion, age, disability, sexual orientation, and gender identity. The equality and antidiscrimination body was considered a well-functioning and effective institution. Merging it with the Commissioner for Human Rights without a strategy to integrate the work of the two bodies effectively is a clear move on the part of government to dissolve the equality body, and ultimately to continue dismantling the legal and institution system created in the decades since the fall of communism as a foundation for the liberal democratic state in Hungary. Orbán's government used the state of emergency it implemented to contain the spread of COVID-19 as an opportunity to bypass democratic decision making and pass legislation without public consultation (Mijatović 2020; ILGA Europe 2020). With this measure, it significantly advanced the implementation of its agenda to curb rights work, terminate formal liberal institutions, and further erode liberal democracy.

The effect of network-based learning through the global or regional networks of peer institutions on the strength of the Hungarian national human rights body was limited at the start, but it has increased in recent years in response to international pressure to improve the country's overall human rights performance. Hungary's NHRI did not apply for accreditation with the Global Alliance for National Human Rights Institutions until 2011, when it came under pressure from the Universal Periodic Review process and put forward for consideration the broadest of the country's independent bodies (Cardenas 2014). Prior to the accreditation process, the government's Minorities Office had been more active on the international stage, particularly at the regional level, participating in NHRI forums like the European Group of National Human Rights Institutions. The Minorities Office was viewed as a body created to show compliance with the European Union's agenda on minority rights promotion and protection in its member states. In that respect, supporters of the governing party and of Orbán's Euroskeptic position initially welcomed the accreditation of the NHRI and its increased access to international peer networks as a move away from showing compliance with the EU (interviews 88, 89, 91, 92). The accreditation body found the Office of the Commissioner for Fundamental Rights only partly in compliance with the Paris Principles and granted it B-status. Although its existence was enshrined in the country's constitution, the Subcommittee on Accreditation expressed concern with the limited scope of the human rights mandate, primarily in terms of promotional powers and pluralism. In addition, the Subcommittee on Accreditation recommends that the candidates for the post of commissioner be selected and removed in a more transparent manner that is formalized through including in relevant legislation. The regular report encouraged the NHRI to develop and formalize different types of cooperation with civil society in the fields of human rights (Subcommittee on Accreditation 2011).

To gain further international recognition from its peers, in 2014 the newly re-structured institution sought re-accreditation. In October 2014 the Sub-committee on Accreditation found the unified NHRI to be largely in compli-ance with the Paris Principles, granting it A-status. It also made a number of recommendations for further strengthening (Subcommittee on Accredi-tation 2014). The Subcommittee on Accreditation commended the effort to incorporate promotional powers in the new mandate and encouraged further legal development to grant the ombudsman power to monitor compliance with international human rights instruments and to encourage government to integrate further in the international human rights system. At the same time, the subcommittee continued to express its concern with the lack of suf-ficient transparency in the process of nomination and appointment of the in-stitution's leader (Subcommittee on Accreditation 2014). These concerns were not adequately addressed by the Commissioner for Fundamental Rights, and the Hungarian government continued to weaken the strength of its NHRI. Hence, the re-accreditation of the institution has been delayed twice.

INSTITUTIONAL EFFECTIVENESS: A BROADER MANDATE BUT A LESS EFFECTIVE INSTITUTION

The effectiveness of the Hungarian Commissioner for Fundamental Rights has fluctuated over the years and has been in clear decline. The most recent institutional mergers, in 2020 and 2021, and the broadening of the institution's mandate to include more rights are not conducive to consolidating a stronger NHRI. Research interviews pointed to the danger of equating a broader spec-trum of formal powers for the NHRI with its effectiveness in carrying out its mandate, pointing to the leadership of the institution as the greatest impedi-ment to its effective operation in recent years (interviews 86, 88, 90, 91, 92, 93).

Political intervention in the NHRI's leadership appointment and decision making has led to a decline in effectiveness and credibility in cross-border networks of peer institutions (interviews 86, 90, 91). The lack of a formal, transparent, and pluralist process of candidate nomination and selection for the commissioner's post has undermined the powers of the institution and its capacity to meet its mandated duties. The lack of transparency in the ap-pointment process of the two institutional leaders (also called ombudsmen) and their deputies (Subcommittee on Accreditation 2012, 2014; Transparency International 2012) give way to political interference in the appointment pro-cess. The appointment in 2013 of Commissioner László Székely has raised concerns in the international community of NHRIs and among civil society in Hungary, due to Székely's past political affiliation with FIDESZ and the Hungarian Civic Alliance and his active career in government since the 1990s. Such political sympathies continue to interfere with the mandated institutional powers that have required it to act as an independent monitoring and accountability body in relation to government. Interviews expressed concern about the high risk of continued political interference in the leadership appointment process in contemporary Hungary, which led to perceptions of the commissioner in office at the time (before September 2019) as having strong political allegiance to the Orbán administration, and as sharing its generally hostile attitude toward human rights promotion and protection (interviews 87, 90, 92, 93).

Confirming the interview partners' expectations, political interference has since continued to shape the NHRI's activity and credibility. Hungary has appointed a new commissioner for fundamental rights, Akos Kozma, who has gained public recognition as a specialist in European law. Interviewees expressed concern that Kozma's experience working for the first Orbán government between 1998 and 2002 had been a clear indication of his future unwillingness to criticize government actions, to hold Viktor Orbán's government to account on rights violations, or to seek to advance a liberal agenda that might sometimes be at odds with the broader direction of government policymaking (interviews 88, 90, 91, 93). In the 2021 report, the Hungarian Helsinki Committee assessed the activities of the NHRI led by Kozma as having "failed to demonstrate adequate efforts in addressing all human rights issues and [having] failed to speak out in a manner that promotes and protects all human rights, similar to his predecessor." Although formally stronger "on paper" due to a wider spectrum of rights promotion and protection on its mandate, the institution has been weakened by political interference in the reform of the Parliamentary Commissioner and in the appointment of the NHRI's latest two leaders.

The decrease in institutional activity, including in the core mandated activities such as complaint handling, confirms the decreased effectiveness of Hungary's NHRI. Moreover, the choice of cases prioritized by the NHRI is an indication of the politicization of the institutional agenda and the alignment with the Orbán administration policy agenda priorities. The NHRI has been active in certain areas that are not politically sensitive, while he has remained inactive and completely silent about high-profile rights considered politically sensitive, such as the extensive discrimination against the Roma in Hungary as well as the rights violations affecting asylum seekers and migrants, or the breach of rights affecting LGBTQ people. In addition, the commissioner did not address the very challenging situation of human rights activists and defenders working in Hungary (Hungarian Helsinki Committee 2021).

The Hungarian NHRI's rights promotion activity has decreased, along with the core institutional work on handling complaint cases. In recent years, the number of complaints lodged with the Commissioner for Fundamental Rights has been unprecedently low, and some members of civil society attribute the decrease to a loss of public trust in the commissioner and an erosion of institutional credibility (interviews 86, 90, 91, 92, 93). It is important to note that, like all rights-focused institutions in Hungary, the Commissioner for Fundamental Rights has operated in a political context openly hostile to human rights (interviews 86, 87, 88, 89). More generally, human rights activists and international observers have expressed concern with the current government's action in helping to mistreat migrants, to consolidate media outlets in the hands of pro-government owners, to restrict funding for NGOs, and to require NGOs that receive foreign funds to brand themselves as such (US Department Of State 2017). In this context, the NHRI has been largely silent to recent rights violations, changes to legal structures, and the general weakening of democratic and rule of law institutions in Hungary.

One such example is the institutional response to the protection of refugees' rights during the large influx of refugees and asylum seekers in 2015 and 2016. While the NHRI considered a large number of cases regarding complaints about the Hungarian authorities' management of borders (2,640 in total in 2016), the broader public institutional response to rights violations was very limited (Commissioner for Fundamental Rights 2016). The rights institution did not openly criticize the government's response to the humanitarian crisis, not did it exercise its right to raise concerns about the adequacy of government policies in front of Parliament. Its response was limited to the issuing of a public communique on the broader need to follow international human rights law and curb consistent violations of the rights of refugees by government officials and the police. In the context of the refugee crisis, the Commissioner for Fundamental Rights was widely regarded as a "toothless" institution (interviews 86, 90, 91, 92, 93). Leaders of several civil society organizations issued repeated calls for more direct involvement of the Commission for Fundamental Rights in preventing refugee rights violations (Eva 2015). They asked the commission to question the government's official actions publicly, and to launch independent investigations into recent bills passed by Parliament to manage migration and refugee flow, which include restrictions of rights not in line with the rights protection principles enshrined in the country's constitution (interviews 86, 90, 91, 92, 93). They pointed also to the need to educate police forces as to what rights refugees have, to prevent confusion and abuse as they enter Hungary and seek asylum (interviews 90, 91). In addition, civil society organizations called on the NHRI and its leader to do on-site inspections to monitor living conditions in temporary shelters, camps, and transition sites for refugees (interviews 86, 91, 92, 93). These institutional duties fall within the remit of the NHRI as the National Preventive Mechanism of Hungary.

In recent years the ombudsman institution has sought to increase its participation in global and regional forums. Nevertheless, the international impact of the Hungarian NHRI has been relatively low, despite its efforts to increase its participation in peer networks. Its international engagement has grown, and its 2014 accreditation gave it the power to participate in decision-making in specialized networks of NHRIs. However, research interviews have shown that its direct involvement with the European Network of National Human Rights Institutions and the Global Alliance of National Human Rights Institutions remains relatively limited (interviews 87, 88, 89). In addition, political interference in the appointment of the last two commissioners, as well as those commissioners' political past, makes peers in the regional and international networks far more reluctant to engage in collaborative work with the Hungarian NHRI. The oldest partnership of the Office of Commissioner for Fundamental Rights is with the European Network of Equality Bodies (EQUINET). Interviews confirmed that the Hungarian institution is a member of several working groups and participates in several meetings during the year (interviews 87, 88, 89). The Hungarian NHRI participated also in a number of working groups organized within the framework of the cooperation platform established by the European Network of Equality Bodies, the Council of Europe, the European Network of National Human Rights Institutions, and the European Union Agency for Fundamental Rights—the working groups focused on hate crime and hate speech, asylum and migration, economic and social rights, and Roma equality (Commissioner for Fundamental Rights 2017).

Despite multiple memberships and active participation in peer networks, interviews with leadership staff of peer networks of NHRIs evidenced that the Hungarian human rights institution was indeed increasingly active in the regional and international peer network, but that other network members expressed uncertainty about the credibility of the Hungarian commissioner's work given his political sympathies (interviews 71, 72, 84, 85). Despite maintaining formal strength over the years, the Hungarian NHRI has significantly decreased in its effectiveness and impact due to political interference. This risk of political interference is particularly high and potentially damaging in young democracies, where the effectiveness of public institutions largely depends on the ability of institutional leadership to remain independent from government and corruption (Transparency International 2012). In these contexts, formal mandate changes unmatched by increased effectiveness or impact on the ground confirm the strategic design of an empty-shell institution. Under the guise of national institutional reform, the political class changed the legal framework in the realm of human rights promotion and protection, weakening the existing NHRI by generating a false front of formal strength that conceals an essentially inefficient body.

The Ombudsman of the Republic of North Macedonia

Established "on paper" at a time of constitutional reform and general enthusiasm surrounding the Republic of Macedonia's independence from Yugoslavia, the creation of the Ombudsman Office of the Republic of Macedonia was intended as a gesture of domestic commitment to a transition toward liberal democracy. The Law of the Ombudsman was passed in the early 1990s, but the institution did not begin its activity until several years later. The development of the North Macedonian Ombudsman Office has been slow and has taken place largely due to international organizations like the UN Development Program, the Organization for Security and Cooperation in Europe, and NGOs such as the Helsinki Committee and Amnesty International. They provided funding and valuable know-how at the time of the institution's establishment, and have continued to do so throughout its lifespan.

Its formal strength has grown over the years, particularly its durability safeguards, but the Ombudsman Office has not been considered a very effective body, having only very limited domestic and international impact. The lack of financial support from government, combined with a system of appointment for the institutional leadership lacking transparency and accountability, has resulted in an increase in formal powers. The 2016 change in government and the Prespa Agreement, signed on 12 June 2018, a bilateral accord with Greece concerning the state's official name, are creating the possibility of further legal and institutional development. Although the research interviews were carried out just prior to the Prespa Agreement, it is fair to expect that further reforms in North Macedonia will result in changes to the strength of the Ombudsman Office as well. The prospect of possible future membership in the European Union will likely offer the country a strong enough motivation to improve the NHRI's formal safeguards for enforcement and to increase the NHRI's impact on the ground, in response to demands by the EU. Only time will tell, however, whether these domestic transformations will lead to sustainable changes in the institution and an increase in its effectiveness.

INSTITUTIONAL WEAKNESS BECAUSE OF
ACCULTURATION IN A POSTCONFLICT ENVIRONMENT

The Constitution of the Republic of Macedonia made provisions for the establishment of the Ombudsman Office as early as 1991 (Constitution of the Republic of Macedonia 1991), although the institution would only begin operations several years later. In 1991, Macedonia held an independence referendum with a 75.7 percent turnout which yielded a 96.4 percent vote in support of the establishment of a sovereign Macedonian state (Nohlen and Stover 2010). Despite a long-standing dispute with Greece over historically contested territory and the name of the country, which was resolved in 2018, the United Nations recognized the Republic of Macedonia as an independent member state in 1993. Human rights were central to the international organizations' programs to promote liberal democracy in the Balkans. The domestic and international context at the time was favorable to the formal establishment of institutions that would signal Macedonia's commitment to continue its transition to democracy and follow in the footsteps of established democracies. Against this background, the ombudsman institution was an important independent body for government oversight, monitoring, and support.

Research interviews revealed that the combination of national lack of expertise in establishing and running an ombudsman body and the lack of political will to create a strong body mandated with human rights promotion and protection were the main causes of significant delay in the process of establishing the institution and making it fully operational (interviews 43, 44, 45, 46, 48, 49). At the start of its activity, support from the United Nations was essential for the creation of the Macedonian Ombudsman Office. At the time, the country was under observation by the Office of the UN High Commissioner for Human Rights, on the mandate of the special rapporteur appointed to assess the human rights situation in the former Yugoslavian republics. Interviews reveal that the creation of an Ombudsman Office in 1997 was a formal sign that the state would seek to keep its human rights commitments and ensure a peaceful transition to democracy by creating both a dedicated legal framework and a specialized institutional structure.

Established in line with the standard duties of a classical ombudsman, the North Macedonian Ombudsman Office's mandate changed over the years, expanding to encompass a broader set of mandated responsibilities. The country's constitution grants the NHRI the power to protect the constitutional and legal rights of citizens when violated by the state administration and other bodies and organizations with public mandates. In the aftermath of

the 2001 Ohrid Framework Agreement between the Republic of Macedonia
and ethnic Albanian representatives (Framework Agreement 2001), Article 77
of the constitution was amended to add a new dimension of responsibility:
protection of the principles of nondiscrimination and equitable representation of communities in public bodies (Constitution of the Republic of Macedonia 2003). In 1997, Parliament voted the first Law of the Ombudsman, formalizing the conditions for the institutional leader's election and dismissal.

The efforts to grow the human rights dimension of the NHRI's durability
and enforcement safeguards began in 2009, as part of the reforms of Gjorge
Ivanov's administration to further the alignment of domestic legislation and
institutional infrastructure with the European Union's general expectations
of states that are candidates for membership (interviews 44, 45, 49, 50). As
a result of these changes, a new legal amendment prescribed special protection of children's rights and established a special department for the prevention of torture and other forms of cruel, inhuman, or degrading treatment or
punishment: the National Preventive Mechanism. Building the financial and
staff capacity of the dedicated NHRI department took time, and the National
Preventative Mechanism officially started its work in April 2011. In response
to feedback from international organizations like the Organization for Security and Cooperation in Europe and the UN Development Program, the
same legal amendments also introduced changes to the manner of financing
the Ombudsman Office from the state budget, reducing its dependency on
direct approval of the Ministry of Finance and thus enhancingts financial and
operational autonomy (interviews 43, 45, 46, 48). Therefore, budget approval
is set up as a two-step process, beginning with a discussion with government
and a vote in Parliament in which the NHRI leadership is allowed to participate. Although the institution's autonomy from government in allocating
funding has increased, this legal amendment does not result in sufficient enforcement safeguards. It does not grant the Ombudsman Office full financial
independence through a dedicated budget line in the state budget and further
curbing of government interference in the decision-making process. In effect,
research interviews have shown that formally, the financial independence of
the institution is indeed greater because of these changes to the mandate. But
they have also highlighted the importance of informal relations between politicians in office and the NHRI's leadership in the negotiation and approval of
the institutional budget (interviews 42, 47, 48, 50).

The impact of the networks of peer institutions on the strength of the
Macedonian Ombudsman Office indicated a degree of norm learning and
willingness to formally comply with the rules of the community of peer bodies. Soon after these institutional reforms, the Macedonian Ombudsman

Office sought recognition from its peer NHRIs and applied for accreditation for its ombudsman in 2011, receiving B-status (Subcommittee on Accreditation 2011). At the time, the Subcommittee on Accreditation expressed concerns regarding the legislative framework of the NHRI and the guarantees for independence from government intervention. The peer review process of accreditation identified the lack of full financial independence as well as the insufficiently transparent appointment and dismissal processes for institutional leadership as real risks to institutional independence. Moreover, the Ombudsman Office did not have a human rights mandate broad enough to ensure sufficient promotional powers, and did not encourage direct engagement with civil society and the international human rights community (Subcommittee on Accreditation 2011). To respond to these recommendations, Parliament passed a new law in September 2016 proposing a number of amendments to the institutional mandate (Law on the Ombudsman 2016). These changes sought to further align the institution with the Paris Principles and Optional Protocol on the Convention against Torture, implementing the Subcommittee on Accreditation's suggestions included in the accreditation report, the recommendations of the Senior Experts' Group of Systemic Rule of Law Issues (the Priebe Report) and the European Commission's Urgent Priority Reforms for the Republic of Macedonia.

The increase in formal strength is likely due to limited internalization of human rights norms. The broader remit enhanced the Ombudsman Office's formal strength as a NHRI, but insufficient funding and staff were allocated to these new responsibilities (interviews 42, 46, 48). The renewed institutional mandate includes also promotional powers in the field of human rights, including the conduct of research, investigations, educational programs, and cooperation with civil society, international organizations, and academia. As national preventive mechanism, NHRI staff can carry out inspections and visits in places of detention without prior approval, and can issue reports and monitor the implementation of its recommendations. Importantly, the National Preventive Mechanism has a special separate budget line in the NHRI's budget. The institution can participate in court proceedings and act as amicus curiae. To enhance the procedures of appointment for NHRI's leadership, legislative changes have made provisions for pluralism of representation and more transparency in the application process. The government is now obligated to consider the NHRI's recommendations, to discuss them in open sessions, and to respond to them every six months (National Preventive Mechanism in the Republic of North Macedonia 2019).

Interviews with civil society representatives in the country provide evidence that normative learning is incomplete and that acculturation might be at work. Members of civil society organizations active in the field of human rights in North Macedonia expressed concern about the inconsistency between, on the one hand, the institutional efforts to enhance formal powers and gain more international visibility and, on the other hand, the relatively limited programs and activities implementing those powers (interviews 44, 45, 46, 50). This is reflected also in the predominant activities of the North Macedonian NHRI. Although the scope of the institution's work has increased with each expansion of mandate, the NHRI's main activity has remained that of complaint handling. The number of complaints has increased every year, from 3,022 in 2008 to 4,346 in 2012 and 4,403 in 2015. In 2015, the largest number of complaints (1,939, or 44.04 percent) concerned rights violations by public services and institutions, while 1,635 (37.13 percent) concerned violations of rights by the central authority, and the remainder of cases dealt with breaches by local authorities and legal entities (Republic of Macedonia Ombudsman 2015). Some commentators attributed the increase in the institution's strength as being partly due to the institutional leader's personal pursuit of more power and credibility among public bodies in Skopje. The lack of sufficient activity to carry out mandated duties has been attributed to a degree of institutional inertia, the lack of human and financial resources, and the lack of strategic leadership (interviews 44, 45, 49, 50). The ombudsman's long tenure (usually eight years, with the possibility for extension and reappointment) and the post's desirability in the North Macedonian context appear to favor a certain unwillingness to broaden the scope of work, and make a change in strategic planning or in the institution's direction less likely.

THE LIMITS OF INSTITUTIONAL EFFECTIVENESS

Despite the increase in de jure strength of the North Macedonian Ombudsman Office over the years, institutional effectiveness has remained relatively low. Some civil society representatives working in the field of human rights across North Macedonia perceived the Ombudsman Office as an institution greatly concerned with its legal status and formal powers, but much less interested in improving effectiveness (interviews 42, 43, 44, 45, 46, 47, 50). Most changes to the mandate of the NHRI were assessed as not having had much of an impact on the ground. One such example is a legal amendment in 2003 that provided for the decentralization of the institution and the creation of ten deputy commissioners across six new regional offices and the main office in Skopje (Constitution of the Republic of Macedonia 2003). This change resulted from the intention to grow the local impact of the institution's work. But research interviews have showed that this amendment, like most changes to the NHRI's mandate, has not made the institution more effective (interviews 42, 43, 44, 45, 46, 47, 50).

Four main factors can explain this lack of effectiveness: a shortage of funding and staff, a lack of transparency and independence from government in the appointment of institutional leadership, a problematic relationship with government, and an inconsistent and challenging relationship with civil organizations active in the field of human rights. First, structural problems, such as limited funding and insufficient staff, have been chronic institutional deterrents to successful operation. Over the years, the Ombudsman Office has continued its activity largely thanks to international support. In fact, it would have probably discontinued its activity about one decade after its founding law was passed, had it not been for the financial and capacity-building support it received from several international organizations working in the country, like the UN Development Program and the Organization for Security and Cooperation in Europe, and international NGOs like the Helsinki Committee and Amnesty International (interviews 44, 46, 47, 48, 49). The lack of institutional capacity continues to be the most important limiting factor of the NHRI's plans to increase effectiveness and impact in the future. Research interviews revealed that the limited capacity of the office and the small number of staff in full-time employment make the North Macedonian human rights institution a less likely participant in twinning projects organized and funded by the European Union to stimulate institutional development in states that have membership candidate status, as those projects tend to be resource-intensive (interviews 42, 48, 49).

Second, as is the case with other NHRIs, the role of leadership is key to determining an organization's effectiveness and its capacity to make an impact domestically and internationally. As a public institution, the Ombudsman Office enjoys unique public status in North Macedonia: in existence since the formation of the independent state, it is one of its most enduring institutions, intended to advance the transition toward liberal democracy. The institutional leader, the ombudsman, usually enjoys high public recognition, being at the helm of the sole institution to which citizens can turn for complaints (interviews 42, 44, 45, 48). The longevity of the appointment makes the ombudsman a long-standing public figure inevitably associated with the public image of the institution itself. Nevertheless, the two ombudsmen the institution has had during its nearly three decades of existence have not succeeded in making the institution more effective, and in fact have jeopardized its legitimacy as an independent body due to their political affiliations (interviews 42, 44, 45, 48, 49). The two ombudsmen who have led the institution so far, Branko Naumoski and Ixhet Memeti, served as Constitutional Court judges prior to their appointment and were well-respected public figures. However, their experience working in the Ministry of Justice and the close ties they have maintained with government have proven to be impediments to the institution's independence and its capacity to hold governments to account. According to members of the civil society involved in domestic human rights work, the North Macedonian public has valid reasons to distrust the Ombudsman Office, particularly due to its lack of autonomy from government (interviews 43, 44, 45, 46, 47, 48, 49). Furthermore, the leadership's lack of specialized expertise in human rights or equality issues, as in the case of Branko Naumoski, is another reason for the public's distrust of the NHRI and its capacity to work effectively.

Political interference in the appointment process and a general lack of transparency in the selection of institutional leadership have remained impediments to institutional effectiveness to this day. Ixhet Memeti has served as ombudsman continuously since 2004, and the two appointment processes leading to his tenure of two terms were considered broadly contentious (interviews 42, 43, 44, 45, 46, 48, 49, 50). Some voices critiquing his first nomination in 2004 see his Albanian ethnicity as having been important at a time when the implementation of ethnic nondiscrimination policies in the labor force was perceived as mechanical and not the result of thorough due process incorporating ethnic diversity among its selection criteria, or an accurate reflection of ethnic diversity in Macedonian society (interviews 44, 45). In addition, the transparency of Memeti's reappointment in 2012 is also contested as it took place on 24 December 2012, a day when violent disagreements in Parliament over the following year's budget resulted in security forces forcefully removing the members of the opposition Social-Democratic Alliance of Macedonia (SDSM). Hostile disputes in Parliament reverberated in the streets, where thousands of pro- and antigovernment protesters clashed in the streets of Skopje (Casule 2012). Despite only half of the members of Parliament being present on the day of the reappointment, and despite members of the opposition and the media being absent, Parliament voted for the budget the government proposed and, during that same session, also appointed Memeti to a second term. Members of the public and of NGOs criticized Memeti's behavior on the day as too passive and complacent about the governing party's undemocratic behavior, and accused him of pursuing his own professional interests to the detriment of a transparent appointment process and higher legitimacy for the Ombudsman Office (interviews 44, 45, 46, 48).

The third barrier to the effectiveness of the ombudsman is the difficulty of the long-standing relationship it has built with the North Macedonian government. Successive governments have allocated insufficient annual budgets to the NHRI and shown themselves unwilling to consider or implement its recommendations (interviews 42, 50). The government has generally been responsive to domestic and international recommendations to create and strengthen the NHRI "on paper." However, this formal endorsement has not been matched by the financial support it needs to carry out its increased responsibilities. On occasion, the government has also decreased the institution's capacity by imposing successive rounds of budget cuts. For instance, in 2016 the budget of the Ombudsman Office amounted to 74,755,000 Macedonian denar (73,250,000 denar for the Office of the Ombudsman and 1,505,000 denar for the national preventive mechanism). The bulk of the budget (65.5 percent) covered salaries and social allowances, while 17.6 percent was earmarked for contractual services, and 17 percent for other costs and expenses (Human Rights NGOs in Macedonia 2016). A similar breakdown of the budget and the line on salaries and social allowances was noted in the 2015 budget, and in 2017 the government cut the salaries further. Research interviews confirm that in the two decades of its existence, the Ombudsman Office has been able to continue its activity largely because of the international obligations the state undertook as part of its commitment to pursue national independence and the transition to democracy (interviews 42, 47, 49, 50). Over the years, the institution has remained almost entirely dependent on financial support from the international community. The UN Development Program, the Organization for Economic Co-operation and Development, and the Council of Europe mission offered financial assistance and capacity-building support, and this assistance only grew when the Ombudsman Office acquired the new mandate of National Preventive Mechanism.

The fourth main factor limiting the institutional effectiveness of the North Macedonian human rights institution is the challenging relationship that the NHRI has fostered with civil society. According to several members of civil society organizations in North Macedonia, the Ombudsman Office has a mixed record of involvement with civil society organizations and international institutions (interviews 44, 45, 46, 48, 49). The most common type of co-operation with NGOs has been on an ad-hoc basis and within the framework of internationally funded projects targeting rights violations in different communities around the country. For the first time in its existence, in 2017 the Ombudsman Office signed a formal agreement with civil society organizations in the form of memorandum of understanding involving ten NGOs, to streamline the efforts to coordinate a response to the current refugee and migrant crisis in Europe (interviews 44, 45).

Overall, representatives of civil society organizations working in the field of human rights promotion and protection in North Macedonia perceive the ombudsman body as too weak an institution to make a real impact on society (interviews 44, 45, 47, 48, 49). One example of its limited domestic impact is the Ombudsman Office's choice to refrain from speaking up against the semi-authoritarian government of Nikola Gruevski, and to support a shared plan of action in partnership with civil society organizations working in the country. The elections that took place on 11 December 2016, with the support of the European Union and following a wave of antigovernment mass protests, offered an opportunity for all independent institutions to speak in favor of democracy and human rights. In this situation, the ombudsman body remained largely silent and limited its contribution to the public debates to a few brief official press releases (interviews 44, 45, 48).

The international impact of the North Macedonian Ombudsman Office has been very limited, and has mostly focused on establishing partnerships with peer institutions in the Mediterranean region. The Association of Mediterranean Ombudsmen facilitated the establishment of cross-border partnerships in the region. In addition, the Ombudsman Office has worked in collaboration with peer bodies in neighboring Balkan states to respond to shared challenges and rights violations. One such successful collaboration is the coordinated response to the problems in refugee camps outside the European Union's borders (interviews 42, 44, 45). The Macedonian NHRI worked in partnership with the Serbian and Croatian ombudsmen as well as other institutions in the Balkans to create a coordinated system of monitoring rights violations in communities of newly arrived refugees in the shared border area (Republic of Macedonia Ombudsman 2017).

Once the dispute over the country's name was resolved in the Prespa Agreement, the European Union was more open to considering the Balkan country's application for accession. In March 2020 it approved the application and began official formal talks with North Macedonia (and Albania). Against this background, we can safely expect that democratic conditionality in preparation for accession will include the defense of human rights and, by extension, also the Ombudsman Office of the Republic of North Macedonia as the country's national human rights institution. As with all Central and Eastern European states, the pre-accession period is likely to bring with it institutional development and overall growth, resulting also in additional resources for the NHRI. Whether the North Macedonian human rights institution will make the most of these resources and seek to improve conditions on the ground remains to be seen. What is certain, however, is that the need for continued work on human rights promotion and protection will remain, not least because the long-term effects of ethnic and religious conflict are still visible in North Macedonian society. Importantly, the so-called European refugee crisis affected North Macedonia greatly, and is likely to continue to do so, given the European Union's border control strategy and refugee management policies. Without a doubt, the need will remain for a strong and effective NHRI to defend human rights in the region, create accountability systems, and ensure that the protection of individuals from rights violations will remain.

Conclusion

National human rights institutions in Central and Eastern Europe have risen out of dramatic regulatory moments linked to the process of state transformation, transitions to liberal democracy, and "membership rites" (Cardenas 2014) in conjunction with strategies for accession to the European Union. In the subregion, human rights ombudsmen have generally increased their formal strength over time. They have broadened their mandates to include a wider spectrum of rights and, in some cases, to encompass promotion powers. Whether in response to domestic pressure to move away from autocracy and transition into becoming liberal democratic states, or as a reaction to international pressure to implement regional and international human rights treaties and harmonize policy in light of accession negotiations for EU membership, governments in the region have generally supported the establishment and continued strengthening of their human rights ombudsmen.

Overall, it is fair to say that for NHRIs in the region higher levels of formal institutional strength, established through stronger institutional powers, have not resulted in increased institutional effectiveness in all countries. Although some institutions in the region, like the Polish NHRI, have consistently been regarded as some of the strongest and most effective in the world, other human rights bodies, like the North Macedonian NHRI, have not been equally successful in increasing their effectiveness. Even when human rights institutions are formally independent from government intervention, their existence is largely dependent on a good working relationship with government and parliament, characterized by willingness to cooperate and consider NHRI's decisions and recommendations. Ultimately, the very activity of NHRIs depends on the willingness of policymakers to honor their commitment to offer financial support and respect the functional autonomy of their human rights ombudsmen.

An important consideration for human rights ombudsmen in the region, and one of the most consequential institutional design choices for the durability of NHRIs around the world, is the key role that leadership plays in determining an institution's ability to weather political changes and threats to its operations. Institutional leaders who are widely recognized by the population, civil society, and the political class as experts in human rights promotion and protection and as influential public figures are the most important predictor of the increased strength and effectiveness of NHRIs. The ability to foster respect and work collaboratively with policymakers is as important as the capacity to create a positive public image of the NHRI as an independent and impartial body that citizens can trust and turn to when their rights have been violated.

Arguably the most significant challenge that NHRIs in Central and Eastern Europe have faced since their establishment in the early 1990s is the current process of democratic backsliding and liberal institutional erosion. States that were considered democratic frontrunners during the transition period have since elected far-right majority parties with illiberal political agendas. Their Euroskepticism and their strongly critical stance toward liberal democracy contribute to a broader narrowing of the space for human rights. Solid legal and constitutional designs and strong formal powers safeguard NHRIs from immediate peril. Nevertheless, human rights bodies today face the risk of political interference by parties that intend to weaken them and diminish their effectiveness. Their sustainable success and continued growth are dependent on their ability to understand their domestic context and respond appropriately to the most pressing needs of their population. The ability of NHRIs to adapt to national realities dominated by income inequality and dissatisfaction with liberal democracy while counteracting domestic and international pressures will be the true measure of their survival and future success.

3

The Strength and Effectiveness of
National Human Rights Institutions
in Western Europe

In the aftermath of World War II, governments in Western Europe were caught between the commitment to advance international human rights, the need to manage postcolonial legacies, and an interest in harmonizing national human rights architectures across borders aligning with international and regional human rights laws, like the Universal Declaration of Human Rights adopted by the UN General Assembly in 1948, and the European Convention on Human Rights formally drafted by the Council of Europe in Strasbourg during the summer of 1949. Often, the establishment of and continued support for national human rights institutions represented an attempt to respond to these international commitments that best suit the national contexts in which they were created. States' choices with respect to institutional models and the formal strength of their national human rights bodies are direct reflections of their effort to abide by international requirements and recommendations while seeking to shape institutions for which they can find the most support from government and the legislative.

Western Europe is home to different institutional models. In some Western European states, the creation of the first rights-focused institutions is tied to their colonial past. These institutions were initially founded because of state commitments to tackle questions of racial discrimination and respond appropriately to public opposition to immigration from former colonies. With the global development of NHRIs after the mid-1990s, the mandates of some of these bodies grew to also include the promotion and protection of human rights. Belgium, Ireland, and the United Kingdom (the Equality and Human Rights Commission) offer prominent examples of commissions with mixed equality and human rights activity. As case studies below will show, institutional growth has not been a smooth process, and the inclusion of human rights in institutional mandates has often been met with resistance. This resistance, motivated by a more contentious view of human rights in certain national contexts, was complemented by opposition to adopting liberal dem-ocratic institutions simply because they have been advanced by international organizations like the United Nations and the European Union.

During the 1970s, two new institutional models appeared—the hybrid om-budsman in the Iberian Peninsula, and the commission model in the Com-monwealth countries. The latter began as antiracism government bodies and were granted a dedicated human rights mandate later. The first institutions with a mixed mandate were established in Southern Europe in the 1970s—the Provedor de Justiça in Portugal and the Defensor del Pueblo in Spain. As discussed earlier, hybrid ombudsmen are also common in Eastern Europe, where, years after the fall of communism, existing classical ombudsmen ex-perienced the expansion of their mandate to encompass human rights duties.

In addition, countries that had chosen to establish classical ombudsmen without dedicated human rights mandates often addressed the institutional gap in the field of human rights protection by having their ombudsmen carry out de facto human rights protection work, usually by handling individual complaints of rights violations. The institutional model of the human rights ombudsman is a design innovation that dates to the "third wave" of demo-cratic transitions (See Huntington, *The Third Wave*, 1991). For instance, that has been the case with the Swedish Equality Ombudsman, whose formal man-date is to handle complaints on different discrimination grounds, until recent talks of establishing a dedicated NHRI. In some cases, classical ombudsmen operating in countries in which no separate human rights bodies have been established have had their mandates expanded to formalize their human rights responsibilities.

Germany, Denmark, and as of 1 January 2022 also Sweden have govern-ment advisory institutes that carry out human rights work, and often also have an international agenda to promote human rights internationally, primarily in Eastern Europe and the Global South. Despite lacking complaint-handling powers, the Danish and German institutions have nevertheless been very ac-tive in leading the global and regional networks of NHRIs, and influential in shaping the strategic direction of development for fellow NHRIs, since early 1990s. Europe is also home to an institutional model that has been influential and unique on the global stage: the Northern Ireland Human Rights Com-mission and the Scottish Human Rights Commission. These human rights institutions have mandates that are more limited in scope (subnational) and hold the status of public bodies in the United Kingdom. Nevertheless, their international impact has been significant, perhaps surprisingly so. Despite being smaller and having subnational mandates, they have held leader-ship positions in regional and global networks of peer institutions and have contributed to shaping their policy agendas. The case studies included below will discuss in greater detail the design and effectiveness of many of the different institutional models introduced here, addressing also the domestic and international determinants of their formal strength, and their effectiveness or lack thereof.

The Relative Weakness of National Human Rights Institutions in Western Europe

The study of NHRIs' formal strength in Western Europe presents us with a unique puzzle. Generally, all NHRIs in Europe and around the world have increased their formal strength over the years. Whether by adopting human rights mandates or by expanding the range of rights within their remit, they have seen their durability and enforcement powers enhanced. Without a doubt, this increase in institutional strength is closely linked to network-based norm learning and socialization processes coordinated by peer institutions under the framework of the United Nations, the Council of Europe, and the European Union.

Nevertheless, many states in the European subregion have NHRIs with weaker durability and enforcement powers than do the newly democratized states in Eastern and Central Europe, despite Western Europe's long-standing history of liberal democracy and institutionalized rights protection. There are several possible explanations for this. In some states, the existence of multiple institutions with overlapping responsibilities relating to human rights has proven a barrier for the consolidation of a single national body with integrated powers and a strong national mandate to support human rights promotion and protection. This is the case in Denmark, where the Danish Institute for Human Rights is a large and very active promotional body that works in parallel with the independent complaint-handling Parliamentary Ombudsman and a specialized Board of Equal Treatment. Another case is the United Kingdom, where in the late 1990s existing equality bodies were merged and granted additional human rights duties, creating a single commission with a significant budget and large staff but with very limited initial expertise in human rights (Lacatus 2018).

Another determining factor for the weaker designs in Western Europe is the primacy of equality and diversity institutions in the subregion, due to the less politically contested nature of these rights (for instance, equal pay or equal rights for minorities). The early creation of equality and antidiscrimination bodies in the subregion is undoubtedly also related to nondiscrimination norms being front and center on the EU policy agenda (European Commission 2019b). The early advancement of diversity and equality as core values of the EU was a direct reflection of the rights-based values underpinning the liberal democratic project that states in Western Europe have advanced since the end of World War II. Over the years, the EU issued five nondiscrimination directives regulating policy with respect to fourteen different grounds of discrimination across member states. To implement these directives, the EU has required all member states to set up dedicated formal institutions to monitor compliance and implementation. Often, states that did not already have dedicated bodies charged with tackling racial or gender-based discrimination in employment created antidiscrimination bodies as government agencies existing within different public ministries (ministries of labor or of justice were common hosts). Some countries had established legal and institutional frameworks for the protection of some types of discrimination—usually on racial or gender grounds—long before the creation of the Charter of Fundamental Rights of the European Union in 2000 and the consolidation of the legal antidiscrimination framework of European Union Directives in the following decade. For instance, the United Kingdom passed its Race Relations Act in 1976 and created a specialized commission in the same year. The United Kingdom had also its Equal Opportunities Commission, which it established in 1975, and granted statutory powers to enforce the Sex Discrimination Act of 1975, the Equal Pay Act of 1970, and other extant gender equality legislation. These commissions formed the formal foundation for the establishment of the Equality and Human Rights Commission in 2007. The case study dedicated to the strength and effectiveness of the NHRIs in the UK will analyze these developments in more detail.

The increased popularity of NHRIs in the 1990s prompted states to join their peers and establish their own dedicated human rights promotional and protection bodies. A common solution at the time for governments in several states in Western Europe was to expand the mandate of existing equality and diversity institutions, granting them new human rights duties. The most prevalent institutional model of mixed human rights and diversity bodies was the human rights commission. When human rights duties were added to their mandates, most equality bodies had existed as government agencies. Their status as public institutions continued even after the mandate expansion, and most human rights commissions are still regarded as such. Some of them have solely human rights promotional powers, and play advisory roles with government without the right to receive complaints or carry out independent investigations. Countries formerly part of the Commonwealth, such as the

United Kingdom and Ireland, and others, including Belgium and the Netherlands, chose to add a human rights mandate to existing institutions and thus to establish human rights commissions that hold the status of public bodies. Although such bodies can be effective in fulfilling mandated duties, their independence is curbed by their dependence on government to approve budgets, oversee leadership appointments, and authorize main institutional activities.

Another explanation for the domestic preferences for certain institutional models can be the colonial pasts of Western democracies. Although a postcolonial critique of human rights is beyond the scope of this book, it is important to acknowledge such a view as a possible interpretation for cultural and social attitudes reflected in the policy and institutional choices of governments in the subregion. In a postcolonial world, the question of human rights promotion and protection is more easily associated with a sense of responsibility toward the protection of "the other" (Agamben 1998). This non-European "other" can be a citizen of a former colony in the Global South. But she or he can also be an immigrant or refugee from one of the former colonies, or from one of the poorer states in Eastern Europe or outside Europe. The rights of these communities require protection, either through international development work or as social and cultural integration assistance when the people have moved to Europe and seek to adapt to life in Western European societies. Given that human rights are viewed as already institutionalized within the state (Cardenas 2014), governments in Western Europe are more likely to think of human rights protection as a necessity in the Global South and, within their own region, in Eastern Europe rather than in their own territories. From this point of view, NHRIs can perform an important duty in protecting and promoting the rights of communities in need of assistance.

The trajectory of institutional development and the balancing act of working with a mixed mandate of human rights and equality have had consequences for the institutions' effectiveness. As research interviews show (interviews 8, 6, 18, 20, 75, 78), the focus of institutional mandates on questions of nondiscrimination and the protection of the rights of "the other" has shaped the public perception of NHRIs. The case studies presented below discuss this development in different national contexts. In countries like Belgium (as in Poland, Hungary, and the Czech Republic), NHRIs are perceived as bodies that no longer protect the rights of all citizens, as they favor the protection of minorities and other communities living at the fringes of society. They are seen as promoting an agenda of inclusion focused on certain "chosen" communities, instead of representing the rights of everyone in the country.

While diversity and equality issues have remained high on national agendas due to the normative priorities defined by the European Union, human

rights have sometimes been relegated to the field of international development practice. In recent years, some states have integrated human rights in
their efforts to assist other countries in curbing human rights violations as
part of their transition to democracy. By extension, institutional structures
dedicated to the domestic protection of human rights have been considered
redundant. Sweden and Denmark are cases in point. The Danish Institute
for Human Rights has an institutional department dedicated to international
development projects in the field of human rights in the Global South. In that
respect, the NHRI becomes a unique vehicle for public efforts to advance liberal democracy abroad. In its turn, Sweden has an ombudsman charged with
issues of equality between men and women, but until 2022 it had no formal
body with a human rights mandate. In response to a 2015 recommendation
by the UN Human Rights Council (Raoul Wallenberg Institute 2017), Sweden
drafted and passed a national human rights strategy, which highlights the
need to establish a NHRI (Minister for Culture and Democracy 2017). The
new Human Rights Institute was created by law in the summer of 2021 and
began its operations in January 2022. As is discussed in more detail below,
institutional establishment is largely also the Swedish government's response
to efforts by the United Nations to counteract the recent rise of the illiberal
far right across the region, and to regenerate in the population an awareness of the importance of safeguarding human rights and not taking them
for granted.

In the past two decades, the extent of activism in domestic human rights
promotion and protection has fallen in old democratic states. This is surprising, as without exception across the region, civil society organizations were
the main drivers of institutional reform in the 1990s and early 2000s, lobbying governments to establish their own independent bodies of human rights
promotion and protection. Since then, the number of specialized human
rights nonprofit organizations with domestic mandates in Western Europe
has decreased. For instance, the few existing civil society organizations in the
Nordic countries carrying out human rights work focus on projects aimed at
countries in the Global South. The lack of strong civil society voices advocating for NHRIs results in weaker domestic pressure on governments to continue supporting and strengthening independent accountability bodies that
monitor human rights violations. That work is now left more to international
actors (such as the European Union and the United Nations), to members of
government and parliament who might be willing to take on human rights
platforms as part of their policy agendas, and to the NHRIs themselves.

Today, the weaker institutional strength of NHRIs is symptomatic of a
broader societal and political disenchantment with human rights (Bell 2003a;

Kjaerum 2003) and of a pushback against multilateralism and liberal democracy. The rise of far-right parties and of populist nationalism grounded in anti-immigrant sentiment creates an environment essentially hostile to human rights. Budget cuts in the public sector as a result of post-recession austerity measures have not been reversed since, and have sometimes been followed by further cuts. In countries that treat NHRIs as public bodies, such as the United Kingdom, these budget cuts have also affected human rights institutions. At the same time, international organizations like the United Nations and the European Union have sought to counteract these developments by continuing the liberal democratic agenda and by offering support for states to continue establishing and supporting NHRIs. One outcome of such efforts is Sweden's current establishment of a NHRIs with a promotional mandate, to complement the complaint-handling activities of the existing system of equality ombudsmen. These competing social and political forces have a direct impact on the capacity of institutions to make a difference in improving human rights in their societies. The following section discusses some of the broader trends in institutional effectiveness in the realm of domestic human rights promotion and protection, and is followed by a more in-depth discussion of institutional cases.

Institutional Effectiveness in Established European Liberal Democracies

A few unifying characteristics stand out in the institutional effectiveness and impact of NHRIs across Western European states. First, strong institutional leaders have been and continue to be instrumental. As the case studies below will illustrate, some institutional figures from Western European bodies have maintained long-term profiles in shaping the international human rights regime and significantly advocating for the advancement of NHRIs. Thus, it is fair to say that one area in which Western European NHRIs have made the most significant impact has been their international leadership in the community of peers.

Not all NHRIs in established democracies are founders and long-standing leaders of the Global Association of National Human Rights Institutions and the European Network of National Human Rights Institutions. Since the formulation of the Paris Principles and the start of the accreditation system, European human rights bodies have been slow to integrate into networks of peer institutions. Nevertheless, a number of NHRIs, like the Scottish Human Rights Commission and the Danish Human Rights Commission, were some of the main national bodies driving the establishment of the European

Network of National Human Rights Institutions, working with the European Union and the Office of the High Commissioner for Human Rights to grant a start-up project to initiate the regional network (ENNHRI 2014a). Through funded projects and the coordination of themed working groups, a few NHRIs have facilitated and contributed to the consolidation of the system of peer networking in Europe as well as globally. By extension, they are actively contributing to the system of support that peer networks make available to NHRIs that seek to strengthen their designs and increase their effectiveness.

Second, compared to peer bodies in Eastern and Central Europe, NHRIs in Western Europe have generally enjoyed larger institutional budgets, even though these financial resources have not always been sufficient. This is not to say that funding has been consistently abundant. Just as in other parts of Europe, and indeed other regions of the world, domestic human rights bodies in Western Europe are dependent on the wavering agendas of changing governments. Financial constraints can often be compounded by electoral cycles and by fluctuations in political agendas and degrees of commitment to rights protection. Although national governments in the subregion have generally been more responsive to institutional needs for adequate financial and staff resources, NHRIs have experienced severe budget cuts, with arguably the most severe ones affecting several institutions after the 2008 economic crisis. This is particularly problematic when human rights institutions lack independence from the executive in the allocation and management of their finances. It makes NHRIs in Western Europe just as vulnerable to changes in government priorities as any other public bodies.

As is discussed in more detail below, the three human rights commissions in the United Kingdom offer good examples. As public bodies, they have suffered significant reductions in financial resources because of government-wide budget cuts. The Northern Ireland Human Rights Commission saw a first budget reduction of 25 percent from 2010 until 2013. It lost two of its four management posts in 2011, and saw its budget cut 11 to 15 percent in 201516 (Northern Ireland Assembly 2014). The relatively small Scottish Commission appears to be the one such body faring better, as it has been able to maintain most of its staff. The Equality and Human Rights Commission began its activity with a large budget that combined those of several commissions that merged. Subsequent budget cuts, including a recent one in 2017, have seen its staff and capacity reduced considerably. For example, in 2016, GANHRI expressed concern at the ways in which cuts equivalent to 70 percent of the Equality and Human Rights Commission's 2010 budget would threaten the effectiveness and independence of the NHRI (Doward 2016).

One of the greatest structural factors limiting the effectiveness of NHRIs in Western Europe is the management of multiple areas of rights promotion and protection included in their remit. Institutions with mixed remits, of which there are several in the region, require adequate financial resources and trained staff for multiple areas of specialization, as well as appropriate management of these resources to make sure that human rights work is carried out effectively. This is a particularly important challenge for equality institutions whose mandates were expanded to also include certain human rights duties. An example of a highly effective NHRI with a mixed mandate and a strong design is the Finnish National Human Rights Institution. Established in 2014 as an independent body under the auspices of the Parliamentary Ombudsman, it consists of the Human Rights Center and the Human Rights Delegation and carries out advising, monitoring, and human rights promotion work. The center is a body of research, education, and promotion of human rights, and the delegation, which is part of the center, consists of representatives of a wide range of civil society actors actively involved in human rights activities. The Ombudsman has the power to handle individual complaints. The integration of the three bodies has made possible the establishment of an effective institution with both promotional and protection powers.

When prompted to create specialized domestic bodies to promote and protect human rights, most governments in Western Europe opted for overall weaker formal institutional designs than those of their counterparts in Eastern Europe. Nevertheless, NHRIs have generally well-developed portfolios of activity, and have successfully carried out the main duties specified in their mandates. Even so, the challenge of assessing their impact on human rights outcomes in their own countries remains significant. Countries in this part of Europe have long-standing traditions of liberal democracy, with generally strong public institutions. Nevertheless, it is fair to say that governments' commitments to liberal values, such as rights protection, have not been consistent and have not always resulted in strong support for NHRIs. This can be an indication that governments are not necessarily more inclined to embrace the existence of independent bodies that can hold them accountable in established democracies. In fact, some Western European states have established new human rights bodies to "tick bureaucratic boxes" for membership in the European Union or in response to recommendations from the United Nations Periodic Review. Even when created as a result of international pressure, these institutions have generally consolidated their positions in the domestic institutional architecture and have come to be recognized for their expertise. Case studies of six NHRIs operating in four Western European countries offer fine-grained insights into the institutional strength and effectiveness of specialized human rights bodies in the subregion.

Case Selection

The remainder of this chapter will present six cases of NHRIs operating in four Western European countries: the Equality and Human Rights Commission of the United Kingdom, the Northern Ireland Human Rights Commission, and the Scottish Human Rights Commission; The Belgian Center for Equal Opportunities; the Danish Institute for Human Rights; and in Sweden, the Equality Ombudsman and the new NHRI currently under development. These institutions illustrate the subregional dynamics of institutional strength and effectiveness across old democracies in Europe. As was the case with the four institutions in Central and Eastern Europe, there NHRIs have generally seen their formal strength increase over time. At the same time, their strength has not increased as dramatically in the past three decades as that of their counterparts to the east.

In some cases, this development has taken the form of a major institutional transformation through a merger of existing bodies and an additional human rights mandate. This has happened in the case of the Equality and Human Rights Commission in the United Kingdom and, to a lesser extent, Sweden's Equality Ombudsman, whose mandate does not include explicit human rights protection duties but who handles cases of rights violations. In other cases, institutions have strong human rights promotional mandates from the very start and have continued to perform their remit effectively, but are coming under pressure to demonstrate to their peers that their work does make a difference when they lack human rights protection powers. This has been the case in Denmark, where the Danish Institute for Human Rights has had a strong human rights promotional mandate since its inception as a human rights institution in the early 1990s. Operating in a domestic environment where complaint-handling work in the realm of rights protection is handled by a number of existing ombudsmen, the Danish Institute has focused on promotional and advisory work as well as a number of international development projects, strengthening its activity in the area of human rights promotion. This is also the pathway that the Swedish authorities are likely to take when they develop their own national institution with a dedicated mandate of human rights promotion and protection. Still, there are some institutions with equality and diversity mandates that carry out human rights-related work but do not have a dedicated human rights mandate. This is the case of the Belgian Center for Equal Opportunities and to some extent also Sweden's Equality Ombudsman.

These cases illustrate variation in the extent to which the main factors identified in the theoretical framework might explain changes over time in institutional strength, such as the role of membership in the global peer network of NHRIs and its accreditation process, as well as the significance of national political and social contexts in shaping institutional strength and effectiveness. Moreover, these case analyses draw from interview data to offer a more in-depth analysis of institutional effectiveness and impact. They offer a closer look at the domestic and international drivers for the success and failure of NHRIs in the subregion. Although their access to financial and staff resources has been generally less limited than that of their Eastern European peer institutions, they have some opposition in national contexts where human rights agendas are considered more contentious, and have enjoyed different degrees of government support over the years. Importantly, NHRIs in Western Europe have been influential in creating and shaping the development of the global and regional networks of peer bodies. Arguably, some of them at times may have made a more notable impact internationally than domestically. This analysis helps to illustrate their contributions to human rights in their own countries as well as internationally.

National Human Rights Institutions Based in the United Kingdom

THE INSTITUTIONAL ARCHITECTURE OF HUMAN RIGHTS IN THE UNITED KINGDOM

In the United Kingdom, the institutional architecture of human rights promotion and protection is arguably more complex than in other countries in the region. This is largely due to the unique geopolitical reality of the devolution of legislative and executive power, and the division of policymaking autonomy across the state. In the realm of human rights promotion and protection, the division of responsibility is negotiated between London and Edinburgh, and between London and Belfast. These policymaking dynamics have reverberated in the strength and effectiveness of the three national human rights institutions operating in the United Kingdom. The scope of their mandates, their institutional reporting system, and their areas of priority are determined by the priorities of central government and, arguably to a higher extent, by policymakers in Holyrood or Stormont. The challenge of tracing the effects of these dynamics is amplified when studying the determinants of institutional effectiveness and impact. Resource management is a two-step process, depending on Westminster's approval and disbursement of budgets for devolved administrations, and on the devolved parliaments and governments allocating adequate funds to their NHRIs. To be effective, the three NHRIs have developed a network of formal and informal relationships that allow them to manage overlapping areas and, when needed, to work collaboratively.

By the end of the 1990s, Great Britain had ratified key regional human rights treaties. The establishment of the NHRI in Northern Ireland was part of the Tony Blair cabinet's efforts to respond to the calls for aligning domestic law with Council of Europe Law, as indicated in the commitment to the implementation of human rights through the Human Rights Act of 1998. This act incorporates the rights set out in the European Convention on Human Rights into domestic British law. The system of rights protection in the United Kingdom has a separate and distinct "devolution dimension," which imposes some constraints on the freedom of the central government to control human rights implementation alone, as devolved legislatures and executives in Northern Ireland and Scotland are also individually required to comply with the European Convention by virtue of specific provisions set out in the devolution statutes.[1] While their authority is more restricted, the Scottish and Northern Irish parliaments can also take measures to give further effect to the United Kingdom's international human rights obligations when acting within the scope of their powers, which included but are not confined to those that arise under the European Convention.

The statutory delegation of powers from the central government to subnational executives and legislatures inside the United Kingdom is a form of administrative decentralization with significant implications for policymaking in the field of human rights, and with an impact on the institutional architecture of human rights implementation. Inside the United Kingdom, NHRIs operate in a unique network-based system made up of two human rights commissions with subnational mandates in Northern Ireland and Scotland, and the Equality and Human Rights Commission, whose mandate covers England and Scotland but not Northern Ireland. It is important to note, however, that all three commissions are considered public bodies, held accountable by the Ministry of Justice for their activity and for their finances.

In 1999, the Blair executive took decisive steps to integrate regional human rights law into British law, implement the European Convention of Human Rights domestically, and make it easier for British citizens to contest

---

1. Sections 6(2)(c) and 24(1)(a) of the Northern Ireland Act 1998; sections 29(2)(d) and 57(2) of the Scotland Act 1998.

human rights violations directly through national law. The same efforts led to
the establishment of the first NHRI on British territory, the Northern Ireland
Human Rights Commission. Embedded in the peace agreement intended
to put an end to the conflict in Northern Ireland, this decision indicated a
commitment on the part of the UK government to a long-standing peace,
cooperative diplomatic relations with the Republic of Ireland with respect to
Northern Ireland, and the implementation of international human rights law
with the goal of ensuring a sustainable peace (Northern Ireland Act 1998).
In this context, the establishment of the NHRI is seen as a viable solution
to monitoring peace implementation, reducing human rights violations, and
providing a framework for transitional justice in a postconflict context (Bell
2003a).

The UK-wide Equality and Human Rights Commission started its activity
in 2007 and resulted from the merger of three existing equality commissions:
the Commission for Racial Equality, the Disability Rights Commission, and
the Equal Opportunities Commission. Staff members at these three commissions had no prior expertise in human rights. The newly formed UK-wide
commission had a mixed equality and human rights mandate. To define its
new priorities of activity, the commissioners reached out to human rights
organizations around the country and conducted consultations on the types
of human rights-focused issues that could be the object of the new commission's future activities. Unlike its Northern Irish equivalent body, which has
sole power over the protection and promotion of human rights in Northern
Ireland, the Scottish Human Rights Commission shares a human rights mandate in Scotland with the Equality and Human Rights Commission based in
Glasgow.

Two framework agreements spell out the terms of the collaboration within
the domestic institutional network, seeking to regulate and facilitate the
working relationship among the Equality and Human Rights Commission,
the Northern Ireland Human Rights Commission, and the Scottish Human
Rights Commission. They define the main purpose of the network in terms
of managerial stewardship based on "close practical collaboration, exchange
of information and, as far as possible, agreement of common positions and
avoidance of conflict" (EHRC, 2010, p. 1). According to the memorandum
signed by the three commissions, each institution retains an autonomous
position inside the network, defined by individual mandates and in relation
to the other two commissions (EHRC 2010). The memorandum encourages
regular formal and informal contact between equivalent staff in the three
commissions in areas of policy work, legal services, and international cooperation. Whenever activities overlap, each commission is expected to alert

others and consider their opinions. The Equality and Human Rights Commission is the national intermediary, as the only NHRI with a country-wide mandate. The Equality and Human Rights Commission retains its powers across the whole of the United Kingdom when it comes to equality issues, while Northern Ireland Human Rights Commission has sole authority over human rights promotion and protection in Northern Ireland. Under the Equality Act (Equality Act 2006), the Equality and Human Rights Commission has the authority to take human rights action in relation to devolved matters that are within the legislative competence of the Scottish Parliament. Since the Scottish Commission began its activity, the Equality Commission will not pursue any human rights activity unless it has obtained the consent of its Scottish counterpart.

Staff members at all three commissions indicate that overall, the three institutions follow a cooperative working model (interviews 2, 5, 6, 7, 9, 10, 11, 13, 17, 21). The multilevel network aims to facilitate cross-institutional learning, organize regular meetings to share information and knowledge, to and consult on specific policy issues as well as shared project-based work. A current legal adviser at the Scottish Human Rights Commission gives the example of the interest that the Northern Ireland Human Rights Commission has shown in learning about the experience of drafting and implementing Scotland's National Action Plan for Human Rights. Whenever institutional leadership deems it appropriate, the three commissions establish joint arrangements to share work on policy areas and programs for which they share responsibility. Formal annual meetings facilitate regular communication among commissioners and senior staff. Over the years, the leaders in each commission have played a significant role in determining the intensity of the collaboration between institutions. In other words, the formal ties within the network have been strengthened or weakened by the informal ties established by the commissioners. This has proven to be of help when commissions have sought to work collaboratively and when individual commissions have sought to exercise their influence internationally.

The support for NHRIs has fluctuated over the years, often responding to political priorities at the time. When they were established, none of the three human rights commissions enjoyed full support from central or devolved governments, although they did receive a lot of support from civil society organizations. Government support was largely motivated by external pressures, such as the pressure to align national law with European human rights law and, in the case of Northern Ireland, the conditions tied to reaching a peace agreement. Although regional contexts can offer room for diversity of opinion informing the support for rights agendas, research interviews have shown that in a British context, human rights norms have historically tended to be perceived as contentious, unlike equality and diversity issues, which are considered more compatible with widely held national cultural values (interviews 4, 13, 16, 17, 78, 79, 80).

In recent history, the public rhetoric advanced by the Conservative Party has shown a party position hostile to the existing national human rights governance in the United Kingdom, enshrined in the Human Rights Act. One such moment was at the Conservative Party conference a few weeks prior to the Scottish independence referendum in 2014, when then Prime Minister David Cameron called for the repeal of the Human Rights Act, with the intention to create a British Bill of Rights (Conservative Party 2015). That prompted warnings from Scotland's First Minister Nicola Sturgeon that it was "inconceivable" that the Scottish Parliament would consent to attempts to amend the act, given that the principles enshrined in it were at the very center of the devolution settlement (MacNab 2015). The contested issue of a bill of rights for Northern Ireland is also a case in point. Under the terms of the Belfast (Good Friday) Agreement of 1998, the Northern Ireland Human Rights Commission was tasked with conducting a consultation on a bill of rights, but this bill never garnered sufficient political support in Westminster to become law. At the time of this writing, it is difficult to assess the long-term effects of Brexit and the impact it will have on the institutional architecture of rights promotion and protection in the United Kingdom. Given the devolved powers of Holyrood, the area of human rights promotion and protection is likely to be an avenue of further action, including on the international stage, which could set Scotland further apart from the rest of the United Kingdom. At the same time, the extent to which these efforts will be successful is hard to predict. In Northern Ireland, the suspension of the devolved parliament from 2017 to 2020 made the NHRI more closely dependent on centralized decision-making, and generally contingent on Westminster's interest, or lack thereof, in making human rights an important part of its agenda.

In 2016 the result of the national referendum in the United Kingdom set in motion the complex political process of the country leaving the European Union. In January 2021 the separation officially took place. Given the legislation changes that the Boris Johnson administration supported during the period of Brexit negotiations with the European Union, however, future changes to human rights legislation and the institutions safeguarding them appear ever more likely. In the first half of 2021 alone, Westminster proposed and voted on two pieces of legislation that curb existing citizens' rights. The proposed Police, Crime, Sentencing and Courts Act 2022 curbs nonviolent protest on the basis of a new noise "trigger" condition, impose conditions on one-person protests in England and Wales, and increase penalties for breaching the conditions placed on protests, in the name of the preservation of public order. The Committee on Human Rights found the bill leading to this act to be in breach of the rights to freedom of expression (Article 10) and freedom of association (Article 11) that are guaranteed by the Human Rights Act 1998, which incorporates the European Convention on Human Rights (Joint Committee on Human Rights 2021). A second law, the Nationality and Borders Act 2022 (originating in Bill 141 of 2021–22) proposes a two-tier protection system, which unfairly distinguishes between refugees depending on their mode of arrival in the UK and proposes measures to manage irregular migration and asylum processes that are contrary to established case law and international refugee law. In bill form, these act have been the subject of little public scrutiny. They are an indication of governments' efforts to further weaken the existing legislative and institutional frameworks for human rights promotion and protection. At this point it is impossible to predict how such changes might impact on the strength and effectiveness of the three human rights commissions in the United Kingdom. However, it is fair to expect that the work they conduct will not receive a great deal more support in the future and might even be affected negatively by future antiliberal institutional and legislative reforms.

The following sections will offer a more in-depth analysis of the strength of the three commissions working in the United Kingdom, and will discuss the determinants of their capacity to make an impact on human rights on the ground.

NORTHERN IRELAND HUMAN RIGHTS COMMISSION

Institutional Strength and Development:
A Strong Institution Born of a Peace Agreement

The Northern Ireland Human Rights Commission came into being as part of the Belfast Agreement, which was signed on 10 April 1998 by the British and Irish governments and most of the political parties in Northern Ireland. The "Good Friday" Agreement put an end to violence and offered a formal framework for how Northern Ireland should be governed. Human rights were considered central to peacekeeping. Section 68 of the Northern Ireland Act 1998 established a semiautonomous institution charged with the promotion and protection of human rights in a postconflict zone, and indicated a commitment on the part of Britain's government to long-standing peace, cooperative diplomatic relations with the Republic of Ireland with respect to Northern

Ireland, and the implementation of international human rights law with the goal of ensuring sustainable peace (Northern Ireland Act 1998).

Research interviews reveal that the decision to establish an NHRI was seen as a key solution to filling a gap in policymaking in postconflict Northern Ireland. At the time, some members of civil society noticed that the primary focus was on passing security measures with an eye to ending the conflict and implementing peace, leaving questions of rights protection and monitoring of rights violations largely uncovered (interviews 4, 8, 11, 19, 21, 78, 79). During a period when NHRIs were diffusing rapidly, the establishment of a similar specialized body in Northern Ireland came as a formal solution to the problem and a concrete institutional safeguard for the implementation of human rights.

Two determining factors in the creation and the definition of the institutional strength of the Northern Ireland Commission were the mobilization of local civil society as well as support from political elites interested in promoting the end of the conflict, and a peaceful consolidation of rights promotion and protection in the region (interviews 8, 11, 21, 78, 79, 80). By design, the Northern Ireland Human Rights Commission has strong enforcement powers and is one of the most pluralist human rights institutions in the world. At the time of its inception, experts selected from among human rights lawyers and academics as well as civil society representatives of communities that experienced human rights violations during the Troubles participated actively in shaping it (interviews 8, 11, 21). Great care was taken to ensure that the institution's leadership included representatives of different social groups that suffered human rights violations during the conflict. The NHRI's diverse composition has continued over the years, and is considered a key enforcement safeguard that makes it more effective in carrying out its transitional justice and human rights mandate (interviews 11, 21).

The postconflict domestic context in Northern Ireland shaped the Commission's enforcement powers, which are reflected in its predominant activities in its first decades of existence. Over the years, the core of the NHRI's work has remained the protection of human rights in a transitional justice context. Recent years have brought an important change in the focus of institutional work, with a new dimension of rights-related work (interviews 4, 11, 21). The birth of a new generation with no living memory of the conflict and violence has spurred a new interest in economic and social rights, also broadening the scope of concerns addressed by the human rights commission. Therefore, more "bread and butter" concerns about issues related to public health, economic differences, and access to housing have become increasingly important in the commission's work (interviews 4, 11, 21). For instance, the Northern Irish human rights institution carried out the first-ever human rights inquiry into emergency care provision in accidents and emergency departments (NIHRC 2015).

The new type of activity is indicative of a greater change of direction in the work that the commission carries out in relation to the communities whose rights it seeks to protect and with government and other public bodies in Northern Ireland. In recent years, the Northern Ireland Human Rights Commission has turned its attention to a participatory approach, moving away from the more formulaic and distant work of complaint handling and inquiries that remained solely "on paper" (interviews 4, 8, 21). The NHRI has sought to change its style of work to include more local and community-level consultations, and it has faced challenges in a post-conflict setting with deep-seated social rifts. Moreover, it has emphasized a novel human rights approach in its work with government and public bodies, as a broader effort to raise awareness of human rights and their general relevance for policymaking across all areas of policy. To this end, it has pioneered training initiatives with government to increase human rights awareness in public decision-making, has run a set of webinars on human rights, and has engaged in work with the police force (interviews 4, 8, 21).

Research interviews have revealed that one of the main priorities of the leadership at the Northern Ireland Human Rights Commission over the years has been to maintain independence from government intervention while continuing to collaborate effectively with other public agencies (interviews 11, 20, 21, 79). This is a greater challenge for NHRIs in the United Kingdom, as they hold public body status. The position of the Northern Ireland Human Rights Commission in the architecture of rights protection in Northern Ireland is unique. While the Equality Commission for Northern Ireland and the Commissioner for Children and Young People receive their funding from the local government, the Human Rights Commission receives its budget from the central Westminster-based government. This setup caused significant tension in the early years of the commission's existence, but the working relationship has improved over the years (interviews 11, 21). In a sense, this financial linkage makes institutional activity less conditioned by the priorities advanced by the government of Northern Ireland. At the same time, it does create an increased risk of dependency on centralized public decision-making and a possible perceived distance from the devolved government with which the commission works more closely (interviews 11, 21, 79). These two dimensions of institutional strength—management of resources and relationship with government—have direct implications for the institution's capacity to carry out its mandate effectively and make an impact domestically and internationally.

AN EFFECTIVE INSTITUTION IN A
POSTCONFLICT SETTING

The Northern Ireland Human Rights Commission is widely considered one of the most effective in the world, despite operating in a postconflict context with a subnational mandate, a small staff, and a budget that has decreased over the years. Three main factors have determined its effectiveness in Northern Ireland—the mitigation of the risk of political interference in the relationship with Westminster, strong institutional leadership, and influential participation in different global, regional, and subregional peer networks of NHRIs. As such, the commission's work has had a significant domestic and international impact.

Research interviews revealed that in the years after its establishment, the Northern Ireland Human Rights Commission operated in a relatively hostile political environment (interviews 19, 11, 21). On the one hand, politicians with unionist sympathies regarded the devolution of human rights work as unnecessary, while civil servants working in Northern Irish public institutions viewed the work of the Human Rights Commission as overlapping with theirs and at best duplicating their own rights promotion and protection work (interviews 11, 19, 21). However, this initial resistance has subsided since, and in the words of the current commissioner, it has become one of "benign indifference" focused primarily on administrative issues and questions of financial accountability (interview 21).

One determining factor for institutional effectiveness, particularly with respect to the activities prioritized among the mandated duties, is the relationship the Northern Ireland Human Rights Commission has fostered with the London-based central government. The government's support of the Northern Ireland Commission has varied over time, but has generally been in decline since the 2010 election and the austerity measures taken by the Cameron government in the aftermath of the financial crisis (interviews 11, 21). The commission enjoyed a relatively large budget during its first years of operation. However, as a public body, it has been affected by different waves of budget cuts in the public sector and has seen its institutional financial resources reduced considerably. It saw a first budget reduction of 25 percent from 2010 until 2013, when it lost two of its four management posts in 2011, and a subsequent 11–15 percent cut in 2015–16 (Northern Ireland Assembly 2014). Overall, these budget cuts have put a strain on institutional resources and have forced the commission to prioritize activities and, to some extent, limit its operations (interviews 4, 11, 19, 21).

Despite financial challenges and a small full-time staff, the Northern Ireland Commission has been effective in carrying out human rights protection

work, such as complaint handling, independent investigations, and exercis-
ing amicus curiae powers to represent victims in courts of law. Arguably the
most publicly visible case in which the NHRI has been involved is the challenge to the law on Termination of Pregnancy in Northern Ireland (NIHRC
2019). The commission began contesting its legality in terms of the European
Convention on Human Rights in 2013, when it brought to court the case of
then twenty-three-year old Sarah Ewart who learned at a nineteen-week scan
that her baby she was carrying had a fatal defect and was refused termination of pregnancy (Carroll 2019). Although the Supreme Court contested the
standing of the Northern Ireland Commission to represent the case, it did
rule in favor of the claim that the abortion ban violated European human
rights law (UK Supreme Court 2018).

What is perhaps most surprising about the impact of the Northern Irish
institution is its successful performance in regional and international peer
networks. Despite its small staff, its commissioners were influential in advising governments and human rights experts in England and Scotland in
initial consultations about the establishment of their own NHRIs. In addition, despite having a subnational remit, the Northern Ireland Human Rights
Commission is unique in the access it has gained to regional and global peer
institutional networks set up specifically for institutions with national mandates. To gain access to those networks, the NHRI in Northern Ireland (and
its Scottish counterpart, years later) benefited from the lack of clearly defined
rules at the Global Alliance of National Human Rights Institutions regarding the access of subnational human rights institutions to the accreditation
system (Lacatus 2018). The global network conditioned the continued acceptance of all United Kingdom–based commissions on their status as a domestic institutional network and on the endorsement of the central government.
Nonetheless, each of the three institutions was assessed independently from
the other two during the accreditation process, and all were granted A-status.
At the same time, the three UK-based bodies share a single vote, one speaking right, and one seat at the Global Alliance of National Human Rights Institutions. In 2008 this result was justified in section 6.6 of the General Observations, stating that "in very exceptional circumstances" multiple national
institutions could seek accreditation, on the condition that they had the written consent of the state government and a written agreement regarding rights
and duties as a member of the Global Alliance of National Human Rights
Institutions, also detailing arrangements for participation in the international
human rights system (ICC 2013).

In addition, the Northern Ireland Commission has taken on leadership roles regionally and in global forums. In 2015 it was elected chair of the

Commonwealth Forum of National Human Rights Institutions. It has also been an active member of the European Network of National Human Rights Institutions over the years, participating alongside the Equality and Human Rights Commission and the Scottish Commission in the organization of several working groups that meet regularly to address issues of relevance for human rights policy in Europe, such as the rights of persons with disabilities, asylum and migration, or European legal structures. These groups provide a platform for mutual learning among members, as well as capacity building and advising, and the facilitation of a regional response from NHRIs on specific thematic areas (ENNHRI 2014b).

Brexit negotiations and related political developments indicated a higher risk of erosion of rights protection across the United Kingdom and an increased risk of reigniting some of the old sources of the conflict in Northern Ireland. At the time, Northern Ireland was ruled directly by Westminster and had no devolved government representation in the Brexit negotiations. While research interviews did not indicate that the lack of devolved government and parliament had an immediate impact on human rights promotion and protection, they did confirm fears of a likely decline in support and a possible change in the focus of institutional activity to consider the implications of Brexit on human rights in Northern Ireland. The Democratic Union Party was the sole regional party involved in national Brexit negotiations with the role of representing the political interests of Northern Ireland. Without a doubt, one of the most contentious aspects of the Brexit negotiations was the drafting of a feasible "backstop solution" to the problem of a hard border between Ireland and Northern Ireland that Brexit would bring with it. In February 2023, the European Union and the United Kingdom signed the Windsor Agreement, which specifies new arrangements to address practical issues linked to the Protocol on Ireland and Northern Ireland. As a result, a hard border between Ireland and Northern Ireland will not be re-established. The protocol, particularly under Article 2, states the UK government's commitment not to reduce certain equality and human rights provisions set out in the Belfast (Good Friday) Agreement. The UK government also committed to ensuring that some of Northern Ireland's equality laws will keep pace with future changes in EU equality laws. Against this complex background which seeks Northern Ireland balancing equality and human rights between EU and UK governing practices, the work of the Northern Ireland Human Rights Commission in human rights promotion and protection is arguably more important than ever for the sustainability of rights protection, human rights promotion, and liberal democracy in Northern Ireland.

THE EQUALITY AND HUMAN RIGHTS COMMISSION

Institutional Strength, Mandate Hybridity, and Aligning with European Union Norms

The creation of a human rights institution with a nationwide mandate in the United Kingdom and the consolidation of its human rights powers were the culmination of a process that had lasted nearly two decades. As early as 1993, members of a few nonprofit organizations had begun lobbying the Labour Party, asking for an independent body for the promotion and protection of human rights. Six years later, a new task force composed of civil servants, academics, and representatives of the existing Equality Commission and leading nonprofit organizations was set up to carry out deliberations from 1999 to 2001, and to oversee implementation of the Human Rights Act. They identified a gap in the formal system of human rights monitoring and implementation in the country, which civil society representatives could not meet. More specifically, there was a high demand from public bodies for training and guidance that neither nonprofit organizations nor Whitehall could provide (Spencer 2008), thus making the creation of a specialized human rights body imperative. The strong presence of a number of human rights nonprofit organizations on the ask force was instrumental in shaping the mandate of the new body and in granting human rights a central role in its vision (Spencer 2008; Crowther and O'Cinneide 2013).

Another important factor determining institutional creation and strength in the case of the Equality and Human Rights Commission was the government coming around to the proposal of creating an institution. Initially, the government had not been open to the idea of creating a stand-alone NHRI and recommended instead that Parliament establish the Joint Committee on Human Rights, which could launch an inquiry into the need to establish a unified body for the promotion and protection of rights (interviews 8, 11, 19, 78, 79, 80). That committee began its activity in 2001, six months after the Human Rights Act had come into force, and it received a significant body of evidence that a culture of respect for human rights within public services was missing and that the Human Rights Act alone was not sufficient for implementation of human rights law in the UK (interviews 8, 19, 78, 79, 80). Around the same time, the British Institute of Human Rights published a report entitled *Something for Everyone*, which spelled out the unmet need for rights protection (Watson 2002) and argued for the need to establish a sole body overseeing human rights. In March 2003, the Joint Committee on

Human Rights reported that the case for a human rights body was "compelling" and moved ahead with presenting a case to establish one (interviews 8, 11, 19, 78, 79, 80). It was not until 2007 that the Equality and Human Rights Commission began its activity as an institution with a broader mandate that also included human rights.

An additional key factor shaping institutional strength was the capacity of the institutional staff to take on human rights work. The long-standing prior expertise in equality and diversity issues made the prioritization of human rights activities a secondary concern. As a result of the merger of three equality commissions, the newly formed commission had a large budget and staff at the start of its activity. At the same time, it lacked a clearly defined human rights agenda at the start, and would not have dedicated human rights duties for several years after its inception. As a former general counsel for the commission stated, in the early days the Equality and Human Rights Commission was "an equality body with an HR framework" (interview 2).

In more than a decade of existence, the NHRI has strengthened its durability safeguards for human rights promotion and protection. Formally, it can apply for judicial review and to intervene in court proceedings. It also has the power to assess public authorities' compliance with their positive equality duties (Equality Act 2006). The Equality and Human Rights Commission inherited from the Disability Rights Commission the power to enter into binding agreements with employers, and it can enforce these agreements through injunctions (Equality Act 2006). While the earlier equality commissions had more limited powers of investigation, this new commission can carry out investigations when it has the "suspicion" of unlawful discrimination taking place (Equality Act 2006). The area in which the new mixed-remit commission has become significantly stronger is its power to bring proceedings against employers in its own name on any issue (Crowther and O'Cinneide 2013). At the same time, it cannot start an investigation into a public authority for violations of the Human Rights Act, and cannot support individual cases in tribunals or courts where the issue falls solely under the Human Rights Act and also under some preexisting British equality legislation (The Human Rights Act 1998).

Arguably the most significant challenge that the Equality and Human Rights Commission has faced over the years has been to position itself as an independent body in the domestic regulatory architecture, defining the parameters of its activities as distinctive from the work of government, other public bodies, and civil society. Research interviews revealed that one of the greatest challenges was to change the perception and mode of its work from the advocacy focus of the three initial equality and diversity commissions to that of a human rights commission that requires de facto independence from public institutions to hold government accountable on human rights violations, carry out impartial investigations, and provide politically neutral advice to public agencies (interviews 2, 3, 4, 5, 78, 80, 81). To a large extent, these challenges continue to be prevalent today. As the analysis of institutional effectiveness will discuss in detail, these structural challenges have been instrumental in shaping the NHRI's capacity to carry out its mandate effectively and to make an impact on human rights behavior.

The durability safeguards granting independence from political intervention have been at the center of recent efforts to continue institutional development (interviews 3, 4, 5, 6, 8, 17, 78, 79, 80, 81). For instance, the first chairman of the Equality and Human Rights Commission was Trevor Phillips, appointed in 2006 directly from his post at the Commission for Racial Equality, which he had led since 2003. An active member of the Labour Party with a prominent political career before his appointment, Phillips was regarded as a political appointee. This view extended to the commission under his leadership, whose activity was not publicly perceived as neutral. Rather, at the start of its existence, the Equality and Human Rights Commission was generally considered a political instrument subordinate to the Labour Party (interviews 3, 4, 6, 78, 79, 80). By 2009 it came under scrutiny by government under suspicion of mismanagement, and half of its commissioners resigned. Generally, research interviews point to this crisis as the moment when, in important ways, the Equality and Human Rights Commission stopped being considered a central institution on the national stage (interviews 3, 4, 6, 78, 79, 80). At the same time, this crisis also marked a turning point for the body. Until 2009, its image was closely tied to its past through the continued legacy of the former equality bodies. After the crisis of 2009, however, the commission sought to carve out a new image for itself, as an independent regulatory body less vulnerable to political interference (interviews 3, 4, 6, 78, 79, 80). Once again, a significant part of this change is linked to the change in leadership. Later commission chairs Baroness O'Neill and David Isaac, came to the position with no prior political experience and have generally emphasized the equal importance of a human rights mandate and the equality and diversity mandate. Recent years have seen the commission gradually strengthen its capacity to carry out human rights work and define its public image as a body with increasing independence from government and a clearly defined mixed expertise in equality and diversity issues as well as human rights promotion and protection (interviews 3, 4, 6, 10, 13, 78, 79, 80). In December 2020, Baroness Falkner of Margravine was appointed as chair of the Equality and Human Rights Committee, after extensive experience serving in public posts and a political career as a member of the Liberal Democrats. Her political past has arguably been one of the main reasons for criticism of some of NHRI's decisions in the first two years of her leadership, linked to allegations of ideological influence by the Conservative Party.

An additional area in which the Equality and Human Rights Commission has weakened over the years is the involvement of civil society in decision-making processes. While at the start, members of civil society were instrumental in setting up the institution and the activities of the preceding equality commissions were centered on advocacy work, the commission has gradually limited civil society involvement. Unlike its Northern Irish counterpart, the Equality and Human Rights Commission does not involve civil society representatives as active participants in decision making or institutional leadership. At the time of research, its collaborative work with civil society was based primarily on partnerships that were project-specific and required input from members of the wider human rights community in the United Kingdom, such as trainings, review of specialized reports, and relevant aspects of institutional strategic plans.

The winding path of institutional development and the slower consolidation of human rights expertise and practice have shaped the NHRI's capacity and effectiveness. It has conducted advisory and reporting work over the years, and has been actively involved in regional and global networks of peer institutions. Nevertheless, its relatively weaker formal strength, which is tied to its lack of full independence from government, has limited its capacity. The next section will discuss the relationship between its institutional strength and its effectiveness, as well as the main factors determining its domestic and international impact over the years.

Institutional Effectiveness: An Institution "Lacking Teeth"

The Equality and Human Rights Commission is generally regarded as an institution that "lacks teeth" and leaves a smaller-than-desired societal mark (interviews 2, 3, 4, 6, 8, 78, 80) despite recent success in building a stronger public profile as an expert human rights body with an increasing capacity to effect change in the realm of human rights. This is largely attributed to its lack of full formal independence from government (interviews 2, 3, 4, 6, 8, 78, 80). During the first years of the commission's existence, the lack of consensus on appropriate boundaries between government and the commission limited its independence significantly (Harvey and Spencer 2012). Unlike the Scottish Commission, which is accountable to the Scottish Parliament, the Equality and Human Rights Commission is accountable not to Parliament but to government, and hence a minister must answer to Parliament for the NHRI's performance. Despite the provisions for de facto autonomy in the 2006 Equality Act, the direct formal subordination of the institution to a ministry allows government to hold the commissioners accountable for their actions and to sometimes micromanage, interfering in a manner that the commission may find intrusive (Harvey and Spencer 2012).

Over the years, the NHRI's subordination to government has caused it additional day-to-day operational difficulties. Its status as a public body, rather than an independent regulatory institution with a set budget, makes it vulnerable to government intervention by holding it financially accountable, with government having the final word on the approval of its main activities. High-level decision making in the NHRI depends on ministerial approval, and political cycles often impact on the nature and pace of its activities (interviews 1, 2, 3, 5, 6, 81). In addition, the ministry under which it operates, currently the Ministry of Justice, has the power of decision over its budget and also has final approval regarding all its projects and activities. The change in political priorities is as consequential as the turnover in ministerial staff members, putting staff of the commission in the position to establish new working relationships and build trust anew every few years (interviews 1, 2, 3, 5, 6). Inevitably, this causes inefficiencies and delays in the commission's activity and limits its overall capacity to make an impact on the government's practices in the field of human rights. This challenge is compounded by change in ministerial oversight over the years, though the inclusion of the commission in the Ministry of Justice granted it more stability as ministerial staff members have legal training and have been likely to understand the nature of its work (interviews 1, 2, 3, 5).

An additional factor impacting negatively on the commission's effectiveness was the decrease in its funding. Like other human rights commissions in the United Kingdom, the Equality and Human Rights Commission was adversely affected by budget cuts. However, these changes have taken place in a manner that is unique to the Equality and Human Rights Commission, which began with a very large budget that combined the individual budgets of the different equality commissions that had merged to form it. Subsequent budget cuts, including a recent one in 2017, have seen its staff and capacity reduced considerably. This has raised concern also among peers in the Global Alliance of National Human Rights Institutions, specifically with respect to the ways in which cuts equivalent to 70 percent of its 2010 budget would threaten the NHRI's effectiveness and independence (Doward 2016).

The choice of institutional model is another important factor affecting the functioning of the Equality and Human Rights Commission. By design, the commission is set up to be effective in addressing a range of equality and human rights issues at the subregional level across England, Wales, and Scotland. To that end, it has decentralized by establishing four separate offices in London, Manchester, Cardiff, and Glasgow. This institutional model represented a formal recognition of the intrinsic diversity of rights-related social problems across the United Kingdom, due to either devolution or distinct social contexts outside London (interviews 2, 3, 4). While staff at these offices perform valuable work, the general perception is that the Equality and Human Rights Commission tends to prioritize issues that are relevant centrally, in Westminster (interviews 2, 3, 4, 8). The case of the office in Glasgow, whose human rights mandate overlaps with that of the Scottish Human Rights Committee, has been cause for concern about institutional inefficiency. To mitigate this risk, the two commissions have established a system of coordination and division of labor, to avoid duplication of effort (interviews 5, 6, 9, 10, 11, 12).

A domain in which the NHRI has been active and impactful, albeit not nearly as influential as the Scottish or the Northern Irish counterparts, is participation in regional and global networks of peer institutions. Being a body with many staff members, especially in its first years of existence, it made its presence felt at the European Network of National Human Rights Institutions. While most institutions in the region usually send one representative to the annual conference or to working group meetings, the Equality and Human Rights Commission was able to send several staff for several years (interviews 2, 6, 8, 9). Thus, it shaped the direction of work in different areas of priority for the regional network. Its involvement in the regional network has continued over the years, but has focused more on areas in which its staff members have direct expertise, such as the human rights legal working group (interviews 1, 3, 5). Looking toward the future, the commission faces a high risk of discontinuing or severely limiting its involvement in international networks due to the possibility of losing its current A-status of accreditation. More than once in recent years, the Global Alliance of National Human Rights Institutions has called on the British body to strengthen both its de jure and its de facto independence, to avoid being downgraded to "B-status" (interviews 1, 2, 3, 6). A lower status would result in the loss of rights the commission has enjoyed in regional and global networks of peers and with the United Nations.

Despite starting as a large body with a sizeable institutional budget and large staff, the Equality and Human Rights Commissions has been seen as less effective in carrying out its mandate than its subnational counterparts in Scotland and Northern Ireland. The merger of the existing equality bodies in the mid-2000s created a new commission that took several years to find its feet as a body with human rights expertise and to disentangle itself from political interference. To ensure compliance with the Paris Principles and with the independence requirements assessed in the re-accreditation process, the NHRI has sought to work toward greater de facto autonomy even when its formal mandate did not grant it full de jure independence (interviews 6, 7, 16, 17). Despite a more clearly contoured profile of human rights practice and internationally recognized expertise on human rights promotion and protection (for instance, the commission submits a specialized report to the Universal Periodic Review), its status as a public body and its formal dependence on ministerial approval for funding allocation and decision-making on main institutional projects continues to be its Achilles heel.

At the time of this writing it is impossible to gauge the full impact of Brexit, the United Kingdom's separation from the European Union, on the strength and effectiveness of the Equality and Human Rights Commission. As a general rule, an NHRI enjoying full formal autonomy from government is more likely to remain on the outside of complex political processes, such as advising the executive and legislative on human rights legislation in a post-Brexit context, and holding policymakers to account on possible human rights violations. The likelihood of mandate changes and an increase in institutional strength in the aftermath of the formal separation of the United Kingdom from the European Union, including that of greater autonomy from government, is low. Hence, the Equality and Human Rights Commission risks becoming further sidelined, ineffective, and even obsolete in a political environment that is largely hostile to human rights. In addition, there is an additional risk brought about by the control government has over the commission's finances and leadership appointment system. This might result in further capture, even lower independence, and a deeper assimilation of the NHRI into the state apparatus.

THE SCOTTISH HUMAN RIGHTS COMMISSION

Institutional Strength in a System of Devolved Governance

In Scotland, the start of the devolution of powers away from Westminster to Holyrood provided a unique opportunity to establish and develop the new Scottish Human Rights Commission in 2006. The prominence of Scottish independence on the political agenda of the Scottish National Party provided an unprecedented opportunity to draw more attention toward human rights, as a chance for the country to advance a social policy platform different from the tradition south of the border. Prior to the devolution of powers and the creation of a parliament and government in Edinburgh, there was little institutionalized tradition of human rights promotion and protection in Scotland. In fact, research interviews showed also that there was a limited understanding among public officials as to how increased efforts to promote human rights could be of direct benefit to Scotland (interviews 12, 13, 15, 16). This might also partly explain the government's initial lukewarm response to the idea of establishing a human rights commission (interviews 12, 13, 15, 16).

As early as 2000, discussions about the possible establishment of an NHRI in Scotland began, but it took until 2006 for the Scottish Parliament to pass the law formally creating the institution. The main domestic actors advocating for the establishment of a human rights commission in Scotland were members of the academic and legal civil society (interviews 12, 13, 14). The proponents of such an institution advocated for the integration of human rights promotion and protection into the strategic political vision of the newly devolved executive and legislative. At first, Holyrood only supported the appointment of a single officeholder as human rights commissioner. Consultations with representatives of the human rights commissions in Ireland and New Zealand were instrumental in drafting a strategic plan for the expansion of the role and the formal institutionalization of human rights promotion and protection (interviews 9, 12).

Prior to the institution's official opening, the staff involved in setting up the Scottish Human Rights Commission advocated for the need to start a commission that could address rights-related issues that were specific to Scottish people. From its inception in 2006 until it became operational in 2008, the formally appointed commissioners and other commission staff consulted with the public across Scotland and identified support for the commission's creation. Their conclusions became instrumental to the legal consolidation of the NHRI and the formulation of a clear mandate and institutional strength (interviews 9, 12, 15, 16). The Scottish Human Rights Commission was created through an act of the Scottish Parliament in 2006 (Scottish Parliament 2006) and started its work two years later. The institution's remit focuses on issues within the devolved powers of the Scottish Parliament and Executive: the promotion of economic, social, and cultural rights in Scotland, as well as rights promotion and protection linked to social care, public health care (for instance, in cases of disability, dementia, and mental illness), the work of the police, and the conditions of people in detention.

The formal strength of the Scottish Commission has not changed during its twelve years of existence. It is more limited than that of the Equality and Human Rights Commission, due to the close connection between the

institutional mandate and Holyrood's devolved powers (which are more limited than those of the central legislative and executive, based in London). At
the same time, in comparison to the Equality and Human Rights Commission and the Northern Ireland Human Rights Commission, the Scottish Human Rights Commission enjoys stronger enforcement powers due to greater
formal independence from political interference (interviews 9, 12, 13, 14, 15).
Although Westminster has the final word on the entire budget for Scotland,
the Holyrood-based Parliament has the final word on the allocation of financial resources to the commission. In that respect, the Scottish commission
is further removed from possible government interference in institutional
decision making than are its peer institutions in the United Kingdom. Having said that, Scotland's NHRI is not immune to the impact of higher-level
decisions taken by the central London-based government indirectly affecting
its budget. As the analysis of institutional effectiveness will discuss in more
depth, Scotland's NHRI has been effective in building a good working relationship with the Scottish authorities, and has had a strong focus on making
an impact. Relative to its size and limited powers, its international impact has
been remarkable.

INSTITUTIONAL EFFECTIVENESS: STRONG IMPACT DESPITE A LIMITED MANDATE

Overall, the Scottish Commission for Human Rights has demonstrated that
it can be effective in carrying out its mandated duties and in partnering successfully with Scotland's public authorities. Three main factors have shaped
its domestic effectiveness and international impact: strong institutional leadership, a good working relationship with Holyrood, and a concerted effort to
align its main activity in the realm of human rights with the goals of Scottish
sovereignty and independence promoted by the Scottish National Party.

The Scottish commission has successfully translated its powers within the
remit of the devolved Scottish administration into a set of strategic guidelines. Its leadership prioritized international institutional activity, during the
first decade of its existence, making an impact on the development of regional
and global networks of peer NHRIs. The institution's prioritization of these
strategic goals has had trade-offs, too, leading to the channeling of most of its
resources toward a smaller set of objectives while leaving uncovered other areas linked to human rights promotion and protection. The close relationship
the Scottish NHRI has built with Holyrood facilitates advising work, while
making far more challenging the work of holding government and public
bodies to account in possible cases of violations. Despite having investigative

powers in its mandate, the institution has yet to dedicate resources to them. As such, it has yet to fully realize its formal mandate to perform investigative work and hold government to account for its activity.

An area of exceptional effectiveness for the Scottish human rights body has been its international activity, engaging with peer institutions as well as regional and international networks of NHRIs and international organizations. The commission's international impact is due to its leadership and their effort to foster ties with peer institutions and secure a more prominent role for the commission in regional and global networks of peer national human rights bodies. Alan Miller, the chair of the Scottish commission (2007–16), held the elected positions of secretary of the International Coordinating Committee of National Human Rights Institutions (currently GANHRI) from 2013 to 2016 and chair of the European Group of National Human Rights Institutions (currently ENNHRI) from 2011 to 2016, and from 2016 to 2019 served as a special envoy with GANHRI. In June 2009, during his tenure as chair of the Scottish commission, it hosted the first joint meeting of the three UK-based commissions together with the Irish Human Rights Commission (SHRC 2009). In October 2010 the Scottish commission organized the Tenth International Conference of National Human Rights Institutions at the Scottish Parliament, which brought representatives from more than eighty countries together at Edinburgh (Scottish Parliament 2009). The conference concluded with the agreement of the Edinburgh Declaration, an innovative instrument calling for more national and international monitoring of businesses' compliance with human rights law, and more efforts to promote corporate responsibility (Scottish Parliament 2009). In addition, the Scottish commission makes submissions to the Treaty Bodies of the UN framework regarding relevant human law, policy, and practice in Scotland; and in June 2009 it was appointed a member of the United Kingdom's independent mechanism responsible for promoting, monitoring, and protecting the implementation of the Convention on the Rights of Persons with Disabilities (SHRC 2009).

Since its inception, the institution has had a small staff. To a large extent, the smallness of the staff has shaped the institution's strategic direction. The Scottish Human Rights Commission has had to prioritize certain areas of work, often defined by the policies the government is interested in advancing. The NHRI has carried out government advisory work, policy-focused research, and promotional activities in the issue areas in which the Scottish government exercises its devolved powers. Arguably its most notable achievement is the development and coordination of Scotland's National Action Plan for Human Rights (SNAP 2013). Published first in 2013, the plan was the first of its kind in the United Kingdom, proposing goals for Scotland in human rights promotion and protection; in its justice, living standards, health and social care, safety, and international obligations; and in the advancement of a broader human rights culture in both policy making and Scottish society more widely.

One of the main explanations for the Scottish NHRI's effectiveness is its good working relationship with Holyrood and the devolved government. Research interviews show that in general, the institution's ties with the legislative and the executive have improved significantly over time and are perceived as more cooperative than the ones between the Westminster-based government and the Equality and Human Rights Commission and the Northern Ireland Human Rights Commission (interviews 13, 15, 16, 18, 19, 21, 79, 80). Nevertheless, the Scottish commission's partnership with Holyrood and Westminster is not without its challenges. Its relationship with the Scottish Parliament is primarily centered on administrative duties (interviews 12, 13, 14, 15). Members of the parliament tend to view their NHRI as a corporate body like any other public agency. Although it is formally independent from the Scottish government, the Scottish Human Rights Commission holds public body status in the United Kingdom. In the opinion of its staff, the public institution status allows Westminster to hold the commission to account on its activities and spending (interviews 12, 13, 14). The corporate body status has also had a direct impact on the institution's finances and its capacity to expand its areas of mandated work. Being a public body, the commission has been hit by the same budget cuts as all public services across Scotland, amounting to about 10 percent of decrease in financial resources over the span of the first eight years of activity. These budget cuts were largely the result of lower centralized resources allocated to the public sector across the United Kingdom, and were implemented without an assessment of institutional performance or an evaluation of institutional needs. Compared to the other two human rights commissions operating on British territories, the Scottish NHRI did not suffer further budget cuts.

Past and current staff speak of the continued challenge they face to increase the awareness of the legislature and the executive about the NHRI's work and about the relevance of human rights beyond advancing a political agenda of Scottish independence. This work is part of a greater institutional effort to advance a more pervasive human rights culture across all public services in Scotland and across all areas of policy work (interviews 12, 15, 16). Ultimately, a greater understanding of the importance of a human rights approach to policymaking might lead to a slightly modified relationship between the Scottish Human Rights Commission and public servants. The current ties are informed by the shared goal of advancing human rights in

Scotland as part of the Scottish National Party's plan to advance Scotland's standing in the world as a nation separate from England and Great Britain. It is the view of several staff members that, if human rights could be decoupled from political agendas, they could become more sustainable by being more easily embedded into policymaking and more immune to future changes in governments' ideological agendas and in the political priorities of majority parties (interviews 12, 16). This would also facilitate a shift in the commission's focus of work: away from expert advisory activities on rights compliance and enforcement, and toward monitoring of government work and accountability building.

An area of low impact for the Scottish Human Rights Commission is its involvement with civil society around Scotland. To address this shortcoming, the commission has sought in recent years to foster a closer engagement with civil society organizations and local communities around Scotland (interviews 14, 16). While it has generally sought to reflect the interest and problems of the Scottish population, it has created a predominant institutional profile as an expert human rights body whose efforts are directed mostly at government and are generally removed from the impact it might make on the ground (interviews 13, 14, 16). In this sense, the National Action Plan represents a good example of collaborative work across civil society, the Scottish NHRI, and the Scottish authorities. This new direction of work is likely to intensify under the leadership of the current chair, Judith Robertson, who joined the NHRI in 2016 after a long-standing career in social justice campaigning and advocating for the rights of many disadvantaged groups.

In the aftermath of Brexit, the long-term impact of the United Kingdom's separation from the European Union remains to be seen. However, the special context that Scotland provides within the UK might bring with it hope for opportunity rather than decline in the field of human rights. In other words, the possibility of Scotland's future independence from the UK brings with it questions of independent treaty ratification and human rights compliance with international human rights law. In this context, the expertise and work at the Scottish Human Rights Commission is key to the process. For instance, the Scottish NHRI and the National Taskforce for Human Rights Leadership, co-chaired by Alan Miller (former Scottish human rights commissioner), were involved in advisory work to the Scottish government, proposing thirty recommendations for the devolved government to strengthen Scotland's human rights framework. In 2021, the government proposed a new human rights bill, aiming to incorporate into Scots law the UN International Covenant on Economic, Social and Cultural Rights, and the International

Convention on the Elimination of All Forms of Racial Discrimination, the Convention on the Elimination of All Forms of Discrimination against Women, and the Convention on the Rights of Persons with Disabilities. The direct involvement of the Scottish NHRI in this process is clear evidence of its impact, bringing the institution a step closer to reaching its goals of raising the profile of human rights in domestic policymaking, and of increasing awareness for rights protection and promotion among public officials and ultimately advancing a broader political culture of human rights.

The Danish Institute for Human Rights

The Danish Institute for Human Rights is among the most long-standing and internationally influential NHRIs in the world. Its formal mandate makes it an exceptionally strong promotional and advisory body. The Danish NHRI has developed over the years to encompass vast legal expertise and research capacity. At the same time, it has relatively weak durability safeguards due to limited protection powers, with no mandated responsibilities to carry out independent investigations related to cases of complaint or to provide legal representation to victims of human rights abuses. Moreover, durability through a solid legal foundation for the institute and safeguards for its resources are not embedded in the Danish Constitution, and are dependent on government approval.

The Danish Institute for Human Rights incorporates in its mandate a rather unusual area of activity compared to those of other NHRIs around the world. A specialized department in the institute carries out international development work focused on human rights promotion and protection in the Global South. Nevertheless, the institute does not have human rights protection duties. and has recently come under repeated criticism by the Subcommittee on Accreditation for making efforts to enhance the international development dimension of activity.

Strong promotional powers have enabled the Danish institute to have a domestic impact through advising government on human rights, and an international one through its action in specialized networks. An area of its exceptional impact has been its contribution to the creation and consolidation of a regional network of NHRIs in Europe. In addition, the institute has been an active participant in the Global Alliance of National Human Rights Institutions (GANHRI) over the years. In peer networks, it has successfully performed leadership roles and has been involved in consolidating and formalizing these peer networks, as well as supporting the development of other peer institutions around the world.

INSTITUTIONAL STRENGTH THROUGH
PROMOTIONAL POWERS

The early days of the Danish institute's development were unusual compared
to those of its peer bodies in the subregion. Established in 1987, the institute
is one of the world's oldest NHRIs with a dedicated human rights mandate.
At the time of its creation, well before the international human rights community had formulated the Paris Principles, only five such institutions existed
in the world (including in France, Canada, and Australia) as part of national
ministries. In May 1987 the Danish NHRI was formally recognized through a
parliamentary decision as a specialized human rights body: the Danish Center for Human Rights. In the early days of activity, the Danish institute had
the same institutional model as its counterparts in Norway and Sweden: it
was a predominantly research institution focused mostly on carrying out historical studies on the Cold War. As a former director of the institute stated
at the beginning of the 1990s, the staff at the Human Rights Center made a
strategic decision to redefine the existing research body as one mandated to
pursue the "domestication of human rights" (interview 28).

The initiative of strong and intentional institutional leadership was the
main factor motivating institutional reform and the creation of the NHRI in
existence today. Participation in the international community of peer bodies helped to shape the strategic direction of the Danish Center, which focused primarily on addressing domestic rights-related policy concerns such
as the protection of refugees and minorities. Staff at the center, in particular
Morten Kjaerum, were actively involved in international efforts to advance
NHRIs as a formal solution to the gap between international human rights
law and domestic implementation. In 1991 the center was one of the only a
handful of institutions participating in the first International Workshop on
National Institutions for the Promotion and Protection of Human Rights,
in Paris (Kjaerum 2003). A cornerstone in the development of NHRIs globally, this workshop led to the first formulation of the Paris Principles, as well
as the formation of the first ever network of human rights institutions. The
Danish human rights institution was also a leading participant at the 1993
World Conference, an event which consolidated earlier efforts and laid the
groundwork for the formation of the International Coordinating Committee
on National Institutions for the Promotion and Protection of Human Rights
(today known as the Global Alliance of National Human Rights Institutions)
(Kjaerum 2003; OHCHR 2010).

Changes in the mandate of the Danish Institute for Human Rights have
taken place in response to the country's efforts to adopt institutions imple-

menting European Union norms and to ratify international rights treaties. In 1995 durability safeguards were strengthened, as the new statute and mandate of the Center for Human Rights were formalized through statutory law. Since then, the formal development of the Danish NHRI has been gradual, with additional duties added to its mandate such as the power to monitor, advise, and report on discrimination on the basis of ethnic background and on the basis of gender and disability (Danish Institute for Human Rights 2019).[2] In June 2004, the Danish government ratified the Optional Protocol to the Convention Against Torture and designated the Parliamentary Ombudsman as National Preventive Mechanism. The human rights nonprofit organization DIGNITY and the Danish Institute for Human Rights function in an advisory capacity in the implementation of the functions of national preventive mechanism. In 2012, the institute's remit expanded further to also include the protection of rights in Greenland. Although the institute has arguably one of the most extensive promotional capacities among NHRIs around the world, it does not have a human rights protection mandate. Although it has a large legal department with ample expertise in human rights law and policy, it cannot receive individual complaints of human rights violations or carry out investigative work on its own initiative.

Arguably the main factor shaping the institutional mandate of the Danish NHRI today is its relationship with national government. An unusual formal feature of the Danish institute is its dual mandate to do international development work in the fields of human rights and equality. While international partnerships are a common institutional trait in NHRIs, the mandate to carry out international development project work with government funding is much more common in the world of nonprofit organizations or in the work of dedicated government agencies. The relationship between the Danish Ministry of Foreign Affairs and the Danish Institute for Human Rights is regulated by a cooperation agreement that is revisited regularly and has recently had two main areas of focus: human rights and sustainable development, and human rights and business. Regular assessments of capacity and activity ensure that the institute's international work aligns with changing Danish priorities in development efforts as formulated in the Strategy for Danish Development Cooperation. This area of activity has been the object of both internal debate and external criticism, for being an area of limited institutional independence and clear dependency on government funding and foreign aid priorities (interviews 29, 30, 33).

---

2. Act no. 374 of 28 May 2003; act no. 40 of 30 March 2004; act no. 553 of 18 June 2012.

Staff at the Danish Institute for Human Rights report being able to work independently from political influence (interviews 28, 29, 30, 31,32, 33, 34). Nevertheless, the institute's formal design does not safeguard it from possible government interference. For instance, government has the power to approve its funding and, through the Ministry of Foreign Affairs, to set its priorities for international development work. Although Denmark's Office of the Auditor General indicated other avenues to allocate funds (Subcommittee on Accreditation 2012), the law has remained unchanged on this issue since the institute was accredited in 2012. Another important element that weakens the formal strength of the Danish NHRI is the system of selection, appointment, and dismissal of its board members. Although the board has representatives from Danish communities of human rights experts, they are appointed through a process that lacks transparency. Vacancies or criteria for selection of the board are not advertised publicly, and the institute's by-laws do not specify any criteria for dismissal or grant board members immunity for legal liability when acting in their official capacity.

The process of re-accreditation coordinated by the Subcommittee on Accreditation and the Global Alliance of National Human Rights Institutions is the main international mechanism with potential impact on the strength of the Danish NHRI. The institution's relationship with the national government, in particular its lack of complete formal independence, was one main area of concern during the process of re-accreditation with the Global Alliance of National Human Rights Institutions in 2018. The accreditation system granted the Danish NHRI A-status in 2007, and confirmed it again in 2012. The re-accreditation process in 2018 raised important questions about the institute's formal compliance with the Paris Principles, given the lack of legal change since the previous round of re-accreditation. The next section will assess the principal ways in which the choices made regarding the institute's formal institutional strength have influenced its capacity to work effectively and make an impact internationally and domestically.

INSTITUTIONAL EFFECTIVENESS
THROUGH PROMOTION OF HUMAN RIGHTS

Three main institutional factors help to explain the powerful impact that the Danish NHRI has had domestically and internationally: a large budget, strong and influential leaders, and the ability to foster good working relationships with the government and with other institutions working in the realm of rights promotion and protection in Denmark. Despite its formal weakness in rights protection and the unusual dimension of international development

work in its mandate, the Danish Institute for Human Rights is widely regarded as one of the most effective and internationally influential NHRIs.
The core promotional work builds on research and analysis, which the institute carries out independently. One of the largest human rights research
centers in Europe, the Danish institute's specialized research department acts
as an international hub of information and expert knowledge on a broader
range of research and practice in the field of human rights.

The NHRI's mandate is conditioned by the institutional framework Denmark has created to protect human rights and equality. Denmark's NHRI
operates inside a complex domestic architecture of rights promotion and
protection, in which cross-institutional collaboration is key for institutional
effectiveness and impact (interviews 29, 30, 32, 33, 34). Different human rights
actors are competing for oversight of different areas of promotion and protection. Despite lacking a rights protection mandate, the Danish Institute for
Human Rights has established itself as an important expert voice for human
rights in Denmark, with particular influence in policymaking both at the earlier stages of policy drafting and once legislation has been drafted and is being
amended and implemented. The Parliamentary Ombudsman and the Equality Board handle casework and complaints. Complementing this work are
legal teams with human rights expertise that advise government on human
rights legislation (interviews 28, 29, 31, 33, 34).

The legal expertise in the Danish NHRI's monitoring department makes
it the main domestic body in charge of legal analysis and reporting (including
contributions to the Universal Periodic Review and treaty body monitoring).
This department closely follows domestic legislation and provides government with expert commentary and analysis with respect to its compliance
with Denmark's human rights and equality commitments (interviews 31, 32).
Over the years, its areas of priority have been migration and asylum policy,
and the integration of Muslim populations and the Roma in Denmark.

An important driver for the Danish NHRI's success over the years has
been its ability to foster an overall good working relationship with different
governments. Institutional leadership has been key in managing this relationship and mitigating risks to the integrity and activity of the NHRI. With
a large budget and constant support for its expanded mandate, the institute
is one of the largest of its kind in the world, with some 150 staff (ENNHRI
2017). But the institute has not been free of threats to its existence and independence. One moment stands out (interviews 28, 31). In 2002, Denmark's
right-wing majority government decided to close the existing Danish Centre
for Human Rights, only to reopen it a few months later under a new name,
the Institute for Human Rights, under the auspices of the Danish Center for

International Studies and Human Rights. This represented a wake-up call for the institute, revealing its formal vulnerability to changes in political support (interviews 28, 31, 32). At the same time, the institute's activity continued, and its strength and effectiveness are seen to have improved since then, due to new responsibilities included in the mandate and increased budgets for new departments—such as the monitoring department, established in the aftermath of the shutdown (interviews 28, 31, 32).

Overall, research interviews show that most of the institute's work is de facto independent from government interference, even when it appears only to react to policy rather than informing and shaping it (interviews 28, 29, 30, 31, 32). Nevertheless, the allocation and administration of funds for the entire institute, and in particular for its international department, makes the institute more vulnerable to having to shape its work to meet government demands. This risk is particularly high given that the international department is dependent on funding from the Ministry of Foreign Affairs and the European Union, with an agenda grounded in the national strategy of international development. In other words, this formal relationship makes the institute's international work part of a national agenda shaped by political priorities and the executive's international commitments.

One area of particularly high impact of the Danish NHRI has been its cross-border activity and involvement in peer networks, to which strong institutional leadership has been key. The Danish Institute for Human Rights has been a constant presence in transnational networks of peer institutions, being instrumental in the creation of GANHRI and ENNHRI. The institute participates in some of the working groups at ENNHRI, where it has spearheaded priorities at the regional level, such as work on rights for the elderly and on the intersection of business and human rights (ENNHRI 2017). It is also a member of the Association of Human Rights Institutes. At the regional level, the institute's former leadership has participated in shaping the course of human rights policy at the European Union by being involved in the Council of Europe and the Fundamental Rights Agency (interviews 28, 32). The closest relationship the Danish NHRI has fostered has been with human rights institutions in other Scandinavian countries. The Scandinavian human rights bodies collaborate on projects and hold annual meetings to exchange knowledge and offer advice and support. In addition, representatives of the Danish institute have been on the advisory committee that has worked with the Swedish government to help create a Swedish NHRI (interviews 28, 31).

The Danish Institute for Human Rights is unusual among NHRIs in Europe and around the world. It is a promotion, advisory, and research body with no independent investigatory or complaint-handling powers. It is subordinated to government in terms of reporting and budgeting. As such, it is considered an institution of medium to weak strength. Nevertheless, its powerful leaders have managed to mitigate the risk of political capture over the years, and have fostered a good working relationship with governments and other institutions with rights promotion and protection mandates operating in Denmark. The institute's international impact is significant, as it has been one of the main actors shaping the global and regional networks of NHRIs, participating in the formulation of the Paris Principles and contributing to the consolidation of the Global Alliance of National Human Rights Institutions and the European Network of National Human Rights Institutions.

The Belgian Center for Equal Opportunities

The institutionalization of human rights promotion and protection in Belgium has been mired in a complex interplay of interregional political differences. The governments of Flanders and Wallonia have had a challenging partnership due to differing regional and federal policy priorities as well as conflicting ideological positions on the question of rights protection, particularly of the rights of migrants. Belgium has a designated NHRI—the Belgian Center for Equal Opportunities and Opposition to Racism (UNIA)—which was selected as the national body with a mandate most closely aligned with the Paris Principles. In 2018, UNIA was granted B-status in the accreditation process coordinated by the Subcommittee on Accreditation. It fell short of full accreditation status due to the lack of legal safeguards warranting its formal independence from government interference, the absence of permanently employed full-time staff, insufficient transparency regarding the leadership appointment process, and no dedicated human rights remit (Subcommittee on Accreditation 2018). In its daily work, UNIA investigates cases of human rights violations brought to its attention, but it does so despite lacking a formal mandate to promote and protect human rights. Belgium's federal government established UNIA in 1993 as a signal of commitment to combating discrimination and human trafficking, safeguarding the rights of foreigners, monitoring migration flow, and advising government on immigration matters. UNIA's institutional strength has increased over the years to include several different grounds of discrimination.

Research interviews point to the complex sociopolitical context in Belgium as the main explanations for UNIA's lack of an explicit formal human rights mandate (interviews 75, 76, 77). Historically, regional ethnic divisions and ideological differences between parties in the regional governments of Wallonia and Flanders have created serious disagreement over rights protection. The conservative parties that have recently dominated the political scene in Flanders have been generally more reluctant to recognize the importance of human rights promotion and protection, especially in reference to the rights of migrants living in Belgium, and the authority of a sole federal body over human rights promotion and protection (interviews 75, 76, 77). While questions of equality and diversity are no less controversial per se, they have been less politically contested in the two regions. Just like the equality and human rights institutions in the United Kingdom, the case of the Belgian NHRI shows that equality and diversity institutions appear much less vulnerable to redefinition in national political debate because their establishment and development are tied to the implementation of European Union antidiscrimination directives, and their activity is defined by set timelines. Against this background, UNIA has been perceived as a federal agency imposed on regional governments, created to represent and protect the rights of migrants and not those of Belgian citizens (interviews 75, 76, 77).

WEAKER FORMAL STRENGTH AND DE JURE HUMAN RIGHTS WORK

UNIA began its operations in February 1993 as a public agency created by the federal government to tackle questions of migrant integration and migrants' rights. The new institution was formed by expanding the competencies of the existing Integration Commissary, whose mandate solely focused on integration of migrants. In the late 1980s the government had created the Integration Commissary in response to large-scale riots in areas with large migrant communities. UNIA integrated in its remit additional duties linked to migrants' integration into Belgian society, such as the fight against racism and against discrimination. Its core responsibilities have remained strategic litigation and the handling of individual complaints in cases of discrimination. Its institutional strength has increased through the expansion of its mandate to include more grounds of discrimination, like the 1995 expansion including powers of litigation in cases of historical negationism as well as human smuggling and trafficking (interviews 75, 77).

UNIA has experienced multiple amendments to its mandate and has survived periods of great institutional reform in the federal institutional apparatus. These changes have not led to stronger durability safeguards in the realm of human rights promotion and protection. The main factor accounting for the increase in its competencies and formal strength was the state's willingness to comply with the European Union's antidiscrimination directives and commit to implementing European law into national legal and institutional

structures. In 2003 its institutional mandate was expanded to include rights
protection related to discrimination on the grounds of disability, age, sexual
orientation, and religious belief. This was accompanied by an increase in its
budget and staff (interviews 75, 77). A further expansion took place in 2007
as a result of a new antidiscrimination law, when UNIA began covering sev-
enteen of a total of nineteen grounds of discrimination integrated in Belgian
law (UNIA 2019). In 2011 the federal government, the regions, and the communities also decided to grant UNIA the mandate of independent mechanism to promote, protect and monitor implementation of the Convention
on the Rights of People with Disabilities (EQUINET 2019). As part of UNIA,
the Convention on the Rights of Persons with Disabilities Service was set up,
with the goal of ensuring promotion, protection, and monitoring of compliance. At the time of this writing, two main areas of expertise are outside
UNIA's remit. Gender-related matters fall under the remit of the Institute for
the Equality of Women and Men, while the Belgian Federal Migration Center
(Myria) is currently the federal center for the analysis of migratory flow, the
protection of the fundamental rights of foreigners, and the fight against human trafficking.

Another important factor shaping UNIA's mandated strength is its relationship with regional governments and its increase of enforcement safeguards through guaranteed greater independence from government interference. The final major change in the Belgian NHRI's formal design took place
in 2014 as a result of a cooperation agreement at the federal level. This was
the moment when UNIA became the sole institution with antidiscrimination
responsibilities at all levels of governance inside Belgium—federal, regional,
and local. UNIA has also increased its research capacity, and is now the main
body in the country that does research and publishes specialized reports on
matters of discrimination and inequality (interviews 75, 76, 77). With the final expansion came also increased formal independence and greater durability through UNIA's inclusion in Belgium's constitution, particularly through
provisions for the institutional mandate and stronger safeguards for the independence of institutional operations (interviews 75, 77). Though UNIA
continued to be a public body, the changes to its mandate offered specific
safeguards for the independence of its leadership appointment system from
government interference, by transferring those powers to the Belgian Parliament, which since 2014 has been responsible for appointing or removing the
twenty-one members of the UNIA's management board.

Despite this increased autonomy from political interference, the latest amendment to UNIA's mandate came with the removal of some of its
power to oversee the rights of migrants, combat human trafficking, and offer

support for immigrant integration in Belgian society. A new institution, the Belgian Federal Migration Center (Myria), was granted the mandate to cover these issues. The decision to separate the two institutions in 2015 stemmed from a complex political controversy over the broader societal relevance of having a stand-alone institution dedicated to safeguarding migrants' rights. The debate saw disagreement between parties that held majorities of votes in the two regions of Belgium, Flanders and Wallonia, which had very different views on the governance of migration and integration of migrants. The conflict over the management of migration has continued to dominate Belgian politics in the years since this institutional split. One example is the 2018 resignation of Theo Francken, the state secretary for migration and asylum in Charles Michel's government, over Belgium's possible participation in the Global Compact for Safe, Orderly, and Regular Migration. Francken is a controversial politician and a prominent figure in the conservative nationalist Flemish party, the New Flemish Alliance. His main claim to public fame centered on his radical views on immigration control, often expressed virulently on Twitter (Laurens 2018).

Research interviews have identified an additional important reason for the contested nature of human rights policy and institutions in Belgium (interviews 75, 76, 77). In the recent past, human rights have been publicly represented as synonymous with the protection of migrants, so they have been placed at the center of political agendas and contentious public debates. This is arguably another main explanation for successive governments' resistance to the idea of establishing a dedicated NHRI with a formal mandate to promote and protect human rights. Since 1999, the UNIA leadership has advocated publicly for the creation of an NHRI and has lobbied with the federal government to either expand the de jure institutional powers to include human rights or establish a new independent body. Despite UNIA's efforts and the recommendations of the international community, no ruling party has so far endorsed this initiative.

Despite lacking durability safeguards through a dedicated human rights mandate, in recent years UNIA has developed stronger enforcement powers through de facto human rights activities. It does human rights work, such as complaint handling and investigations, though it is not formally included in its mandate (interviews 70, 71, 75, 76, 77). In 2018, UNIA reapplied for accreditation as a separate institution, and received B-status because it lacked a de jure human rights mandate. The Global Alliance of National Human Rights Institutions took note of the institutional separation and assessed it as a move to weaken the human rights dimension of UNIA's mandate. This was one of the main criticisms that the Subcommittee on Accreditation offered

UNIA. The reaccreditation process acknowledged the very challenging national and interregional contexts in which UNIA works and the structural challenges it faced due to its lack of permanent full-time staff. Nevertheless, it recommended a set of guidelines for formal strengthening of the Belgian institution. At the time of research, UNIA staff gave no indication of sufficient political will to amend the center's mandate, or to strengthen its powers and make it more effective (interviews 70, 71, 75, 76, 77).

IMPACT ON HUMAN RIGHTS WITHOUT A DEDICATED MANDATE

Two main factors shape UNIA's capacity to make a domestic impact on human rights outcomes: a dedicated staff that, despite working on a part-time basis, continues to do casework and does not shy away from taking on complaints about human rights violations; and the center's capacity to maintain a neutral public image as a nonpartisan institution doing expert advisory and legal work. The cultivation of an apolitical image has helped UNIA to maintain credibility in the eyes of the public of both Flanders and Wallonia, as well as across regional and federal governments. At the same time, its political neutrality has an important trade-off, as the center has chosen not to collaborate with civil society in activism and human rights work on the ground, for fear of being associated with certain political and ethnic agendas (interviews 70, 71, 75, 77).

Despite having strengthened its formal mandate and undergone the accreditation process with the Global Alliance of National Human Rights Institutions, UNIA remains a dedicated diversity and equality body. Nevertheless, the center's work has shown that it has de facto powers to protect human rights. Some staff members with legal expertise have handled numerous cases of complaints about human rights violations (interviews 70, 71, 75, 76, 77). Cases of particularly high visibility in Belgium are linked to discrimination on linguistic grounds, which is a culturally and politically sensitive issue there, given the ethnic and language-based differences between the Flanders and the French-speaking part of the country. No institution has linguistic discrimination in its remit, but UNIA has received individual complaints about such cases and has been the sole public body handling them.

Within its core areas of responsibility, the Belgian NHRI has been effective in carrying out its mandate. First, the institution has created a public image for itself as the expert body to which individuals can turn for complaints about hate speech, crime, and discrimination (interviews 75, 76, 77). In the first year of its existence alone, it received more than two thousand complaints, and the number has doubled since then. Staff at UNIA inter-preted this increase as a sign of higher public trust in the center's work thanks mainly to its extensive experience with strategic litigation (interviews 75, 76, 77). Moreover, UNIA staff have found the institution's mixed rights mandate both a blessing and a challenge (interviews 75, 77). When litigation cases consider different dimensions of discrimination, the complexity of casework increases greatly. At the same time, the NHRI's multilevel mandate and ex-pertise in a range of rights have equipped it well to view complaints from an intersectional perspective, and to offer the more appropriate legal response to complex cases. What makes UNIA particularly effective in the Belgian national context is its power to carry out work at different levels: regional, federal, local, and institutional. Its staff sees its multidimensional design as a sign of its greater capacity to make an impact (interviews 69, 70, 75, 76, 77).

One of the main determinants of UNIA's effectiveness today is its ability to maintain a consistently neutral public image as an expert body with the power to conduct impartial investigations and handle individual complaints (interviews 75, 76, 77). Surveys prior to 2017 showed that some in the Belgian political class view it as "the institution of Muslim migrants" (interviews 75, 76, 77). This view appears to be more widely endorsed and increasingly ad-vanced by far-right parties. To counteract it, the center has sought to limit its work with NGOs to consultation on cases and rights promotion projects (interviews 75, 76, 77).

UNIA has had a limited impact on peer NHRIs internationally, but it has stayed engaged with peer networks and European institutions by being a long-standing member of the management board of EQUINET, and by more limited involvement with the European Network for National Human Rights Institutions. It has also long been involved in the leadership of the European Union's Fundamental Rights Agency, and on the management board of the European Commission against Racism and Intolerance, based at the Council of Europe.

In addition, UNIA's reintegration into the Global Alliance of National Hu-man Rights Institutions through its new accreditation in 2018 was seen as international recognition of its work in the area of human rights, as well as an acknowledgment of its efforts to advance human rights promotion and protection in Belgium and to motivate government to grant it a formal hu-man rights mandate and support its full compliance with the Paris Principles (interviews 75, 77). At the same time, the case of UNIA highlights the key role that NHRIs can play in the process of accreditation and gaining the endorse-ment of their peers for de facto institutional work. In other words, it points to the growing need for international assessments to move away from being a mere technical assessment of formal compliance. Some adaptation of the assessment process to national contexts would allow a better understanding of the limitations that NHRIs face domestically even in countries with long-standing democratic traditions. This might ultimately lead to an accreditation process that is more closely aligned with the needs of the NHRIs, and which can offer accredited institutions better guidance in how to increase their formal strength and effectiveness.

The Institutional Architecture of Human Rights Promotion and Protection in Sweden

THE CREATION OF A NEW NATIONAL HUMAN RIGHTS INSTITUTION

On 9 June 2021, the Swedish Parliament voted to create a dedicated body for human rights promotion and protection: the Swedish National Institute for Human Rights. In January 2022, the Swedish Institute for Human Rights began its operations. This was the culmination of a decade-long process, motivated by pressure from international organizations and by specific recommendations from the states involved in the Universal Period Review process of 2015. The Swedish NHRI will be based in Lund and housed at the Raoul Wallenberg Institute, an established human rights research institute led by Morten Kjaerum, former director of the Danish Institute for Human Rights.

The country with the longest standing tradition of establishing government accountability institutions and citizen complaint bodies, Sweden has a complex public architecture of rights protection institutions. In this context, the creation of a new body dedicated to the promotion and protection of human rights has long been the subject of public debate. Some commentators find it surprising that Sweden has taken so long to align itself with other states in establishing a dedicated NHRI (interviews 24, 40, 69). Others are not equally supportive of the idea of adding another institution to the domestic architecture, and do not see a real need for a dedicated human rights institution. As long as the decision stems only from a desire to show compliance with the United Nations recommendations for Sweden to demonstrate more willingness to align itself with other states around the world and to continue acting as a "model" liberal democracy across the borders, the dedicated human rights institute runs the risk of lacking sufficient public and political support (interviews 28, 36).

The decision to open formal discussions about the establishment of a new institution with a human rights promotional mandate was determined mainly by external pressure from international organizations. The initiative to begin consultations was motivated by the 2015 Universal Periodic Review process, which resulted in a strong recommendation for Sweden to establish an NHRI in full compliance with the Paris Principles (Human Rights Council 2015). Despite having been involved in supporting and advising other states on the creation of their own NHRIs, Sweden had yet to create one of its own. During on the Universal Periodic process, this was found to be a rather paradoxical reality. Given Sweden's history of institutionalizing rights protection and formally monitoring government activity through ombudsmen, the UN called on it to continue setting an example. In effect, research interviews have found that the predominantly external motivation for the creation of a NHRI might have acted as a deterrent to setting up a strong and effective body that would be operational soon after its legal founding (interviews 28, 35, 36).

One deterrent to the establishment of an NHRI in Sweden is the view among political elites that human rights promotion and protection are not needed there, and that violations of human rights are not part of its reality. In the immediate aftermath of the Universal Periodic Review, the center-right government in power at the time did not see much value in a dedicated human rights body, given that Sweden is an established liberal democracy with a well-developed equality and diversity ombudsman system (interviews 28, 35, 36, 37). Human rights and compliance with UN recommendations were not high national priorities.

The lack of political interest might also be grounded in the belief that the human rights situation in Sweden has always been very good and will continue to be so, and that human rights outcomes there ought not require monitoring (interviews 36, 37, 40). This point of view sees human rights violations as endemic in the Global South, where developed countries can make a difference by providing assistance and expertise. Civil society associations in Sweden with human rights mandates are in effect nonprofit organizations with mandates to act in the field of international development.

Domestically, human rights violations have tended to be associated with poor integration of outsiders, usually migrants and refugees from the Global South, into Swedish society. Better integration programs and controlled migrant intake are seen as appropriate institutional responses to these human rights violations (interviews 36, 37, 40). Hence, the underlying expectation is that effective migration management through integration policies offer a necessary and sufficient solution to the question of domestic rights promotion and protection in Sweden.

One key factor in the effort to establish a new NHRI in Sweden was the openness of a new minister of culture to the initiative. Responding to international recommendations, the Swedish government in 2019 launched a public consultation for a proposal to create an NHRI. The initiative was supported by the minister of culture and democracy from 2014 to 2019, Alice Bah Kuhnke, who put forth a strategy for human rights and advanced a clear plan for the creation of a Swedish NHRI. The fact that all other Scandinavian countries had established NHRIs appropriate to their domestic context (Finland created its Human Rights Center in 2012, and restructured its parliamentary ombudsman body to accommodate a stronger human rights institution, while Norway established a new NHRI in 2015) created momentum in Sweden for more public support for this idea. After two years of expert consultation regarding the best suited institutional model in Sweden, coordinated by the Ministry of Culture, the government endorsed the idea of a functionally independent NHRI under the auspices of government (interviews 35, 36, 37). While questions about full de jure independence can arise given the NHRI's subordination, the decision to adopt this format was based on a lengthy process of expert evaluation and consultation of the Justice Ombudsman about the suitability of extending the NHRI's mandate to include human rights promotion and protection. The consultation process recommended the creation of an independent body operating under the umbrella of the national government rather than a new body affiliated with the country's parliament. In 2019 the Swedish government held public consultations with several civil society groups (Government of Sweden 2019) and found domestic support for the initiative and a call for institutional independence and sufficient resources (Nätverket för en svensk människorättsinstitution 2021). In March 2021 it introduced a bill in Parliament, to establish the Human Rights Institute.

Before a dedicated NHRI was proposed, the Equality Ombudsman held the status of an NHRI in Sweden. To understand better the national context leading to the decision to establish a separate dedicated institution, and to develop an understanding of the institutional solutions Sweden has found to tackle human rights in past decades, the next section briefly reviews the development of the existing network of ombudsmen and their strength and effectiveness. The story of Sweden's institutional development offers valuable insights into the national processes that have shaped the creation of NHRIs in liberal democracies. Especially valuable for this book are the insights into the determinants of institutional development and increasing institutional strength over the years. This section cannot review the changes in effectiveness and impact on human rights outcomes that occur after the very recent establishment of the Swedish NHRI; but it will briefly consider the formal strength and effectiveness of the Swedish Equality Ombudsman, which held NHRI status in Sweden its accreditation in 2011 and until the newly established

Human Rights Institute is itself accredited (the Swedish NHRI applied for its first-ever international accreditation status in April 2023).

To comply with European Union norms, Sweden established several equality and diversity bodies. In the 1980s it established its first Equality Ombudsman, with a mandate focused on gender equality, particularly discrimination in the labor force. In the early 2000s, three new equality and diversity ombudsmen were created, with remits in the areas of ethnic discrimination, disability, and sexual orientation. These ombudsmen had remits that covered new grounds of discrimination, including discrimination in the educational system as well as in the provision of goods and services (Diskriminerings Ombudsmannen 2016). In the mid-2000s, efforts to unify the legislation began, institutional-izing and centralizing antidiscrimination and equality work. By 2009, Parlia-ment had passed new legislation encompassing seven areas of rights protec-tion, including gender identity, freedom of expression, and religion. In 2015, at the Equality Ombudsman's recommendation, the law also included protec-tion against discrimination in access to goods and services (Diskriminerings Ombudsmannen 2019). The 2009 Law on Antidiscrimination laid the legal foundation for the establishment of a single Discrimination Ombudsman, as a result of the merger of all four existing ombudsmen.

Unlike that of most peer institutions around the world, the institutional development of the ombudsmen in Sweden has not been motivated by learning from participation in global or regional peer networks of NHRIs. That said, the Swedish ombudsmen have enjoyed some limited recognition through accreditation (B-status) and membership with limited rights in the Global Alliance of National Human Rights Institutions. Despite not having an explicit human rights mandate, a representative of the Swedish ombuds-men was present at the International Workshop on National Institutions for the Promotion and Protection of Human Rights, held in Paris on 7–9 October 1991, which was instrumental in the creation of NHRIs and in the early con-solidation of a global network of peer NHRIs. Shortly thereafter, the Subcom-mittee on Accreditation granted the Swedish ombudsmen accreditation; all four ombudsmen shared the responsibility of participating in the peer net-work. Re-accreditation was delayed by two years, due to the extended dura-tion of the merger, and the Equality Ombudsman reapplied for accreditation in 2010. One year later, the Equality Ombudsman received B-status because it lacked a sufficiently broad human rights mandate and independence from government (Subcommittee on Accreditation 2011).

An important factor determining the strength of the Swedish Equality Ombudsman is the special nature of the NHRI's independence from government. Despite being subordinate to government by law, the Equality Ombudsman enjoys the statutory independence legally granted to all public bodies in Sweden (interviews 36, 37). A characteristic in Sweden is the public authorities' sociolegal autonomy from ministries. Sweden has a system of public administration that operates outside ministries with full power of decision over its own activities, embedded in a system of governance in which specialized ministries have much smaller of staff and responsibilities than those in other countries. In other words, public authorities have the legal guarantee of constitutional independence regardless of their formal integration in the broader public institutional architecture (interviews 35, 36, 37, 40). In the memory of former staff members at the ombudsman's office, the sole instance of government intervention to constrain the institution's activity was the early removal of Ombudswoman Katri Linna in 2011 (interviews 35, 36). This dismissal had no significant impact on institutional activity but was evidence that, despite functional independence, the ombudsman as an institution can be vulnerable to some degree of political intervention.

The Swedish Equality Ombudsman is considered an effective complaint-handling body with primary expertise in handling equality and diversity complaints. To the extent that complaint cases refer to rights violations with a human rights dimension, the Swedish Ombudsman's work can be said to contain some degree of de facto human rights protection (interviews 36, 37, 49). However, most of its activity is focused on its main mandate of safeguarding, monitoring, and reporting on equality and diversity issues. The Equality Ombudsman is also the main institution in charge of raising awareness of discrimination, following relevant academic research to inform the wider population about its rights and to recommend best measures. The institution's more recent promotional work has focused on generating an Internet-based set of resources, such as specialized reports, leaflets, brochures, and video materials, to which employers and individuals can turn for specialized information (Diskriminerings Ombudsmannen 2019). As such, it is considered a well-respected hub of specialized information and legal expertise (interviews 35, 37). However, the institution has a limited involvement with civil society, usually offering expert advice and specialized guidance on legislation and specific cases of violations.

Historically, the main source of structural inefficiency in the Equality Ombudsman's work stemmed from the merger of the former equality ombudsmen more than a decade ago. Much like the equality and diversity bodies that formed the Equality and Human Rights Commission in the United Kingdom, the former Swedish ombudsmen took several years to create a common institutional culture and to align their work so as to integrate all competencies in rights protection. Another source of inefficiency was the change made in the ombudsman's relationship with government by moving its main affiliation to different ministries, such as the Ministry of Labor, the Ministry of Integration and Equality, and more recently the Ministry of Culture. However, staff who worked at the Ombudsman Office at the time did not recall these changes as hierarchical, or as obstructions (interviews 35, 36). The Equality Ombudsman continued its advisory work with government with respect to legislation on diversity and equality, and also regarding the integration of safeguards against discrimination in all legislation. Despite these institutional transformations, the office of the Swedish Equality Ombudsman has enjoyed continuous support from successive governments and has not suffered budget cuts.

The Equality Ombudsman's international activity is significant in diversity and equality communities. Over the years, the office has been consistently active in EQUINET and has often found itself in the position of mentoring and advising peer institutions in other countries on equality legislation. As European Union member states developed their national legislation to implement EU directives, the Equality Ombudsman was able to draw upon Sweden's own experience of developing relevant legislation earlier than any other country in the region. Moreover, a particularly important cross-border relationship that the Swedish ombudsman has maintained over the years has been the close collaboration with equality ombudsmen in other Nordic countries. Learning and support across institutions occurs informally through continual staff contact, and also formally at regular annual meetings for the subregional network. It is no surprise that this special partnership, present in many other aspects of social and political life, also exists in the realm of human rights protection and promotion.

Conclusion

Given the long traditions of liberal democracy in Western Europe, it is perhaps not surprising that all states in the region have designated bodies mandated to promote and protect various rights of their citizens. What is surprising, however, is that the long-standing respect for liberal values and rights protection in these democracies has not resulted in continuous government support for strong formal institutions that can monitor human rights performance, aid in rights implementation, and hold public bodies accountable on rights violations. This inconsistent commitment to formalizing the promotion and protection of human rights through NHRIs may be due to a sense that a complex system of domestic democratic institutions is indeed already in place in Western European states (Cardenas 2014), and that there is thus no need for more national instruments to enforce human rights. The finding that there is less support for NHRIs among the longer-established democracies provides an interesting parallel to the finding that the more securely democratic states tend to be less eager to join international human rights treaties (see, for example, Moravcsik 2000 on the European Convention on Human Rights, or Simmons and Danner 2010 on membership in the International Criminal Court).

This chapter has explored reasons for the variations in institutional strength of NHRIs in the Western European subregion, with a focus on their relative formal weakness. Moreover, chapter 4 investigated the implications of this weakness the institutions' effectiveness and impact. Somewhat paradoxically, a main reason for weaker institutional mandates is the long tradition of liberal democracy in the region. It has spurred the creation of varied domestic architectures of specialized rights promotion and protection bodies, with mandates that include complaint handling and casework, primarily in the areas of diversity and equality. Whether implementing EU directives in rights promotion and protection or responding to domestic demands to establish complaint-handling mechanisms, states in Western Europe have sought to integrate NHRIs into their existing domestic networks of liberal institutions.

The success of states in establishing strong NHRIs has varied, but a broader subregional trend is visible. Most NHRIs in Western Europe have been established on the foundations of existing public equality and diversity bodies, and have remained relatively weak in terms of their human rights mandates and their formal independence from political interference. While a few NHRIs are fully independent from government, such as the Finnish Parliamentary Ombudsman and the recently established NHRI in Norway, more human rights institutions in the subregion—including the ones discussed in this chapter—have maintained some degree of affiliation with the executive, continuing the association of the equality and diversity bodies they have replaced.

Regardless of their current level of strength and their institutional model, all NHRIs in Western Europe have strengthened their formal designs over the years. Moreover, even as their formal powers have not been as strong as those of some peer institutions in Eastern Europe, they have generally been able to carry out their mandates successfully, and to have some impact on human

rights on the ground. The extent of government support for NHRIs has varied from government to government, with left-wing cabinets being generally
more favorable. But most institutions in the subregion have had sufficient
funding to carry out their activities, even when hit hard by budget cuts during the 2008 economic recession, and have enjoyed relatively good relationships with their respective national executives. More recently, governments
in established European democracies have slowly begun to realize that there
is an increasing need to strengthen the rights protection mechanisms in their
territories in relation to certain policy areas. This process started less than a
decade ago, and has intensified in recent years, particularly as a reaction to
increasing south-to-north migration and growing numbers of refugees. In
this context, NHRIs have played key roles in mitigating the impact of policy on migrant communities, and in advising governments, monitoring the
implementation of international human rights law, and reporting to treaty
bodies on countries' performance.

Recent election results in several European countries indicate a decline
in overall public and political support for liberal democratic institutions,
and a rise in far-right (generally, populist and nationalist) disenchantment
with liberal internationalism and multilateral solutions to shared transborder
problems. It is fair to expect that in this context, NHRIs will feel the impact negatively. Nevertheless, the track record of resilience and continued
strengthening that most NHRIs have shown in recent decades promises their
continued success. Chapter 4 will discuss broader patterns in the regional and
global development of NHRIs, and will seeking to uncover the conditions for
stronger and more effective promotion and protection of human rights in
Europe and beyond.

4

European and Global Patterns of Socialization: A Quantitative Exploration of Institutional Strength

Since the early 1990s, national human rights institutions have spread around the world with surprising speed. With the encouragement of international organizations such as the United Nations and the European Union, governments adopted new bodies dedicated to the promotion and protection of human rights in their territories, or have adapted existing institutions to also encompass human rights mandates. NHRIs have become formally stronger. The norm cascade triggered by the active global promotion and advancement of NHRIs has resulted in an exceptional expansion from 20 such structures before 1990 to approximately 130 in 2015 (Linos and Pegram 2016b). Many countries also have institutions with de jure or de facto powers to implement human rights domestically—whether as unaccredited ombudsmen, as is the case in several countries in Central America, or as public agencies integrated in government ministries or commissions with too few resources to enter the accreditation process, as is the case for a number of human rights bodies in the Asia-Pacific region and on the African continent.

In 1999, six European countries had strong institutions, and by 2004 that number had more than doubled, to fourteen. By 2014 it had increased to a total of twenty-two NHRIs with strong formal designs. In the span of twenty years, the number of weak and medium institutions halved, with some weak institutions reaching medium strength and some medium-strength ones becoming stronger. During that time, the upward trend was reflected in the dimensions of institutional strength: on average, NHRIs in Europe strengthened their safeguards for institutional durability even higher than the safeguards for enforcement. This indicated the European governments' commitment to establishing stronger institutions "on paper," granting them stronger powers and securing their existence through legal documents.

Europe has arguably the most developed system of regional human rights governance, with a diverse set of regional instruments set up in parallel with the global regime to safeguard the promotion and protection of rights in the region. Human rights provisions are embedded in regional human rights treaties overseen by the Council of Europe, complementing the foundational liberal values advanced by European Union in its framework of supranational legislation, like the Charter of Fundamental Rights and the European Convention on Human Rights and the Treaty on the Functioning of the European Union. In addition, in 2012 the European Council adopted its Strategic Framework on Human Rights and Democracy, accompanied by an action plan to implement the framework (Lerch 2019). These documents lay out principles, objectives, and priorities with a particular focus on improving the integration of human rights in the EU's international policymaking as well as in its foreign policy practices.

With the efforts to consolidate the legal framework of human rights regionally and globally came a stronger interest in closing the gap between legislation and implementation. The concern with minimizing the distance between the principles embedded in law and the action to implement them domestically is particularly pertinent, as several European framework policies are not legally binding instruments for member states. Formally strong NHRIs have increasingly come to be seen as providing a viable solution for domestic implementation, being regulatory bodies that operate as intermediaries between international organizations and national governments, with functional independence and the capacity to advise governments but also monitor their work and hold them to account. The rising interest in strengthening the domestic regulatory structures to implement regional and international human rights law has resulted in stronger support for NHRIs across "greater Europe" (including EU member states, states with candidate status, and states included in the European Neighborhood Policy area).

The European Union intensified the action to include NHRIs in the performance reports assessing the progress of states that were candidates for EU membership. It also integrated a human rights dimension into partnership agreements with states just outside EU borders, into the allocation of development aid, and into the conditions to bilateral trade agreements. The EU's Action Plan on Human Rights and Democracy had as a first objective to support NHRIs, advancing its engagement with A-status institutions to strengthen their involvement in consultation processes (such as the Human Rights Dialogues), supporting B-status bodies to prepare them for accreditation and cooperation with regional and international networks, and facilitating cooperation between NHRIs in the EU and their counterparts in partner countries (Council of the European Union 2015).

To explain these regional and global trends, this chapter proposes to measure the strength of NHRIs and apply the analytical framework described in chapter 1 first to regional data and later to global data. It discusses the main factors that affect institutional design for human rights implementation and the causal mechanisms at work in institutional change across borders and over time. The regional analysis finds strong evidence in support of socialization and conditionality hypotheses. In other words, membership in peer networks like the Global Alliance of National Human Rights Institutions (GANHRI) and state ratification of human rights treaties under the remit of the Council of Europe are associated with stronger NHRIs. In addition, conditionality tied to the prospect of membership in the European Union and positive change in newly democratizing states are associated with stronger NHRIs, particularly those with safeguards for durability. The second part of the analysis in this chapter shows that the findings of the regional analysis could be extrapolated to the global level, too. Socialization effects linked to membership in GANHRI remain meaningful determinants of institutional strength. Both the ratification of international human rights treaties and the cost-benefit calculations of national governments in newly democratized states are associated with stronger NHRIs. Unlike the qualitative analysis, the regional and global analyses do not explore the effectiveness of NHRIs in making an impact on human rights outcomes regionally or globally. The main reason for this gap is the lack of systematic, quantitative data on the domestic and international impact of national human rights over time. At the same time, this book aims to inspire future data collection efforts and further research on the topic.

Institutional Strength in Europe: Data, Indicators, and Coding

The development of the dependent variable was based on coding publicly available documents for each NHRI and each country. Data was collected for the period 1994–2017. The cutoff points for institutions established after 1994 is the year immediately after the year of institutional establishment (e.g., the Serbian NHRI was created by law in 2005 and was coded as nonexistent until 2009, when I introduced data on institutional safeguards into the data set). The time interval and the selection of fifty countries included in the study are closely tied to the availability of sources; while all the institutions publish reports and their publication is stipulated in institutional mandates, not all the institutions publish them annually. Some publish reports covering their activities over two or three years, and in some years no reports were published at all. Most of the institutions had no formal reporting systems before the mid-1990s, and some went without them well into the 2000s, when the Paris Principles were introduced. Most NHRIs make such information public on their official Internet pages, in their national languages and usually also in English. The materials were consulted directly in their original form in the following languages: Danish, English, French, Portuguese, Romanian, Spanish, and Swedish. Translation of material in Bulgarian was provided by a native speaker, and automatic translation was used for small passages of text in Greek that were not otherwise available (see appendix for details).

Information from available reports was complemented and corroborated by information from institutional mandates, relevant legislation, and country constitutions. In the rare cases where constitutions or relevant laws were not available on institutional web pages, other sources were consulted, such as the International Labour Organization online database of national labor, social security, and related human rights legislation, NATLEX (NATLEX, International Labour Organization 2013). For countries in the data set that were candidates for EU membership, country reports issued by the European Commission offer assessments of ombudsman-type and human rights institutions (European Commission 2015b). For states with candidate status prior to earlier waves of EU enlargement, data was collected from available country reports (European Commission 2015b). In the cases of Serbia and Montenegro, which were members of the Federal Republic of Yugoslavia until 2003 and of the nation called Serbia and Montenegro until 2006, a single ombudsman-type institution (with separate regional offices dealing with separate ethnic groups) was coded for both countries until 2006, the moment of their official independence and the establishment of separate NHRIs for each new state. Whenever two institutions with national human rights mandates exist in one country (for instance, in Romania, Bulgaria, the Netherlands, and Malta), I selected the one that was established first.

Building on the definition of institutional strength presented in chapter 1, the operationalization of institutional strength as a ranked categorical variable is made up of two main dimensions of institutional strength: durability and enforcement. These two dimensions are each made up of three distinct subdimensions that capture the main mandated characteristics of NHRIs. Legal embeddedness, institutional mandate, and de jure powers of promotion and protection make up the broader dimension of institutional durability (see table 1.1). Three other subdimensions—institutional autonomy from government intervention, predominant activities of human rights promotion and protection, and pluralism of representation across societal groups—constitute the dimension of institutional enforcement. These sub-dimensions were defined on the basis of formal features identified in the mandates and reported operations of national human rights organizations around the world, including institutions with and without accreditation. In their turn, these six subdimensions capture measures of formal institutional strength and predominant areas of activity along eleven different indicators of institutional strength (table 4.2).

Original data was collected on eleven ordered categorical indicators ranking NHRIs as weak, medium, strong, or nonexistent. Included in the study are formal bodies that, by design or through their activity, promote and protect human rights, such as ombudsmen and *defensores*, human rights commissions, and NHRIs. Civil society organizations and informal institutions were excluded. Data was collected through textual analysis of publicly available institutional documentation (annual reports and institutional mandates), country constitutions, and national legislation (see appendix).

A model was fit with institutional strength as an ordered categorical variable obtained through multidimensional scaling across the eleven indicators grouped in two main dimensions of institutional strength for NHRIs. Separate models with institutional durability and institutional enforcement as dependent variables captured possible differential effects of independent variables on the two dimensions of institutional strength for NHRIs. An expert survey of heads of NHRIs and others with extensive knowledge of NHRIs was also conducted, to assess the institutional design of weak and medium-strength NHRIs as well as of institutions without accreditation, which may not have documentation for all years of interest in our study. Nineteen out of thirty-five experts we contacted (55 percent) completed the survey. Both the textual analysis and the surveys made use of the coding scheme included in the appendix to this book. A list of sources of annual reports and relevant institutional legislation for the over-time data in the regional analysis can also be found in the appendix.

To capture the effects of various determinants on institutional strength, the models presented below also include independent variables (table 4.1). The variables that measure membership in one of the networks of countries in our sample—GANHRI, the European Union, and candidate countries with EU conditionality—are operationalized as binary (0 for nonmembership and 1 for membership). Membership in the European Neighborhood Policy is coded as a binary variable (European Commission 2019a). These variables allow us to observe the effects of independent variables on NHRI strength over time, as some countries joined the three networks between 1994

TABLE 4.1. Variables included in the three models (see also appendix)

Short variable names	Long variable names
NHRI strength	Institutional strength
NHRI enforcement	Institutional enforcement safeguards
NHRI durability	Institutional durability safeguards
GANHRI membership	Membership in Global Alliance of National Human Rights Institutions
EU membership	European Union membership
ENP membership	Membership in European Neighbourhood Policy
EU conditionality	European Union conditionality
European HR treaties	European human rights treaties
Global HR treaties	Global human rights treaties
Common law	Country with common-law system
Newly democratized	Newly democratized country
Freedom House	Freedom House score of states' regime type
Polity	Polity IV score of states' authority characteristics
GDP/cap	Gross domestic product per capita
Trend	Variable taking into account time trend in data

and 2017. As a measure of states' commitment to the regional human rights regime promoted by the Council of Europe, the models include an indicator measuring the number of ratified European human rights treaties (Council of Europe 2019). The models also include a measure of commitment to the global human rights regime, operationalized through a variable consisting of the number of ratified global human rights treaties. Freedom House data is used to measure different levels of democratization (Freedom House 2016). As a measure of whether a country is a new democracy, data was compiled to generate a binary variable that assigns the value of 1 to countries that transitioned from communism to democracy since 1989. Based on existing scholarship, democracies in general (Linos and Pegram 2016b) and the democratic frontrunners among new democracies (Moravcsik 2000; Schimmelfennig and Sedelmeier 2004) are expected to have stronger NHRIs. Moreover, lower- and middle-income countries are more likely to engage in institutional borrowing (Wayland 2004), even when their governments do not intend to enforce those institutions (Van de Walle 2001). The models also include a binary control variable, indicating whether a country has a common system of law (Linos and Pegram 2016b).

A Model of Institutional Strength in Europe

I model change in the institutional strength of NHRIs in fifty states located in "greater Europe" (European Union member states, states with candidate

TABLE 4.2. Indicators and respective coding scheme for coding of variable "strength of national human rights institutions"[a]

Institutional strength 1–4 scale: 4. strong 3. medium 2. weak 1. nonexistent	Dimension	Subdimension	Definition	Indicator	Ranking
	Durability	Legal embeddedness	Degree of inclusion of institutional establishment and mandate in the country's legal framework	Legal embeddedness	(4) country constitution (3) inclusion in national law (2) other type of official document such as presidential decree (1) nonexistent
		Mandate	Degree to which NHRI mandate contains human rights	Human rights mandate	(4) broad human rights (3) partial human rights, or rights mixed with other issues, such as equality remit or mixed remit (2) no human rights (1) nonexistent
		Promotion and protection ("on paper")	Mandated duties to promote and protect human rights	Promotion	(4) research and education (3) annual institutional reporting (2) limited or no such activity (1) nonexistent
				Protection	(4) power to impose fines litigation and legal representation (3) complaint handling and independent investigations (2) no such powers (1) nonexistent
	Enforcement	Autonomy from government	Degree of formal autonomy from government interference	Sources of institutional funding	(4) parliament through yearly budget (3) government (2) other sources like donations (1) nonexistent
				Government representation in decision making	(4) none or very limited (3) government participates but has no power of decision (2) government incorporates NHRI or has power of decision (1) nonexistent

(continues)

TABLE 4.2. (*continued*)

Institutional strength	Dimension	Subdimension	Definition	Indicator	Ranking
				Leadership appointment structure	(4) the institution alone (3) parliament (2) government (1) nonexistent
				Formal reporting	(4) to parliament (3) to government or ministry (2) other (1) nonexistent
		Promotion and protection ("predominant")	Predominant types of activities prioritized by the institution	Promotion	(4) research and education (3) annual institutional reporting (2) limited or no such activity (1) nonexistent
				Protection	(4) powers to impose fines, litigation, and legal representation (3) complaint handling and independent investigations (2) no such activity (1) nonexistent
		Pluralism of representation	Extent to which representatives of NGOs and civil society representatives are included in the decision-making process	Civil society/NGO representation	(4) representation on board or council of NHRI (3) project collaboration (2) public consultation (1) nonexistent

TABLE 4.3. Three quantitative models of institutional strength in greater Europe

	Model 1 Strength	Model 2 Durability	Model 3 Enforcement
GANHRI membership	0.893***	1.446***	0.193
	(0.301)	(0.275)	(0.252)
EU membership	0.938**	0.237	0.606
	(0.450)	(0.368)	(0.404)
EU conditionality	2.056***	1.603***	1.622***
	(0.427)	(0.351)	(0.352)
ENP membership	0.103	0.552	0.405
	(0.388)	(0.358)	(0.329)
Global HR treaties	0.280	0.268	0.291
	(0.409)	(0.301)	(0.484)
European HR treaties	0.126	0.103	0.241**
	(0.094)	(0.071)	(0.111)
Freedom House	0.123	0.130	0.417
	(0.289)	(0.286)	(0.260)
Newly democratized	2.837*	1.898*	2.416
	(1.537)	(1.122)	(1.855)
Common law	0.323	0.938	−0.805
	(2.281)	(1.686)	(2.681)
GDP/cap	−0.001**	−0.001*	2.570
	(0.000)	(0.000)	(0.000)
Trend	0.256***	0.213***	0.196***
	(0.028)	(0.025)	(0.024)
N	1200	1200	1200

Prob > chi2 = 0.000, ***$p < 0.01$, **$p < 0.05$). Standard errors in parentheses.

status in 2017, and states included in the European Neighborhood Policy area), during the period from 1994 to 2017, fitting a series of pooled ordered logit models. Given that NHRIs have registered a natural increase in their strength since 1994, the impact of the time trend on the strength of NHRIs is included in the models through a variable accounting for the trend. The analysis explores the effects of the main international determinants—membership in GANHRI through accreditation, EU membership, Council of Europe influence, and EU membership conditionality—on institutional strength (model 1 in table 4.3) and the two separate dimensions of institutional strength (models 2 and 3 in table 4.3).

SOCIALIZATION PROCESSES IN GREATER EUROPE

The analysis offers valuable insights into possible causal processes explaining the strength of NHRIs in greater Europe. The results indicate that over time, countries that are members of GANHRI have stronger institutions than do countries that are not members. This result furthers the conclusions of recent research on the design of NHRIs (Linos and Pegram 2016b) and on their strength (Lacatus 2019). Membership in GANHRI, granted through the accreditation process and maintained through periodic re-accreditation, matters for formal design and also for institutional strength. Given that the analysis studies change in institutional strength over time, our findings show that the positive impact of GANHRI membership is also felt over time. The sample of countries included in the analysis also includes unaccredited institutions, so the results add further evidence that a country's decision to seek accreditation and join the global network of peer bodies is associated with an increase in institutional strength over time.

These results offer important evidence in support of the socialization thesis for institutional change. In the context of this study's multilevel analysis, the quantitative findings confirm the existence of regional socialization effects of which we have also found evidence at the country level, in the case studies presented in chapters 2 and 3. Made possible by participation in GANHRI or by networking at the regional level in the European Network of National Human Rights Institutions, positive change in the formal strength of NHRIs is possible over the years. The regional analysis provides additional backing for explanations of institutional strength that emphasize cross-border learning facilitated by membership in peer networks and resulting in acculturation or persuasion. Although they are analytically distinct, processes of acculturation and persuasion are hard to disentangle in the reality of the world around us. This is partly due to the need for institutions to pass the test of time, and the need to see whether learning is complete, leading to institutional transformation and the internationalization of norms through persuasion. Interpreting regional effects along two dimensions of institutional strength—durability and enforcement—advances our understanding of the extent to which states in greater Europe have indeed strengthened their NHRIs by having embraced human rights norms.

Qualitative evidence increases our confidence in this quantitative finding, and mitigates the potential for endogeneity effects (e.g., only strong NHRIs join GANHRI). Until 2018, GANHRI used a three-tier membership system based on accreditation levels determined by the assessed compliance with the Paris Principles. Weaker human rights institutions, which we expect might have lower compliance with the Paris Principles, would be granted C-level of accreditation, while institutions stronger compliance would be granted B-status. The strongest level of compliance would be granted A-status. Every five years, all GANHRI member institutions would undergo a re-accreditation process intended to assess their performance and make recommendations for their strengthening. While some institutions may have chosen to apply for GANHRI accreditation and membership once they gained more formal strength, the majority have seen their strength increase after they joined the global network.

To that end, models 1 and 2 show that the impact of GANHRI remains significant and positive on institutional strength, particularly its durability. The effect of GANHRI membership on enforcement safeguards is positive but not statistically significant. While the influence of the global network could explain the stronger independence and autonomy from government, it could not account for states granting NHRIs stronger enforcement safeguards. The "shallower" commitment to enforcement safeguards, reflected in the predominant activities of NHRIs to promote and protect human rights, may be due to incomplete learning and persuasion. At the institutional level, these findings point to institutional isomorphism due to acculturation processes, rather than to the complete internationalization of norms about the appropriate design of independent national bodies charged with the promotion and protection of human rights.

The results provide some evidence in support of the thesis that regional membership-based participation in peer state networks can lead to persuasion and norm learning, but this evidence is inconsistent and relatively weak. From this perspective, the EU can be a promising case for persuasion and norm learning, but this evidence does not hold along the two disaggregated dimensions of institutional strength. EU membership has a positive and statistically significant effect on institutional strength, as evidenced by model 1, but these effects lose statistical significance when measured on the two disaggregated dimensions: durability and enforcement. This result might be an additional confirmation that, once countries have joined the EU, they do not necessarily maintain the same level of commitment to its normative values for the longer term (Conant 2014). At the same time, the impact of membership in the European Neighborhood Policy on institutional strength is positive but does not reach the level of statistical significance. These findings support the conclusions of prior scholarship regarding the EU's weaker influence on human rights promotion and protection in countries that are geographically more distant and have a less credible promise of future membership (Börzel and Risse 2012; Schimmelfennig 2012).

This analysis finds evidence of norm learning through international mechanisms coordinated by the Council of Europe, in the case of safeguards for enforcement. Although the statistical effect is small, the commitment of states to European human rights treaties is associated with an increase in the institutional safeguards for enforcement. This might be an indication that the Council of Europe's efforts to advance human rights in the region and promote their institutionalization through NHRIs have been successful. States that ratify regional human rights treaties make efforts to establish NHRIs on their territories and to support their continued development over time. The stronger statistical effects on enforcement safeguards can be an indication of the states' keener commitment to the implementation of human rights in their territories.

INCENTIVE-SETTING THROUGH EUROPEAN UNION
MEMBERSHIP CONDITIONALITY

Incentive-setting is a key mechanism that can set in motion institutional change in states with a credible chance of joining the EU. Imposed for the first time on the states aiming to become members in 2004, democratic conditionality laid out a set of demands for states in Central and Eastern Europe to carry out legal and institutional reforms in different policy areas, such as rule of law, independence of the courts, and corruption control. These requirements include assessments of institutional performance in the case of NHRIs, commending progress and making recommendation to national governments to offer them continued support.

The results of the analysis offer strong evidence that EU membership conditionality has a positive and statistically significant effect on institutional strength and on the dimensions of durability and enforcement. Even as the effect of EU membership does not reach the level of statistical significance, as is the case with its effect on the institutional durability and enforcement safeguards discussed above, the impact of EU democratic conditionality on institutional strength in Central and Eastern European states remains positive and significant. These findings lend additional empirical evidence to existing scholarship on the impact of EU conditionality on institutional strength, and on compliance with EU demands on legal harmonization and alignment with human rights practices as a requirement for granting candidate member status (Sedelmeier 2009b). They also offer additional quantitative evidence in support of the qualitative findings presented in chapter 2 of this book.

To some extent this finding might not be surprising, as states with accession candidate status make great efforts to meet the EU's requirements before starting negotiations with the EU and during the years leading to full membership. One can expect that states will seek to establish new NHRIs or strengthen existing ones to show their commitment to human rights promotion and protection. This certainly has been even more the case for states like the postconflict countries in the Balkans, where human rights violations were a central concern due to war-related crimes and the large wave of migrants and refugees. More generally, in biannual progress reports on virtually all candidate states since the 2004 wave of accession, the European Commission repeatedly expressed concern about the treatment of ethnic and religious minorities, violations of the rights of detained and incarcerated persons, and states' conduct toward persons with disabilities. To that end, the European Commission often recommends that states support the existence of strong and effective human rights ombudsmen or commissions to address such violations. As discussed earlier, governments can choose to expand the institutional mandate of existing ombudsmen and commissions to include provisions for torture prevention, equality, and diversity on several grounds, as well as protection of the rights of people with disabilities.

Moreover, it is important to consider that the effect over time of EU conditionality on institutional strength is often indirect in nature. The EU began imposing conditions for accession prior to the 2004 wave of enlargement. While addressing some areas of rights violations was high on the European Commission's agenda, other measures of institutional and legal development were also viewed as crucial to meeting accession requirements. Meeting demands in policy areas linked to liberal democratic consolidation led states to turn to existing ombudsmen and strengthen their institutional mandates. For instance, accession conditionality was linked to the need for states to promote the rule of law, control corruption in public institutions, and strengthen their judiciary. In addition, efforts to tighten existing legal frameworks and increase the independence of courts have resulted in more effective relationships between those state organs and NHRIs.

This quantitative result also reinforces the conclusions of the qualitative research in Central and Eastern European countries presented in chapter 2 of this book. The statistical analysis shows that the conclusions of the qualitative research can be extrapolated across Europe. Democratic conditionality is an important regional predictor of stronger NHRIs in greater Europe. In other words, coercive policy is not effective only in specific conflict situations such as cases of violent ethnic cleansing in Bosnia and Kosovo, or human rights violations in Estonia and Latvia (Schimmelfennig 2006, pp. 257–60). Rather, the results speak more generally to the instrumental role that coercive policies play in human rights promotion and protection at the regional level.

THE IMPACT OF DOMESTIC LEVELS OF DEMOCRACY
ON INSTITUTIONAL STRENGTH

As discussed in chapter 1, the political preferences of domestic actors are key predictors of institutional strength. Whether states have a recent or a long-standing tradition of liberal democracy provides an important explanation for their support of their NHRIs. By the same token, changes in political preferences over time have also influenced the degree of their support for further strengthening NHRIs. In some instances, institutional reforms have in fact resulted in formally weakening a human rights body, sometimes temporarily and in other cases for the longer term. Examples are discussed in more detail in several case studies from both newly democratized states and old democracies in Europe. These effects are also visible in the regional quantitative analysis.

The results of this analysis show that states' early efforts to democratize can be marginally significant predictors of an increase in institutional strength over time, in terms of durability safeguards. That is to say that European governments in power during periods of transition to democracy tend to support the establishment of formally strong institutions meant to withstand possible attempts by future governments to destabilize processes of democratization. By this logic, changes in institutional strength can be tied to domestic political calculations that take into account the costs and potential benefits of institutional change when supporting the "lock-in" of democratic reforms (Moravcsik 1995; Simmons 2009). Whether responding to in-country public pressure to establish liberal institutions, as was the case in Poland and the Czech Republic, or indicating to international institutions and the EU their intention to consolidate liberal democracy, as was the case in Croatia, governments in Central and Eastern Europe have tended to create NHRIs with the strongest designs in the region and the world. As a result of mandate expansion and the pressures of membership conditionality in several states, NHRIs in the region strengthened their formal powers and often also their effectiveness.

By comparison, European states with long-standing democratic traditions have experienced less institutional growth as reflected in the formal strength of their NHRIs. The qualitative analysis shows that NHRIs in Western Europe have varying levels of strength which have not increased much over time. NHRIs in old democratic states have also suffered in past years as institutional effectiveness has diminished due to budget cuts, economic recession, and growing political resistance to liberalism. The quantitative analysis presented above supports the conclusions of the qualitative analysis, showing that the effect of overall levels of democracy on the strength of NHRIs in greater Europe does not reach statistical significance. In other words, the results indicate that more significant growth in institutional strength occurs in periods of democratic transition, while old democratic states in Europe have not sought to increase the formal strength of their national human rights bodies.

Some NHRIs have enjoyed good relationships with their governments, as is the case in most Scandinavian countries, while others have fought to broaden their mandates beyond equality and diversity to gain recognition for their rights work, as is the case in the United Kingdom and Belgium. Nevertheless, the findings of this analysis point to a higher overall risk for NHRIs in Western Europe to see their stability and effectiveness further curbed in the future. Given the relatively limited political will to continue growing and supporting NHRIs in the past twenty years, it is fair to anticipate a continued decline in broader support for human rights and for liberal democracy more generally. Against this background, national human rights bodies with weaker formal safeguards for durability and enforcement will likely have less strength to fend for themselves and preserve their independence from political interference. They will be more vulnerable to political attempts to curb their strength and effectiveness.

A Global Analysis of Institutional Strength

This section takes a broader analytical perspective and proposes a global analysis of institutional strength in 187 countries around the world. It is the first analysis of its kind, and the first global data set that measures institutional strength globally. The challenges faced by any researcher seeking to code the formal features of institutions around the world are numerous. NHRIs in Europe, and their counterparts in South America and some states in Southeast Asia as well, are generally better at reporting their activities in detail and on a regular basis, usually annually. Limitations on the availability of data sources, due to the inconsistent publication of annual institutional reports, have caused challenges for data collection at the global level. Surveys have helped to fill some of the informational gap, but they can only offer a snapshot of the processes of institutional development and effectiveness.

Despite these data-related limitations, the global analysis represents an important step in advancing our understanding of institutional strength in NHRIs, and its significance for understanding changes in human rights outcomes around the world. They show that in effect, measuring states' commitment to the promotion and protection of human rights not just in binary terms (whether a state has established an NHRI, regardless of whether the

TABLE 4.4. Variables included in global models of NHRI strength

Short variable names	Long variable names
NHRI strength	Institutional strength
NHRI enforcement	Institutional enforcement safeguards
NHRI durability	Institutional durability safeguards
GANHRI membership	Accreditation coordinated by United Nations OHCHR-based Subcommittee for Accreditation
PTA hard	Preferential trade agreements with hard human rights conditionality
Global HR treaties	Global human rights treaties
EU conditionality	European Union conditionality
Postcommunist	Country with communist regime prior to 1989
Intrawar	Country involved in civil war
Interwar	Country involved in intrastate war
Common law	Country with common-law system
Log GDP/cap	Log of gross domestic product per capita
Log world population	Log of world population

institution has any power) but through a more nuanced measure of institutional strength allows new insights into the effect that these specialized bodies can have on human rights outcomes globally. This section will begin with a discussion of the data, and will continue with the analysis of institutional strength and its determinants at the global level.

DATA, OPERATIONALIZATION, AND VARIABLES FOR THE GLOBAL MODELS

In the global data set, the institutional strength indicator remains the same as in the regional analysis. Additional explanatory factors in the global models of institutional strength (table 4.4) capture the main international and domestic factors that could explain variation in institutional strength across countries around the world. To capture the effects of membership in transnational peer institutional networks—the Global Alliance of National Human Rights Institutions—I propose a binary measure: 0 for nonmembership and 1 for membership. To measure incentive-setting and indirect coercion effects, the models also include binary measures of a state having signed a preferential trade agreement (Hafner-Burton 2005, 2009) and for the effects of EU membership conditionality on institutional strength (Lacatus 2019). As a measure of state commitment to human rights based on the argument that treaty membership is often endogenous to countries' human rights practices

(Cole 2012; Landman 2005; Simmons 2009), the models include also a control variable that measures a country's total number of ratified human rights treaties, and also controls for the effects of deep optional commitments to international human treaties (Cole 2012). Control variables were included for population size and country income, and to capture whether a country had engaged in international or civil wars and whether it had a system of common law. To test whether NHRIs influence human rights outcomes over and above treaty effects, the models include dummy variables for countries that undertook these optional commitments. They also include a measure of whether or not a country is postcommunist (Easterly 2001; Cole and Ramirez 2013). The appendix details the sources of data for the above independent and control variables included in the global models of institutional strength. It also contains the results of post-estimation tests.

A Model of NHRI Strength at the Global Level

I fit a series of pooled logit models using an original data set of indicators of national human rights strength for 187 countries. The appendix to this book contains summary statistics, information about data sources, and the results of post-estimation tests and robustness checks. Given the cross-sectional nature of the data, the values of coefficients represent the average effect of explanatory variables over the outcomes when the explanatory variables change between countries by one unit. The analysis explores the effects of the main international determinants: membership in the GANHRI through accreditation, preferential trade agreements with human rights conditionality, the ratification of global human rights treaties, and EU membership conditionality—on institutional strength (model 1) and the two separate dimensions of institutional strength (models 2 and 3).

SOCIALIZATION PROCESSES AT THE GLOBAL LEVEL

The results of the analysis illuminate possible causal processes explaining the strength of NHRIs around the world and expanding the regional and country-level insights presented so far in this book at the global level. Table 4.5 presents the results of the regression analysis for three models (1, 2, and 3), capturing the effects of GANHRI membership on the strength of NHRIs, their durability, and enforcement safeguards. The analysis provides evidence that the accreditation-based membership in GANHRI has a positive and significant effect on institutional strength and its two dimensions of durability

TABLE 4.5. Three quantitative models of institutional strength at the global level

	Model 1 Strength	Model 2 Durability	Model 3 Enforcement
GANHRI membership	2.407***	2.688***	2.102***
	(0.369)	(0.388)	(0.346)
PTA hard	0.698*	0.585*	0.615*
	(0.316)	(0.312)	(0.314)
Global HR treaties	0.188***	0.182***	0.210***
	(0.053)	(0.052)	(0.052)
EU conditionality	0.063	0.255	−0.327
	(0.613)	(0.586)	(0.576)
Freedom House	0.482	0.077	0.450*
	(0.240)	(0.273)	(0.238)
Postcommunist	1.079**	0.177	1.300***
	(0.435)	(0.403)	(0.433)
Intrawar	−0.668*	−0.293	−0.786**
	(0.390)	(0.391)	(0.380)
Interwar	−0.082	−0.098	−0.233
	(0.625)	(0.588)	(0.587)
Common law	0.797*	0.670	0.775*
	(0.464)	(0.450)	(0.456)
Log GDP/cap	0.058	−0.019	0.138
	(0.104)	(0.103)	(0.102)
Log world population	0.066	0.104	0.032
	(0.088)	(0.087)	(0.087)

Prob > chi2 = 0.0000, n = 187, *** for $p < 0.01$, ** for $p < 0.05$, * for $p < 0.10$.
Standard errors reported in parentheses.

and enforcement. This finding furthers the conclusions of recent research on the diffusion and design of NHRIs (Kim 2013; Lacatus 2018; Linos and Pegram 2016b), showing that states holding membership in the global peer network of NHRIs through accreditation and periodic re-accreditation have overall stronger NHRIs compared to countries that have nonaccredited institutions for the promotion and protection of human rights.

Particularly important in the context of this book is that UN-coordinated institutional accreditation, which was an important determinant of institutional strength in Europe, remains a key determinant of stronger NHRIs at the global level as well. The impact of membership in the global network of NHRIs on both dimensions of institutional strength, durability and enforcement, can be an indication of socialization effects due to learning from peer institutions and the efforts to create more alignment of institutional designs with the Paris Principles across all institutions in the network. More specifically, the small difference in the magnitude of the effects that GANHRI membership has on durability and enforcement, with a higher value for the impact on durability, may indicate a stronger global tendency toward isomorphism due to acculturation processes, rather than the complete internalization of norms about the appropriate design of independent national bodies charged with the promotion and protection of human rights. Given the small difference between the two results, one would be best served by further analysis of institutional strength, whether using case studies or quantitative data at the regional level, to get a deeper understanding of the extent of norm internationalization and learning in different regional and domestic contexts.

Additionally, this analysis supports the hypothesis that socialization at the global level matters in explaining the strength of NHRIs. The integration of states into the international human rights regime through the ratification of international human rights treaties has a positive and statistically significant impact, albeit small, on all dimensions of institutional strength. More specifically, the results of the analysis indicate that states which are more integrated into the global human rights regime through treaties are more likely to establish strong institutions to oversee the domestic implementation of international human rights law than are states that have ratified fewer such treaties. The impact of states' integration in the global human rights regime through treaty ratification was not a statistically significant predictor of institutional strength at the regional level in Europe. The earlier analysis at the regional level found that the independent European regime of human rights treaties overseen by the Council of Europe did have a positive and statistically significant effect on enforcement safeguards across institutions in greater Europe. This difference is an indication that a strong regional human rights regime can take precedence over the global human rights regime in shaping the formal domestic institutional mechanisms states create for implementation of human rights on the ground. Nevertheless, states' commitments to the global human rights regime through treaty ratification can be an indication of their intention to align themselves with peer states in the international community. Furthermore, states that commit to stronger international human rights treaties appear to pledge more strongly to implement international human rights law by establishing stronger formal bodies to protect and promote human rights domestically.

INCENTIVE SETTING THROUGH
INTERNATIONAL CONDITIONALITY

The regional analysis found that democratic conditionality linked to membership in the European Union is an important determinant of institutional strength in greater Europe. However, the global analysis no longer confirms this result. In other words, internationally, countries that have been subjected to EU membership conditionality do not have stronger NHRIs than states that have not been in that position. Thus, an important predictor of institutional strength at the regional level, democratic conditionality tied to the credible promise of membership in the EU, does not explain stronger institutional powers internationally. This result might be explained by the relatively small number of countries with EU conditionality compared to the total number of countries around the world (of which 187 countries were included in the analysis). The existence of many states with stronger NHRIs outside Europe could also explain these results, as could more impactful factors determining the strength of NHRIs on a global level. One such factor is conditionality tied to preferential trade agreements.

The global analysis does find some evidence that human rights conditionality tied to preferential trade agreements has a positive and statistically significant effect on the formal strength of NHRIs, and particularly on their enforcement safeguards, though those effects are relatively small. This result partly confirms the findings of existing research about the importance of considering conditional ties, including trade, when exploring states' decisions about human rights implementation (Hafner-Burton 2009). In other words, conditionality linked to being part of preferential trade agreements is a possible predictor of national human rights enforcement strength; but the impact it has on a state's decision to support stronger human rights enforcement institutions is small.

DOMESTIC FACTORS: THE COMMITMENT OF
TRANSITIONS TO LIBERAL DEMOCRACY

Unlike the findings of the analysis at the regional level in Europe, the global analysis finds only marginal support for an explanation of institutional strength due to the democratic identity of the states that host these institutions. In other words, in this model, democracy levels in a country are only marginal predictors of whether it will have NHRIs in its territory with stronger formal powers of enforcement. In this respect, the results of the regional and the global analyses align. This raises important questions about the distance between the commitments states make to establishing stronger NHRIs, and their more general endorsement of liberal democracy. Although the statistical effects are small and thus cannot support definitive causal statements, the analysis provides valuable insights into the possibly surprising roles that

NHRIs might play in domestic environments. If long-standing democracies around the world do not necessarily endorse stronger NHRIs, it is important to ask why human rights enforcement institutions do not enjoy strong domestic support in national settings where, at least in principle, the political cost of endorsing liberal institutions ought to be smaller.

The reverse can also be true. When states with weaker democratic performance endorse the establishment of strong NHRIs, is this "window-dressing" to please the international community? We can also ask the question differently, stressing the positive dimension of such a decision. Earlier sections present some of the success stories in which NHRIs are protagonists, where formerly communist states established NHRIs with strong formal mandates that survived transitions to democracy and became ever stronger and more effective national accountability bodies. The results of the analyses in this book point to the important strength NHRIs can have in aiding the transition to liberal democracy and social transformation. While this may not be the case in all transitional states around the world, the findings of these analyses present important evidence of a global trend worth considering.

Supporting the conclusions above, and much like the results of the regional analysis, the global models find that postcommunist states are more likely to have strong NHRIs, although at the global level the positive impact is stronger on enforcement safeguards. This effect can be tied to political behavior linked to the desire to "lock in" the process of democratic transition (Moravcsik 2000), where governments in transitional states are motivated to safeguard the consolidation of liberal democracy through the establishment of formally strong institutions that are more likely to withstand the pressures of the political and social transition away from authoritarianism. In the absence of incentives for states to make that transition, such as the concrete prospect of EU membership, governments seeking to move away from a communist past appear to rely on formal institutional mechanisms like stronger NHRIs.

Another domestic factor that is a global determinant of institutional strength is the experience of civil war (during 2011 and in the years just prior to the year of measurement, as measured by the data). Statistical results indicate that civil wars have a negative impact on states' abilities to establish and support formally strong NHRIs. This finding offers additional support to the existing scholarship on peace and human rights (Bell 2003b; Parlevliet 2005; Lacatus 2018; Lacatus and Nash 2019), which highlights the significant challenges that human rights actors face in conflict and postconflict settings. At the same time, in these domestic contexts the role of NHRIs is key to monitoring and enforcement of human rights during peacekeeping and peace implementation. Evidence of this is the establishment of new NHRIs through peace agreements all around the world—for instance, in Colombia, Bosnia and Herzegovina, Northern Ireland, Afghanistan, and Liberia. Given local challenges in postconflict environments, international institutions are essential to the establishment of strong NHRIs and to their operations, sometimes well into the transitional process in the aftermath of the conflict.

Conclusion

The statistical models in this section build on the theoretical framework and the operationalization of institutional strength presented earlier in this book. They offer explanations for the patterns of variation in the strength of NHRIs in Europe and globally. The regional analysis finds that as NHRIs become members of GANHRI, their strength is more likely to increase. This is a clear indication of strong socialization effects through peer networking both regionally and globally. In addition, the analysis finds strong support for a significant impact of EU conditionality on both dimensions of strength. It finds also that commitment to regional human rights treaties is associated with stronger safeguards of institutional enforcement. This can be an indication of the influence that the Council of Europe has had on the development of domestic human rights mechanisms, offering support for NHRIs to become more effective in fulfilling their mandates. At the same time, positive changes in democratic outcomes in newly democratizing states are associated with stronger NHRIs, and particularly with safeguards for durability. This is evidence of efforts to increase the durability of NHRIs over time as part of domestic elites' strategy to safeguard democratic progress and mitigate the risk of institutional decline in the event of future democratic backsliding.

Unlike the regional model that includes data over time, the global model of NHRI strength is cross-sectional, due to the limitations intrinsic to the global institutional strength data linked to the lack of rigorous regular reporting on institutional activity and changes in mandated strength. The findings of the global analysis confirm some findings of the regional analysis, especially regarding socialization effects being key to increased institutional strength. Peer network–based learning, through membership in GANHRI, is the key determinant of institutional strength internationally. Ratification of global human rights treaties has a smaller effect, indicating that the establishment of stronger NHRIs might also stem from states' normative commitment to implementing international human rights law with the help of strong human rights bodies. Unsurprisingly, the effects of EU membership conditionality are not significant at the global level. At the same time, postcommunist states generally have stronger NHRIs than do old democracies or autocratic states. This provides additional evidence in support of cost-benefit calculations driving compliance with international norms in states that seek to secure a successful transition to liberal democracy.

Conclusion

In his State of the Nation address on 18 February 2018, Hungary's prime minister, Viktor Orbán, spoke of Nils Muižnieks, the Council of Europe's commissioner for human rights. He said Muižnieks "recently let slip that some years ago they secretly launched a program to breed a Soros-like human race, or, as they modestly put it—if I can pronounce the term—*Homo sorosensus*. . . . I realized that from their point of view, from the viewpoint of the Soros types, we indigenous people who have our own countries, our own culture and our own religion—things for which we will fight tooth and nail—are individuals beyond redemption" (Ra'ad 2018). Mired in untruth and conspiratorial discourse, Orbán's interpretation of human rights is in equal measure racist, nativist, illiberal, and Euroskeptical. Anchored in the rhetoric of far-right populism, this statement encapsulates what is likely the greatest threat that the human rights regime faces in Europe and around the world today. A strong distrust among domestic political elites of international cooperation and the institutions promoting the liberal global order fuels political agendas that are driven by antagonism between international institutions and national interests and values.

In 2011, Article 9(3) of the new Fundamental Law of Hungary proposed a significant change to the process of appointing the commissioner for fundamental rights, providing that the president of Hungary nominates a candidate to Parliament for election as commissioner. Additionally, section 7(4) of act 111 of 2011 calls for the commissioner for fundamental rights to seek advice from government before proposing a candidate for deputy commissioner responsible for protection of minority rights. Effectively, this legal change weakens the formal strength of the NHRI by removing some of its autonomy in the process of institutional leadership appointment, and by tying it to majority political decision making. Ultimately, this results in further centralizing the power of the president and reinforcing the dominance of majority political parties.

Despite acquiring a broader human rights mandate (and hence an overall stronger mandate) as a result of legal and institutional reforms, the overall strength of the Hungarian NHRI was weakened by granting the president rather than the parliament or the NHRI itself the power to nominate the commissioner. This ultimately resulted in decreased institutional effectiveness. When institutional leadership is not independent from political interference, the activities of NHRIs are much more likely to support political and ideological agendas rather than to hold governments to account for their human rights records and their commitment to international laws. For instance, the Office of the Commissioner for Fundamental Rights in Hungary chose not to question or speak up against legislation like the Foreign Funded Organizational Act, against the government decision not to ratify the Istanbul Convention (meant to prevent and combat violence against women and domestic violence), or against laws that fail to protect the rights of vulnerable groups like ethnic minorities, LGBTI, migrants, or asylum seekers. As a result of these institutional changes, in June 2021 the Global Alliance of National Human Rights Institutions downgraded the accreditation status of Hungary's NHRI from A to B, confirming the international human rights community's loss of trust in the commissioner's strength and effectiveness.

Since the research for this book began in October 2012, human rights have been increasingly challenged around the world. Recent elections in several countries in Europe and around the globe have favored the promotion of far-right illiberal parties that, once in power, consolidated their efforts to wear away at the existing human rights architecture. These are signs that the commitment to human rights may be shrinking. Many NHRIs have also not been spared. Even when they remain formally stronger than other institutions, such as courts, in the face of external pressures (see, for instance, the situation of constitutional courts in Hungary and Poland), their long-term resilience is not guaranteed. Changes in governments' support for institutional activity and fluctuations in policymakers' respect for the independence and integrity of NHRIs often result in decreased capacity of NHRIs to fulfill their mandates.

This book is an attempt to understand and explain the interplay of domestic and international factors underpinning the development of NHRIs, as well as their capacity to make an impact on the ground through their work. As I conclude, I want to make a broader case for a more dynamic and contextualized view of NHRIs as bodies that are foundational to our liberal democracies and are highly dependent on support from both domestic governments and international organizations. Institutions with rights-centered mandates are not simply weak or strong in one context or another. Their initial formal designs are not static. In fact, they develop and change as a result of continuous interactions with peer institutions in other countries, as well as with a range of domestic actors including public institutions and civil society members. Importantly, a more contextualized view of NHRIs allows us to study them in relation to both domestic and international factors, helping us to understand how their formal strength and effectiveness can change over time. While most NHRIs have seen their legal mandates strengthen, an increasing number are seeing their effectiveness curtailed by hostile governments.

When NHRIs are formally strong, are independent from political interference, and have strong and influential leadership, they can make important domestic and international impact and can maintain a balanced and collaborative relationship with politicians, public institutions, and the government. As some of the institutions introduced in earlier chapters of this book—the Northern Ireland Human Rights Commission, the Scottish Human Rights Commission, and the Danish Institute for Human Rights—have shown, NHRIs that are formally strong can make a difference domestically and internationally in some of their areas of expertise, even when they operate in challenging national contexts, with small budgets, and with only a handful of staff members.

In most democratic and transitional states, human rights continue to be at the center of liberal democratic projects for some of the political elites. At the same time, increasingly strong political voices on the right mount virulent critiques of liberal values and their destructive effects on national identity. NHRIs have been caught in the political crossfire. They are usually the most important domestic bodies charged with closing the gap between international human rights law and human rights performance on the ground. Against this political background, their status—as intermediaries connecting international organizations with national governments—is both a blessing and a curse. When the domestic and international environment is optimal, NHRIs receive support from both international organizations and national governments, working effectively and independently in collaboration with both. If, on the other hand, the risk of political interference is very high and the activity and effectiveness of a institution decreases as a consequence, its sole hope for survival lies in having a strong legal and constitutional foundation guaranteeing its formal powers and generally safeguarding it from being dissolved.

Institutional Strength and the Key Role of
International Organizations

Key to the survival and increased strength of NHRIs over the years has been their capacity to form peer networks under the auspices of international organizations and to seek guidance and support from their peers. Since the mid-1990s, the support NHRIs have received from international organizations (regional and global in scope) and peer networks has been growing, with new and more diverse mechanisms to engage in cross-institutional learning and information exchange, as well as more refined tools of assessing compliance with the Paris Principles as part of the accreditation process. At the global level, the accreditation granted by the Global Network of National Human Rights Institutions is an opportunity for continued peer feedback and learning as well as a form of international recognition that comes with increasing benefits, such as speaking rights in the Universal Periodic Review process and the chance to lead peer networks globally and regionally. Regionally, the European Network of National Human Rights Institutions fosters cross-institutional learning and aims to build capacity for member NHRIs, in addition to supporting and raising their profile in Brussels and at EU institutions.

In general, how much support NHRIs receive from international institutions and the peer-based networks they form goes far in predicting how strong and resilient they are and, importantly, whether they can continue to make an impact on governments' human rights performance. But their good functioning is to a significant extent also dependent on the degree of domestic support they receive from national governments. Thus, NHRIs walk a fine line between national governments' interests and international institutions. Their future success rests on their capacity to link the domestic with the international while maintaining independence from political interference and remaining true to the human rights norms they uphold. To that end, formal strength is key.

The history of each NHRI is unique, shaping some of the institutional feats as well. Nevertheless, NHRIs share formal characteristics due mainly to similarity in the challenges governments face in younger democracies as compared to old democracies. Writ large, democratic transitions away from autocracy tend to motivate pro-democratic governments to establish formally stronger liberal institutions to safeguard the transition and to signal domestically and internationally their commitment to consolidating liberal democracy. At the same time, these NHRIs are subject to external pressures from political interference—as is the case with the Polish and Czech human rights ombudsmen—and are not impervious to democratic backsliding. The transformation of the Hungarian commissioner discussed above is a case in point. As state power becomes more centralized in the hands of the president and the majority party, legal and constitutional reforms can change the effectiveness of even a formally strong NHRI, creating opportunities for political interference in the appointment of institutional leadership, and ultimately changing the areas of institutional priority and activity.

In their turn, national human rights bodies in old democracies operate in national environments with often well-developed legal and institutional frameworks for the rule of law, citizen complaint handling, and promotion of diversity and equality rights. Governments overall have fewer domestic incentives to establish a single body dedicated to human rights, and instead often create mixed rights-protection bodies, like the Equality and Human Rights Commission in the United Kingdom, or the Equality Commission in Belgium. When Western European states have strong NHRIs, they don't usually do so because of pressure to align with the Paris Principles. They tend to support stronger NHRIs in their territory because they want them to "lead by example" and increase their influence in international human rights forums.

Institutional Effectiveness and Institutional Leadership

It is important to note that differences in the mechanisms that determine mandated powers across institutions in the two subregions—Central and Eastern Europe, and Western Europe—are more marked than the dissimilarities in the tools used by national actors to curb institutional effectiveness. More specifically, the motivation for establishing formally weaker institutions might be different across countries, but the formal tools used to curb the enforcement capacity and actions of NHRIs bear visible similarities across European states. The multilevel empirical analysis in this book will show that there are similarities in European governments' responses when they seek to either support or curtail the activities of NHRIs. While institutional adaptation to change in the levels of support for their activities can be different from one institution to another, governments tend to use similar tools when they seek to limit the effectiveness and impact of NHRIs. This political interference can be direct when a human rights body is directly subordinated to government, or when the majority party in Parliament has an illiberal agenda. Such limiting action can commonly take the form of budget cuts or of refusal to cooperate with the human rights body on policy or its recommendations. The institution's leader plays a key role in mitigating the risk of external interference by cultivating a constructive relationship with public institutions.

When political influence is the most damaging to an institution's effectiveness, it seeks to capture the leadership of the NHRI by intervening directly in the appointment of its commissioner.

As domestic guardians of human rights, NHRIs are not immune to the pressures that liberal democratic structures face today. The analyses in this book show that even the most independent of institutions with some of the strongest institutional mandates, like those of the Polish and the Czech ombudsmen, can struggle to carry out their duties when governments actively seek to curb their effectiveness. As the case of the Hungarian Office of the Commissioner for Fundamental Rights shows, an NHRI can grow formally stronger over time and see its effectiveness decline at the same time. Once a majority party or coalition with an illiberal policy agenda is successful in appointing a commissioner who endorses, or at least does not oppose, the government's position on human rights, the institution becomes toothless. It loses the fundamental power of holding government to account on human rights violations. It also loses the credibility with civil society, and with the citizenry more generally, that is required of a body with the power to carry out independent investigations in complaint cases opened by individual citizens against public institutions. Finally, it loses the trust of peer institutions in other countries, thus limiting the institution's international impact and rendering futile its participation in regional and global peer networks.

Reflections on Institutional Strength and Effectiveness in Other Regions

This book's multilevel approach to the study of institutional strength and effectiveness in greater Europe and around the world offers valuable insights that can be extrapolated to the study of NHRIs in other regions. A principal focus on the influence of the United Nations and the global network of peer institutions is particularly salient for the study of the formal strength and effectiveness of NHRIs in regions other than Europe, which lack a strong regional human rights regime and a transnational organization like the European Union with membership rules tied to democratic conditionality. In these regional contexts, the role of UN-supported regional and subregional networks of peer institutions becomes arguably ever more important—coordinating cross-institutional learning, offering capacity-building assistance, and ultimately advancing formal compliance with the Paris Principles.

The Asia Pacific Forum offers a very interesting example. The oldest and the most consolidated regional network of the four in existence today, it promotes NHRIs as essential complaint-handling and investigative bodies

in a region that lacks a dedicated regional court or a protection system in
the realm of human rights (Asia Pacific Forum 2020; Gomez and Ramcharan
2020). For the study of NHRIs in the region, the models of strength and effectiveness proposed in this book would enhance our understanding of the
impact that peer learning coordinated by the UN has on institutional development. Importantly, it would offer a systematic framework to explain
institutional effectiveness and impact in domestic environments with more
widespread opposition toward human rights as an essentially Western liberal
framework of regulating the relationship between national governments and
their citizens.

As Levitsky and Murillo have shown, the study of institutional weakness
and strength is particularly important when investigating the weakness of
liberal democratic institutions in Latin America and other parts of the Global
South (2009, 2013). In Latin America, the Office for the High Commissioner
for Human Rights and the Organization of American States have supported
the creation of NHRIs, mostly by expanding the mandates of existing ombudsmen to include human rights protection and promotion. In addition,
recent international efforts target the consolidation and formalization of the
existing regional network of NHRIs, through the establishment of a secretariat (interviews 24, 83). The Network of National Institutions for the Promotion and Protection of Human Rights in the Americas is the smallest of all
regional networks, with fifteen full member institutions as of 2020. Despite
operating in national environments with a high degree of informality and
political instability, some of the NHRIs in the region are very strong and, in
some cases, effective (Pegram 2013, 2011).

The definitions and analytical models of institutional strength and effectiveness proposed in this book could also be useful when studying NHRIs
on the African continent, where research is very limited and based almost
exclusively on single-case studies. The influence of the United Nations has
been the most powerful voice in support of the establishment of NHRIs in
African states. In line with our argument, the UN (through the Program of
Advisory Services and Technical Cooperation in the Field of Human Rights,
and the work of the National Institutions Unit of the Office of the High Commissioner for Human Rights) and the African Commission have actively promoted the establishment and consolidation of NHRIs in the region as the
main instrument for human rights promotion and protection (Tsekos 2002;
Murray 2007b).

The Network of African National Human Rights Institutions is weaker
than its European and Asian counterparts (interviews 24, 83), even if its
membership at the time of writing this book (thirty-five bodies) is larger than

those of its counterparts in Latin America (fifteen member institutions) and the Asia-Pacific area (twenty-six member institutions). Nevertheless, the effectiveness of most efforts to advance strong and independent NHRIs has been, at best, uneven across the region. A few NHRIs have been effective in curbing human rights violations. For instance, the Nigerian Human Rights Commission has maintained autonomy of action from political interference, despite not enjoying strong government support and reporting directly to the Ministry of Justice (Agbakwa and Okafor 2002). In general, however, most NHRIs in the region have been weak and ineffective (Tsekos 2002; Ibhawoh 2019). The efforts of international and regional organizations have had the unintended consequence of uncritically offering support to formally weak institutions and, by extension, legitimizing political regimes that commit human rights violations (Tsekos 2002; Ibhawoh 2019). These NHRIs are rendered "empty shells," serving the interests of national governments in rallying domestic support and gaining international acceptance, with limited domestic impact on human rights performance (Tsekos 2002; Ibhawoh 2019).

Closing Remarks

Systems of governance and policymaking require formal structures of checks and balances. Nowhere is this necessity as vitally important as in the realm of human rights promotion and protection. National human rights institutions were created to fulfill this very role, operating as intermediaries at the intersection of international institutions and domestic political interests. In other words, they contribute to filling the implementation gap between international institutions with their human rights treaties and domestic governments that might be reluctant to give up some of their sovereignty to show compliance with human rights policy. When formally strong, NHRIs are more likely to carry out their mandated duties effectively, assisting, monitoring, and holding domestic governments to account on their compliance with the international human rights treaties they have ratified. When impactful, NHRIs contribute to curbing human rights violations, facilitate norm learning for domestic policymakers in the realm of human rights, and play leadership roles in international networks of peer accountability bodies.

As has been discussed throughout this book, to understand the strength and effectiveness of NHRIs as intermediaries seeking to close the human rights governance gap, we must consider the important role that international organizations have played in institutional development and effectiveness. This book finds that socialization through global and regional peer networks supported by the UN Office of the Commissioner for Human Rights is key to having stronger and more impactful NHRIs, which can thus learn from their peers how to navigate the tension between international and domestic pressures, and how to work in partnership with national governments to increase their own institutional strength and effectiveness. Specialized working groups within networks build capacity in different areas of expertise, and shape the future development of participating human rights institutions.

At the same time, socialization alone does not tell the complete story. Institutional learning is motivated both by genuine interest on the part of staff and by a system of external incentives. Membership in the two networks directly relevant to the analyses in this book—the Global Alliance of National Human Rights Institutions (GANHRI) and the European Network of National Human Rights Institutions (ENNHRI)—is linked to compliance with the Paris Principles and is confirmed through the accreditation process. Good compliance is linked to a system of incentives that opens the door to human rights forums at the United Nations and to the possibility of regional and global leadership in the peer networks. An additional system of incentives is in place for states in Central and Eastern Europe, linked to democratic conditionality and the promise of membership in the European Union. These incentives motivate national governments to offer support to NHRIs as part of their efforts to meet the standards of democratic conditionality imposed by the EU. They also empower NHRIs to request continued support from government and, at the same time, to independently monitor government activity and investigate human rights violations.

Nevertheless, what we see from this book is that external incentives for national governments are not a sustainable tool for the long-term success of strong NHRIs. As the case studies show, several EU member states, including democratic frontrunners in Central Europe and some countries with long-standing traditions of liberal democracy in Western Europe, have NHRIs whose effectiveness has declined over the years, sometimes along with their formal strength. In light of the recent rise of far-right parties in Europe and the worldwide increase in contestation of the Western liberal democratic tradition, many commentators express deep concern about what the future will bring. Particularly worrisome is the future of the multinational post–World War II consensus regarding the need for formal structures that safeguard the protection of rights. While scholarly research does not lend itself to prediction, it does allow a deeper understanding of the present and a more nuanced grasp of the past. With that in mind, this book is an attempt to broaden our understanding of the resilience of some of our liberal-democratic institutions by studying change in the institutional strength and effectiveness of NHRIs in Europe and beyond.

Acknowledgments

At various stages of research, I have benefited from the suggestions, comments, and insights of friends, colleagues, and mentors. I especially wish to thank Emmanuelle Blanc for her incredible patience when she read the full draft manuscript and offered careful feedback. I want to thank Cathy Boone, Christina Boswell, and Peter Trubowitz for continued support and mentorship.

This research began during my doctoral studies at the London School of Economics. I wish to thank Mathias Koenig-Archibugi, Jon Pevehouse, and Ulrich Sedelmeier for their feedback and guidance. Tom Pegram was generous with his time and offered thoughtful feedback on drafts of papers related to this research. Different stages of research and writing were made possible by funding from a number of institutions, principally the London School of Economics, the UK Economics and Social Research Council, the University of Edinburgh, Queen's University Belfast, and Queen Mary University of London. At the University of Chicago Press, I would like to thank Chuck Myers, Erika Barrios, and Renaldo Migaldi.

In writing this book I have accumulated many debts, but none is greater than the one I owe to my family—particularly my husband, Alex Nogues, and my parents, Floarea and Ion. I have benefited enormously from their patience and unwavering support.

Appendix

TABLE A1.1. Summary statistics for all variables included in the regional analysis

Variable	Obs.	Mean	Standard deviation	Min	Max
NHRI strength	1,200	2.750	1.158	1	4
NHRI durability	1,200	3.233	1.469	1	5
Enforcement	1,200	3.245	1.546	1	5
GANHRI membership	1,200	0.371	0.483	0	1
EU membership	1,200	0.438	0.496	0	1
EU conditionality	1,200	0.438	0.496	0	1
European HR treaties	1,200	20.7	10.132	0	33
Global HR treaties	1,200	14	2.264	8	18
Freedom House	1,200	1.53	0.743	1	3
Newly democratized	1,200	0.38	0.486	0	1
Common law	1,200	0.12	0.325	0	1
Intrawar	700	1.53	0.742	1	3
Interwar	500	0.038	0.191	0	1
GDP/cap	1,200	17016.96	18596.18	318.02	119225.4

TABLE A1.2. Models including controls for intrastate wars and interstate wars as well as different measures of levels of democracy, polity IV, as robustness checks

	Model 1 Strength	Model 2 Strength	Model 3 Durability	Model 4 Enforcement
GANHRI membership	1.069*	0.772**	1.259***	0.044
	(0.569)	(0.310)	(0.282)	(0.258)
EU membership	−0.770	0.574	−0.213	0.169
	(1.401)	(0.468)	(0.383)	(0.410)
EU conditionality	−1.139	1.739***	0.993***	1.062***
	(0.719)	(0.469)	(0.379)	(0.372)
ENP membership	−21.509	0.144	0.559	0.491
	(1124)	(0.396)	(0.368)	(0.331)

(*continues*)

TABLE A1.2. (*continued*)

	Model 1 Strength	Model 2 Strength	Model 3 Durability	Model 4 Enforcement
Global HR treaties	0.578	0.221	0.217	0.122
	(0.520)	(0.462)	(0.336)	(0.529)
European HR treaties	0.123	0.096	0.046	0.253**
	(0.130)	(0.102)	(0.077)	(0.117)
Freedom House	−0.875			
	(0.724)			
Newly democratized	1.635	2.589	1.609	1.804
	(2.341)	(1.616)	(1.171)	(1.847)
Common law	−1.265	0.035	0.850	−1.376
	(2.749)	(2.575)	(1.887)	(2.924)
GDP/cap	0.001	−0.001	−0.001	7.690
	(0.001)	(0.001)	(0.001)	(0.001)
Trend	0.489***	0.249***	0.212***	0.194***
	(0.081)	(0.029)	(0.026)	(0.025)
Intrawar	0.746			
Interwar	(0.855)			
	−3.142			
	(0.945)			
Polity IV		0.113**	0.169***	0.027
		(0.047)	(0.043)	(0.043)
n	500	1,117	1,117	1,117

Prob > chi2 = 0.000; (***$p < 0.01$; **$p < 0.05$; *$p < 0.10$). Standard errors in parentheses.

Supplementing the regional analysis in chapter 4, table A1.1 includes descriptive statistics for all the variables included in the statistical models. Table A1.2 includes four models as robustness checks, including alternative variables to the ones included in the main analysis in chapter 4. Due to lack of Polity IV data on all countries included in the data set, models 2 through 4 (table A1.2) have fewer observations (1,117 instead of 1,200). The results of the analysis are broadly the same as the ones reported in the main analysis. In addition, the missing observations available on interstate and intrastate data for many of the years in the data set reduces the number of observations in model 1 to 500 (table A1.2). Robustness checks show that the impact of the variable measuring democracy remains similar, but other results change slightly. I do not include Polity IV in the main models because, given the smaller *n*, the reduction in data points is likely to be an explanation for the change in estimation results. In addition, table A1.3 shows the results of multicollinearity tests for all independent variables included in the analysis.

As an additional robustness check for the effect of the time trend on the results of the analysis, I also include a test for the primary assumption of "stationarity," which is missing in time series analysis (table A1.4). To check

TABLE A1.3. The results of multicollinearity tests show no evidence of multicollinearity.

Variable	VIF	SQRT VIF	Tolerance
GANHRI membership	1.55	1.25	0.644
EU membership	3.42	1.85	0.292
EU Conditionality	1.66	1.29	0.601
ENP membership	2.36	1.54	0.424
European HR treaties	4.86	2.20	0.206
Global HR treaties	2.41	1.54	0.415
Freedom House	3.71	1.93	0.270
Newly democratized	2.50	1.58	0.399
Common law	1.45	1.20	0.690
GDP/cap	2.93	1.71	0.341

TABLE A1.4. Results of models with differenced time variant variables

Variable	Strength	Strength	Durability	Durability	Durability	Enforcement
GANHRI	1.665***	1.632***	1.803***	1.779***	1.149***	1.166*
membership	(0.474)	(0.459)	(0.453)	(0.553)	(0.669)	(0.656)
EU membership	−1.515***	−1.514***	−1.659***	−1.611***	−1.313***	−1.363***
	(0.423)	(0.420)	(0.457)	(0.450)	(0.345)	(0.361)
EU conditionality	−0.749***	−0.761***	−0.819***	−0.845***	−0.656***	−0.640***
	(0.213)	(0.215)	(0.234)	(0.237)	(0.165)	(0.164)
Freedom House		1.171**		0.707		0.719
		(0.517)		(0.468)		(0.879)
GDP/cap		−0.000		−0.000*		0.000
		(0.000)		(0.000)		(0.000)

Prob > chi2 = 0.000; (***$p < 0.01$; **$p < 0.05$; *$p < 0.10$. Standard errors in parentheses.

the assumption of whether variables maintain a constant mean and variance across different frames, I ran models with differentiated variables for the main independent variables in our study, which are time variant, and also models that include control variables that are time variant. I find no unit root in the case of the main independent variables driving our analysis. In the expanded models, the results show that two control variables—GDP/cap and Freedom House—are not statistically significant for some of the models, thus indicating a certain nonstationarity across panels in these control variables. Second differencing eliminated the trend in Freedom House, and reduced the trend in GDP/cap. This nonstationarity and the time dependency are further addressed in the main analysis by including a "trend" variable that controls for the effect of a time trend in all models.

Robustness Checks for Global Analysis

Table A1.6 includes a set of robustness checks, presenting models with different measures of levels of democracy, Polity IV. The results of the two analyses
are broadly the same as the ones reported in the main analysis. As table A1.6
shows, the impact of the variable measuring democracy remains similar, but
other results change slightly. I do not include Polity IV data in the main models because of the smaller *n*. The reduction in data points is likely an explanation for the change in the magnitude of estimation results.

Brant Test Results for Models Included in the Analysis

Devised by Brant (1990), the Brant test is commonly used to assess whether
the observed deviations from what the proportional odds model predicts
are larger than what could be attributed to chance alone. A significant test
statistic provides evidence that the parallel regression assumption has been
violated. It is important to keep in mind, however, that in models with small
sample sizes, this assumption is often violated. Table A1.7 presents the results
of the Brant test for the dependent variable NHRI strength. Table A1.8 presents the results of the Brant test for the dependent variable NHRI durability.
Table A1.9 presents the results of the Brant test for the dependent variable
NHRI enforcement. The Brant test results show that in the statistical models
included in this book, the parallel regression assumption is not violated by
the main explanatory variables and the majority of control variables.

TABLE A1.5. Summary statistics for all variables included in the global analysis in chapter 4

Variable	Obs	Mean	Std. dev	Min	Max
NHRI strength	187	2.519	1.142	1	4
NHRI enforcement	187	3	1.485	1	5
NHRI durability	187	3.118	1.469	1	5
Physical integrity	187	2	.769	1	3
Civil and political right	187	3.027	.918	1	4
GANHRI membership	187	.54	.5	0	1
PTA hard	187	.508	.501	0	1
Global HR treaties	187	11.711	3.707	2	18
EU conditionality	187	.096	.296	0	1
Postcommunist	187	.219	.415	0	1
Log GDP/cap	187	9.115	1.232	6.525	12.142

TABLE A1.6. Models for NHRI strength, NHRI durability, and NHRI enforcement at the global level

	Model 1 Strength	Model 2 Durability	Model 3 Enforcement
GANHRI	3.067***	3.055***	2.726***
membership	(0.431)	(0.431)	(0.406)
PTA hard	0.605*	0.315	0.556
	(0.343)	(0.335)	(0.338)
Global HR treaties	0.146**	0.153**	0.165***
	(0.059)	(0.059)	(0.058)
EU conditionality	−0.064	0.056	−0.641
	(0.662)	(0.625)	(0.647)
Polity IV	0.103**	0.064**	0.120***
	(0.033)	(0.032)	(0.034)
Postcommunist	0.737	−0.029	1.017**
	(0.456)	(0.429)	(0.453)
Intrawar	−1.017**	−0.629	−1.065**
	(0.425)	(0.420)	(0.409)
Interwar	−0.091	−0.032	−0.197
	(0.631)	(0.609)	(0.610)
Common law	0.812	0.581	0.844*
	(0.509)	(0.499)	(0.495)
Log GDP/cap	−0.272**	−0.370**	−0.094
	(0.152)	(0.152)	(0.147)
Log world population	0.057	0.095	0.007
	(0.115)	(0.113)	(0.114)

Prob > chi2 = 0.0000, n = 132, *** for $p < 0.01$; ** for $p < 0.05$; * for $p < 0.10$. Standard errors reported in parentheses.

TABLE A1.7. NHRI strength: Brant test of parallel regression assumption

	chi2	p > chi2	df
All	31.280	0.091	22
GANHRI membership	4.580	0.101	2
PTA hard	3.160	0.206	2
Global HR treaties	1.140	0.566	2
EU conditionality	0.600	0.741	2
Freedom House	2.510	0.286	2
Postcommunist	7.540	0.023	2
Intrawar	0.480	0.785	2
Interwar	1.170	0.558	2
Common law	2.470	0.291	2
Log GDP/cap	0.960	0.619	2
Log world population	1.500	0.473	2

TABLE A1.8. NHRI durability: Brant test of parallel regression assumption

	chi2	p > chi2	df
All	19.640	0.606	22
GANHRI membership	4.890	0.087	2
PTA hard	3.510	0.173	2
Global HR treaties	0.050	0.977	2
EU conditionality	0.190	0.909	2
Freedom House	0.900	0.638	2
Postcommunist	0.240	0.887	2
Intrawar	0.920	0.632	2
Interwar	0.450	0.800	2
Common law	0.260	0.878	2

TABLE A1.9. NHRI enforcement: Brant test of parallel regression assumption

	chi2	p > chi2	df
All	44.090	0.094	33
GANHRI membership	9.070	0.028	3
PTA hard	3.590	0.310	3
Global HR treaties	5.820	0.121	3
EU conditionality	1.720	0.633	3
Freedom House	3.700	0.296	3
Postcommunist	14.790	0.002	3
Intrawar	6.630	0.085	3
Interwar	2.030	0.566	3
Common law	1.810	0.613	3
Log GDP/cap	0.800	0.850	3
Log world population	2.330	0.506	3

Sources for Coding of Dependent Variable

To create the main dependent variable and its constitutive dimensions—durability and enforcement—I coded publicly available documents for each NHRI and each country (table A1.10). Data were collected for the period 1994–2017. The cutoff point for institutions established after 1994 is the year immediately after the year of institutional establishment (e.g., the Serbian NHRI was created by law in 2005 and was coded as nonexistent until 2009, when I introduced data on institutional safeguards into the data set). The time interval, and the selection of the fifty countries included in the study, are closely tied to the availability of sources. While all institutions publish

TABLE A1.10. Sources for coding of dependent variable (NHRI strength)

Country	Institution	Annual reports	Institutional mandate laws	Country constitution (when applicable)
Albania	Avokatii Populiit	http://www.avokatipopullit.gov.al/en/reports	http://www.avokatipopullit.gov.al/en/ligji-p%C3%ABr-avokatin-e-popullit-0	http://www.avokatipopullit.gov.al/en/kushtetuta
Algeria	Commission nationale des droits de l'homme	http://cndh.org.dz/index.html	http://cndh.org.dz/FR/images/Textes_de_loi/Textes_nationaux_ref/loi%203-11-2016.pdf	http://cndh.org.dz/FR/images/Textes_de_loi/Textes_nationaux_ref/Articles_de_la_Constitution_relatifs_au_CNDH.pdf
Armenia	Human Rights Defender	http://www.ombuds.am/en/home.html	http://www.ombuds.am/en/legislation/the-law-on-the-ombudsman.html	http://www.ombuds.am/en/legislation/constitution.html?chapter=46
Austria	Austrian Ombudsman Board	https://volksanwaltschaft.gv.at/en/about-us	https://volksanwaltschaft.gv.at/downloads/974v3/AOB_Ombudsman_Act.pdf	https://volksanwaltschaft.gv.at/downloads/a78uj/b-vg-fassung-vom-26-08-2016-english.pdf
Azerbaijan	Human Rights Commissioner (Ombudsman)	http://www.ombudsman.gov.az/en/	http://www.ombudsman.gov.az/upload/editor/files/Azeri_Constitutional_law_HR_Commissioner_2010_en(1).pdf	http://www.ombudsman.gov.az/upload/editor/files/Constitution(1).pdf
Belarus	n/a			
Belgium	Interfederal Center for Equal Opportunities and Opposition to Discrimination and Racism	https://www.unia.be/en/publications-statistics/publications?keywords=annual+report&require_all=category	https://www.unia.be/en/law-recommendations/legislation/interfederal-centre-for-equal-opportunities-cooperation-agreement	
Bosnia and Herzegovina	Institute of Human Rights Ombudsmen	http://ombudsmen.gov.ba/Dokumenti.aspx?id=27&tip=1&lang=EN	http://ombudsmen.gov.ba/documents/obmudsmen_doc20130410 0342457 eng.pdf	http://ombudsmen.gov.ba/Default.aspx?id=14&lang=EN
Bulgaria	Ombudsman	http://www.ombudsman.bg/reports/	http://www.ombudsman.bg/regulations/ombudsman-law	http://www.ombudsman.bg/regulations/constitution

(continues)

Country	Institution	Annual reports	Institutional mandate laws	Country constitution (when applicable)
Croatia	Ombudsman	http://ombudsman.hr/en/reports		
Cyprus	Commissioner for Administration and Human Rights	http://www.ombudsman.gov.cy /ombudsman/ombudsman.nsf /page17national_en/page17national _en?OpenDocument	http://www.ombudsman.gov.cy/ombudsman /ombudsman.nsf/page52national_en /page52national_en?OpenDocument	
Czechia	Public Defender of Rights	https://www.ochrance.cz/en/reports /reports/	https://www.ochrance.cz/en/law-on-the -public-defender-of-rights/	
Denmark	Danish Institute for Human Rights	https://www.humanrights.dk/publica tions?field_kategori_udgivelse _tid=33&date_filter%5Bvalue%5D% 5Byear%5D=&field_emne_tid=All	https://www.humanrights.dk/about-us /acts-bylaws	
Egypt	National Council for Human Rights	http://www.nchregypt.org/index .php/en/	http://www.nchregypt.org/index.php/en /about-us/establishment.html	
Estonia	Chancellor of Justice	http://www.oiguskantsler.ee/en /annual-reports-0	https://www.riigiteataja.ee/en/eli /507042016001/consolide	https://www.riigiteataja.ee/en /eli/521052015001/consolide
Finland	Finnish Human Rights Institution	http://www.ihmisoikeuskeskus.fi /in-english/publications/	http://www.ihmisoikeuskeskus.fi/in-english /who-we-are/human-rights-centre/ https://www.oikeusasiamies.fi/en /parliamentary-ombudsman-act	https://www.oikeusasiamies.fi /en/constitutional-provisions -pertaining-to-parliamentary -ombudsman-of-finland
France	Commission nationale consultative des droits de l'homme	http://www.cncdh.fr/fr/publica tions?f1%5B0%5D=im_field_type _de_document%3A308	https://www.legifrance.gouv.fr/affichTexte.do ?cidTexte=JORFTEXT000000327887&dateTe xte=20180424	
Georgia	Public Defender's Office	http://www.ombudsman.ge/en/	http://www.ombudsman.ge/uploads/other /5/5299.pdf	http://www.ombudsman.ge /uploads/other/1/1475.pdf
Germany	German Institute for Human Rights	http://www.institut-fuer-menschen rechte.de/en/publications/	https://tinyurl.com/ya4rx3f8	

Greece	National Commission for Human Rights	http://www.nchr.gr/index.php/en/2013-04-03-11-07-36/115-reports	http://www.nchr.gr/index.php/2013-04-03-10-13-40/2013-04-03-10-15-59
Hungary	Commissioner for Fundamental Rights	https://www.ajbh.hu/en/web/ajbh-en/annual-reports	https://www.ajbh.hu/en/web/ajbh-en/act-cxi-of-2011	https://www.ajbh.hu/documents/14315/121663/basic_law.pdf/6083c0af-bf9c-48b7-9988-9e05660d31d6
Iceland	n/a		
Ireland	Irish Human Rights and Equality Commission	https://www.ihrec.ie/publications/	https://www.ihrec.ie/about/ihrec-act-2014/
Italy	n/a		
Israel	n/a		
Jordan	The National Centre for Human Rights	http://www.nchr.org.jo/User_Site/Site/Home_Page.aspx	http://www.nchr.org.jo/User_Site/Site/Site/View_Article.aspx?type=1&ID=323&name=NCHR%20Law%20&lc=0
Latvia	Ombudsman of the Republic	http://www.tiesibsargs.lv/en/pages/research-and-publications/annual-reports	http://www.tiesibsargs.lv/en/pages/about-us/ombudsman-office/bylaws
Lebanon	National Human Rights Institution	https://www.alkarama.org/en/articles/lebanon-parliament-approves-law-instituting-national-human-rights-institution-and-national	
Libya	National Council for Civil Liberties and Human Rights	https://lib.ohchr.org/HRBodies/UPR/.../LY/A_HRC_WG.6_22_LBY_1_Libya_E.doc	https://lib.ohchr.org/HRBodies/UPR/.../LY/A_HRC_WG.6_22_LBY_1_Libya_E.doc	
Lithuania	Seimas Ombudsmen Office	http://www.lrski.lt/en/reports.html	http://www.lrski.lt/images/dokumentai/Law_of_the_seimas_ombudsmen_VIII-950_ENG_2015.pdf	http://www.lrski.lt/en/legal-acts.html

(continues)

Country	Institution	Annual reports	Institutional mandate laws	Country constitution (when applicable)
Luxembourg	Commission consultative des droits de l'homme	https://ccdh.public.lu/fr/publications.html	https://ccdh.public.lu/fr/legislation.html	
Macedonia	Ombudsman	http://ombudsman.mk/en/annual_reports.aspx	http://ombudsman.mk/en/competence/law_on_the_ombudsman.aspx	http://ombudsman.mk/en/competence/constitution_(article_77).aspx
Malta	Office of Ombudsman	https://www.ombudsman.org.mt/category/annual-reports/	https://www.ombudsman.org.mt/about-us/legislation/#_ftnref1	http://justiceservices.gov.mt/DownloadDocument.aspx?app=lom&itemid=8566
Moldova	People's Advocate Ombudsman	http://ombudsman.md/en/rapoarte/anuale/	http://ombudsman.md/en/	
Montenegro	Protector of Human Rights and Freedoms	https://www.crin.org/en/library/custom-search-publications?promo=1&search_api_language=current	http://www.gov.me/files/1187944648.pdf	
Morocco	People's Advocate of the Republic of Moldova	http://ombudsman.md/	http://ombudsman.md/ro/link-type/reglementari-institutionale	
Netherlands	Equal Treatment Commission (until 2010); Netherlands Institute for Human Rights	https://mensenrechten.nl/mission-and-ambition	https://mensenrechten.nl/publicaties/detail/17477	
Poland	Commissioner for Human Rights	https://www.rpo.gov.pl/en/content/report	https://www.rpo.gov.pl/en/content/act-commissioner-human-rights	https://www.rpo.gov.pl/en/content/constitution-republic-poland
Portugal	Provedor de Justica	http://www.provedor-jus.pt/?idc=16	http://www.provedor-jus.pt/site/public/archive/doc/Lei_Organica_da_Provedoria_de_Justica__com_template_.pdf	http://www.provedor-jus.pt/site/public/arlic/archive/doc/Constituicao_da_Republica_Portuguesa.pdf
Romania	Avocatul Poporului	http://www.avp.ro/index.php?option=com_content&view=article&id=50&Itemid=174&lang=ro-ro	http://www.avp.ro/mnp/legi/lege9_mnp.pdf http://www.avp.ro/linkuri/lege35.pdf	http://www.avp.ro/linkuri/constitutia.pdf

Country	Institution			
Serbia	Protector of Citizens	http://www.ombudsman.org.rs/index.php?option=com_content&view=category&layout=blog&id=11&Itemid=13	https://www.osce.org/serbia/16577?download=true	http://www.predsednik.rs/en/documents/constitution-republic-serbia
Slovakia	National Center for Human Rights	http://www.snslp.sk/?locale=en#page=2427	http://www.snslp.sk/CCMS/files/Act_on_Centre.pdf	
Slovenia	Human Rights Ombudsman	http://www.varuh-rs.si/publications-documents-statements/annual-reports/?L=6.	http://www.varuh-rs.si/legal-framework/legal-documents-of-ombudsman/?L=6	http://www.varuh-rs.si/legal-framework/constitution-laws/?L=6
Spain	El Defensor del Pueblo	https://www.defensordelpueblo.es/informes/resultados-busqueda-informes/?tipo_documento=informe_anual	https://www.defensordelpueblo.es/ley-organica-3198/	http://www.senado.es/web/conocersenado/normas/constitucion/detalleconstitucioncompleta/index.html#1c2s1
Sweden	Equality Ombudsman	http://www.do.se/om-do/vad-gor-do/arsredovisningar/	https://www.riksdagen.se/sv/dokument-lagar/dokument/svensk-forfattningssamling/lag-2008568-om-diskrimineringsombudsmannen_sfs-2008-568	
Syria	n/a			
Tunisia	Comité supérieur des droits de l'homme et des libertés fondamentales	http://www.csdhlf.tn/presentation-2/?lang=fr	http://www.csdhlf.tn/cadre-juridique/?lang=fr	
Turkey	n/a			
Ukraine	Ukrainian Parliament Commissioner for Human Rights	http://www.ombudsman.gov.ua/	http://www.ombudsman.gov.ua/en/page/applicant/legislation/acts/	http://www.ombudsman.gov.ua/en/page/applicant/legislation/constitution/
UK/Great Britain	Equality and Human Rights Commission	https://www.equalityhumanrights.com/en/adrodd-corfforaethol/annual-reports	https://www.equalityhumanrights.com/en/equality-act/equality-act-2010	

reports, and while the publication of annual activity reports is often stipulated in the mandates of the NHRIs, not all institutions publish them annually. Some years have no annual reports at all, and sometimes NHRIs group activities of two or three years in a single report. Most NHRIs had no formal reporting system prior to the mid-1990s, when the Paris Principles were introduced. Most make such information public on their official web pages, and do so in the original language as well as, in most cases, English. Materials were consulted in their original versions in the following languages: Danish, English, French, Portuguese, Romanian, Spanish, and Swedish. Translation from Bulgarian was provided by a native speaker, and automatic translation was used for small bodies of text in Greek which were not available in translation.

Information from available reports was complemented and corroborated by information from institutional mandates, relevant legislation, and country constitutions:

1. In the rare cases where country constitutions or relevant laws were not available on NHRI web pages, I consulted the International Labour Organization online database of national labor, social security, and related human rights legislation, NATLEX, available at http://www.ilo.org/dyn /natlex/natlex4.home?p_lang=en.

2. For countries in the data set that had accession candidate status to EU membership, I consulted the country reports issued by the European Commission during the pre-accession period, which offer assessments of ombudsman-type and human rights institutions. For countries with candidate status in 2014, reports are available at https://neighbourhood-enlargement.ec.europa. eu/countries_en. For states with candidate status prior to earlier waves of enlargement, country reports are available in the online archive at the bottom of this web page: https://ec.europa.eu/neighbourhood-enlargement /countries/package_en.

3. In the cases of Serbia and Montenegro, which were part of the Federal Republic of Yugoslavia until 2003 and of Serbia and Montenegro until 2006, I coded the single ombudsman-type institution for both countries (the ombudsman office had separate regional offices dealing with separate ethnic groups) until 2006, the moment of their official independence and of the establishment of separate NHRIs for each independent state.

4. Whenever two institutions with national human rights mandates exist in one country (for instance, in Romania, Bulgaria, the Netherlands, or Malta), I selected the one that was established first.

I collected original data on eleven ordered categorical indicators of NHRI strength in fifty European countries for the period 1994–2017. Along each of the eleven indicators, institutions are coded as weak, medium, strong, or nonexistent (table A1.11).

To assess institutional design of weak and medium strength NHRIs as well as of institutions without accreditation, which may lack documentation for all years of interest in our study, I conducted an expert survey with heads of NHRIs and others with extensive knowledge of NHRIs. Nineteen out of thirty-five experts I contacted (55 percent) completed the survey. Both textual analysis and surveys made use of the coding scheme included in the appendix. A list of sources of annual reports and relevant institutional legislation for the over-time data in the regional analysis can be found in table A1.10, grouped by country and NHRI (all links were last accessed on 24 April 2018):

Data Sources for Independent Variables and Control Variables

The main independent variables in the models measure membership in one of the networks of countries in our sample—GANHRI, EU, and candidate countries with EU conditionality—and are operationalized as binary: 0 for non-membership and 1 for membership. Membership in the European Neighborhood Policy is coded as a binary variable. These variables allow us to observe the effects over time of independent variables on NHRI strength, as some countries join the three networks from 1994 to 2017. As a measure of states' commitment to the regional human rights regime promoted by the Council of Europe, I include an indicator that measures the number of European human rights treaties a country has ratified. I also include a measure of commitment to the global human rights regime, operationalized through a variable consisting of the number of global human rights treaties ratified by countries included in our data set. Freedom House data is used to measure different levels of democratization (Freedom House 2016). As a measure of whether a country is a new democracy, I use a binary variable that assigns the value of 1 to countries that have transitioned from communism to democracy since 1989.

Countries with common-law (or mixed with common-law) systems: CIA World
    Factbook
https://www.cia.gov/library/publications/the-world-factbook/fields/2100.html
Last accessed 3 August 2018

Data on intrastate wars and interstate wars: Correlates of War Database
http://www.correlatesofwar.org/data-sets
Last accessed 3 August 2018

TABLE A1.11. Indicators and respective coding scheme for coding of variable "strength of national human rights institutions"

Institutional strength 1–4 scale: 1. nonexistent 2. weak 3. medium 4. strong	Dimension	Subdimension	Definition	Indicator	Ranking
	Durability	Legal embeddedness	Degree of inclusion of institutional establishment and mandate in the country's legal framework	Legal embeddedness	4) country constitution (3) inclusion in national law (2) other type of official document such as presidential decree (1) nonexistent
		Mandate	Measure of degree to which NHRI mandate contains human rights	Human rights mandate	(4) broad human rights (3) partial human rights or mixture with other issues, such as equality remit or a mixed remit (2) no human rights (1) non-existent)
		Promotion and protection ("on paper")	Mandated duties to promote and protection human rights	Promotion	(4) research and education (3) annual institutional reporting (2) limited or no such activity (1) nonexistent
				Protection	(4) power to impose fines, litigation, and legal representation (3) complaint handling and independent investigations (2) no such powers (1) nonexistent
	Enforcement	Autonomy from government	Degree of formal autonomy from government interference	Sources of institutional funding	(4) parliament through yearly budget (3) government (2) other sources, e.g., donations (1) nonexistent

Dimension	Description	Sub-dimension	Response options
		Government representation in decision making	(4) none or very limited (3) government participation with no power of decision (2) government incorporation of NHRI with or without power of decision (1) nonexistent
		Leadership appointment structure	(4) institution alone (3) parliament (2) government (1) other or nonexistent
		Formal reporting	(4) to parliament (3) to government or ministry (2) other (1) no formal reporting system or nonexistent
Promotion and protection ("predominant")	Predominant types of activities prioritized by the institution	Promotion	(4) research and education (3) annual institutional reporting (2) limited or no such activity (1) nonexistent
		Protection	(4) power to impose fines, litigation, and legal representation (3) complaint handling and independent investigations (2) no such activity (1) nonexistent
Pluralism of representation	Extent to which representatives of NGOs and civil society rep resentatives are included in the decision-making process	Civil society / NGO representation	(4) representation on board or council of NHRI (3) project collaboration (2) public consultation (1) nonexistent

Data on GRP per capita: World Bank Open Data
https://data.worldbank.org/
Last accessed 3 August 2018

Data on levels of democracy: Freedom in the World data, Freedom House
https://freedomhouse.org/report-types/freedom-world
Last accessed 3 August 2018

Data on levels of democracy: Polity IV, Center for Systemic Peace
http://www.systemicpeace.org/polityproject.html
Last accessed 3 August 2018

Information on NHRI accreditation: United Nations Office of the High Commissioner for Human Rights
https://nhri.ohchr.org/EN/Pages/default.aspx
Last accessed: 3 August 2018

Information on the members of the European Neighbourhood Policy
https://ec.europa.eu/neighbourhood-enlargement/neighbourhood/overview
_en
Last accessed 3 August 2018

Information on candidacy status to EU membership
https://ec.europa.eu/neighbourhood-enlargement/countries/check-current-status_en
Last accessed 3 August 2018

European Human Rights Treaties

The source for country-specific ratification ("signature with ratification") information is the Council of Europe: https://www.coe.int/en/web/conventions
/search-on-treaties/-/conventions/chart/signature.

1. Convention for the Protection of Human Rights and Fundamental Freedoms
2. Protocol to the Convention for the Protection of Human Rights and Fundamental Freedoms
3. European Social Charter
4. Protocol no. 2 to the Convention for the Protection of Human Rights and
   Fundamental Freedoms, conferring upon the European Court of Human
   Rights competence to give advisory opinions
5. Protocol no. 3 to the Convention for the Protection of Human Rights and
   Fundamental Freedoms, amending Articles 29, 30 and 34 of the convention

6. Protocol no. 4 to the Convention for the Protection of Human Rights and Fundamental Freedoms, securing certain rights and freedoms other than those already included in the convention and in the first protocol thereto

7. Protocol no. 5 to the Convention for the Protection of Human Rights and Fundamental Freedoms, amending Articles 22 and 40 of the convention

8. European Agreement Relating to Persons Participating in Proceedings of the European Commission and Court of Human Rights

9. Protocol no. 6 to the Convention for the Protection of Human Rights and Fundamental Freedoms Concerning the Abolition of the Death Penalty

10. Protocol no. 7 to the Convention for the Protection of Human Rights and Fundamental Freedoms

11. Protocol no. 8 to the Convention for the Protection of Human Rights and Fundamental Freedoms

12. European Convention for the Prevention of Torture and Inhuman or Degrading Treatment or Punishment

13. Additional Protocol to the European Social Charter

14. Protocol no. 9 to the Convention for the Protection of Human Rights and Fundamental Freedoms

15. Protocol amending the European Social Charter

16. Protocol no. 10 to the Convention for the Protection of Human Rights and Fundamental Freedoms

17. European Charter for Regional or Minority Languages

18. Protocol no. 1 to the European Convention for the Prevention of Torture and Inhuman or Degrading Treatment or Punishment

19. Protocol no. 2 to the European Convention for the Prevention of Torture and Inhuman or Degrading Treatment or Punishment

20. Protocol no. 11 to the Convention for the Protection of Human Rights and Fundamental Freedoms, restructuring the control machinery established thereby

21. Framework Convention for the Protection of National Minorities

22. Additional Protocol to the European Social Charter Providing for a System of Collective Complaints

23. European Agreement relating to persons participating in proceedings of the European Court of Human Rights

24. European Social Charter (revised)

25. Protocol no. 12 to the Convention for the Protection of Human Rights and Fundamental Freedoms

26. Protocol no. 13 to the Convention for the Protection of Human Rights and Fundamental Freedoms, concerning the abolition of the death penalty in all circumstances

27. Additional protocol to the Convention on Cybercrime, concerning the criminalization of acts of a racist and xenophobic nature committed through computer systems
28. Protocol no. 14 to the Convention for the Protection of Human Rights and Fundamental Freedoms, amending the control system of the convention
29. Council of Europe Convention on Action against Trafficking in Human Beings
30. Protocol no. 14bis to the Convention for the Protection of Human Rights and Fundamental Freedoms
31. Council of Europe Convention on Access to Official Documents
32. Council of Europe Convention on preventing and combating violence against women and domestic violence
33. Protocol no. 15 amending the Convention for the Protection of Human Rights and Fundamental Freedom
34. Protocol no. 16 to the Convention for the Protection of Human Rights and Fundamental Freedoms

International Human Rights Treaties

Source: http://indicators.ohchr.org/

1. International Convention on the Elimination of All Forms of Racial Discrimination
2. International Covenant on Civil and Political Rights
3. International Covenant on Economic, Social and Cultural Rights
4. Convention on the Elimination of All Forms of Discrimination against Women
5. Convention against Torture and Other Cruel, Inhuman, or Degrading Treatment or Punishment
6. Convention on the Rights of the Child
7. International Convention on the Protection of the Rights of All Migrant Workers and Members of Their Families
8. International Convention for the Protection of All Persons from Enforced Disappearance
9. Convention on the Rights of Persons with Disabilities
10. Optional Protocol to the Covenant on Economic, Social and Cultural Rights
11. Optional Protocol to the International Covenant on Civil and Political Rights
12. Second Optional Protocol to the International Covenant on Civil and Political Rights, aiming at the abolition of the death penalty
13. Optional Protocol to the Convention on the Elimination of Discrimination against Women

14. Optional protocol to the Convention on the Rights of the Child concerning the involvement of children in armed conflict
15. Optional protocol to the Convention on the Rights of the Child concerning the sale of children, child prostitution and child pornography
16. Optional Protocol to the Convention on the Rights of the Child concerning a communications procedure
17. Optional Protocol to the Convention against Torture and Other Cruel, Inhuman, or Degrading Treatment or Punishment
18. Optional Protocol to the Convention on the Rights of Persons with Disabilities

Research Interviews for Qualitative Data Collection

During November 2016 and September 2019, I conducted research interviews in person, via phone, Skype, and email. These interviews and follow-up conversations included a range of professionals in eight countries, like members of staff at eleven national human rights institutions, government staff, members of civil society active in human rights-related work. Table A1.12 presents the list of all interviews I conducted including some details about the position, the institution or the area of work for each interview partner. I also included details about the mode(s) of communication for each interview partner.

TABLE A1.12. Research interviews informing the qualitative analyses

Interview number	Interview date	Current or former position, and location of interview	Method of communication
1	4 November 2016	Research manager, Equality and Human Rights Commission, United Kingdom	Email and phone
2	8 November 2016	Former general counsel, Equality and Human Rights Commission, United Kingdom	In person and Skype follow-up
3	11 November 2016	Former senior lawyer, Equality and Human Rights Commission, United Kingdom	Email and in person
4	16 November 2016	Academic and long-standing research consultant and collaborator with the three UK-based commissions, United Kingdom	Email and phone
5	18 November 2016	Human rights director, Equality and Human Rights Commission, United Kingdom	Email and in person
6	15 November 2016	Former director of Domestic and International Human Rights Programme, Equality and Human Rights Commission, United Kingdom	Email and Skype
7	17 November 2016	Research officer, Scottish Human Rights Commission, United Kingdom	Email and phone
8	21 November 2016	Academic and long-term research and policy consultant with the three UK-based commissions, United Kingdom	Email and in person
9	6 December 2016	Former commissioner, Scottish Human Rights Commission, United Kingdom	Email, Skype
10	7 December 2016	Director of strategic planning and policy, Equality and Human Rights Commission, United Kingdom	Email and Skype
11	8 December 2016	Former special adviser to British Government, the Northern Ireland Office, and the Equality and Human Rights Commission	Email and Skype
12	13 December 2016a	Former chair, Scottish Human Rights Commission, United Kingdom	In person
13	13 December 2016b	Legal officer, Scottish Human Rights Commission, United Kingdom	In person
14	13 December 2016c	Manager, participation and wider engagement, Scottish Human Rights Commission, United Kingdom	In person
15	14 December 2016a	Former commissioner, civil society engagement, Scottish Human Rights Commission, United Kingdom	In person
16	14 December 2016b	Commissioner, Scottish Human Rights Commission, United Kingdom	In person

TABLE A1.12. *(continued)*

Interview number	Interview date	Current or former position, and location of interview	Method of communication
17	15 December 2016	Former director of legal policy, Equality and Human Rights Commission, United Kingdom	In person
18	14 March 2017a	Senior scholar, United Kingdom and United States	In person
19	14 March 2017b	Senior scholar, United Kingdom	In person
20	14 March 2017c	Senior human rights scholar, United Kingdom	In person
21	25 April 2017	Chief commissioner, Northern Ireland Human Rights Commission, United Kingdom	Email and phone
22	10 January 2018a	Senior legal officer, United Nations OHCHR Switzerland	In person
23	10 January 2018b	Senior staff, United Nations OHCHR Switzerland	In person
24	10 January 2018c	Former human rights commissioner and former leadership in GANHRI, United Kingdom	In person
25	24 March 2018a	Senior academic in human rights law, United States	In person
26	24 March 2018b	Senior academic in human rights, United States	In person
27	25 March 2018	Senior scholar of human rights and former policy adviser with United Nations, United States	In person
28	16 April 2018	Former director, Danish Institute for Human Rights, Denmark	In person
29	17 April 2018a	Program co-lead, Danish Institute for Human Rights, Denmark	In person
30	17 April 2018b	Program co-lead, Danish Institute for Human Rights, Denmark	In person
31	17 April 2018c	Program director, Danish Institute for Human Rights, Denmark	In person
32	17 April 2018d	Senior administration and lawyer, Danish Institute for Human Rights, Denmark	In person
33	18 April 2018a	Legal adviser, Danish Government, Ministry of Justice, Denmark	In person
34	18 April 2018b	Senior administration, Danish Institute for Human Rights, Denmark	In person
35	26 April 2018	Senior legal adviser, Ministry of Justice, Sweden	In person
36	27 April 2018	Director and senior academic, Research Institute, Sweden	In person

(continues)

Interview number	Interview date	Current or former position, and location of interview	Method of communication
37	3 May 2018	Senior lawyer and executive, Sweden's Equality Ombudsman	In person
38	3 May 2018a	Human rights lawyer, Macedonia	In person
39	3 May 2018b	Senior academic and adviser to the ombudsman, Macedonia	In person
40	4 May 2018	Senior researcher, Fundamental Rights Agency, Austria	Phone
41	4 May 2018	Senior academic and government adviser, Sweden	In person
42	8 May 2018a	Senior lawyer, ombudsman, Macedonia	In person
43	8 May 2018b	Senior legal adviser and Programme Director, Macedonia	In person
44	9 May 2018a	Director, human rights civil society organization, Macedonia	In person
45	9 May 2018b	Director, human rights civil society organization, Macedonia	In person
46	9 May 2018c	Senior researcher, regional organization country office, Macedonia	In person
47	10 May 2018a	Senior academic and member of national equality commission, Macedonia	In person
48	10 May 2018b	Director, international organization national office, Macedonia	In person
49	11 May 2018a	Senior staff member at regional organization country office, Macedonia	In person
50	11 May 2018b	Human rights adviser and legal specialist, Macedonia	In person
51	15 May 2018a	Senior leadership, civil society organization, Poland	In person
52	15 May 2018b	Senior legal leadership, ombudsman office, Poland	In person
53	15 May 2018c	Senior policy officer, international organization country office, Poland	In person
54	16 May 2018	Senior researcher, international nongovernmental organization country office, Poland	In person
55	17 May 2018a	Human rights lawyer and senior leadership, international nongovernmental organization country office, Poland	In person
56	17 May 2018b	Law scholar, ombudsman legal adviser and former staff, Poland	In person
57	17 May 2018c	Human rights lawyer and head of human rights organization, Poland	In person
58	17 May 2018d	Senior research and program director, regional organization, Poland	In person

Interview number	Interview date	Current or former position, and location of interview	Method of communication
59	21 May 2018a	Senior lawyer, ombudsman office, Czech Republic	In person
60	21 May 2018b	Program lead and lawyer, ombudsman office, Czech Republic	In person
61	21 May 2018c	Senior lawyer, ombudsman office, Czech Republic	In person
62	22 May 2018a	Senior policy officer, government, Czech Republic	In person
63	22 May 2018b	Legal scholar and legal adviser to the ombudsman, Czech Republic	In person
64	22 May 2018c	Legal scholar and historian of human rights, Czech Republic	In person
65	23 May 2018a	Senior leadership, civil society organization, Czech Republic	In person
66	23 May 2018b	Senior policy officer, civil society organization, Czech Republic	In person
67	23 May 2018c	Head of rights-focused civil society organization, Czech Republic	In person
68	11 June 2018a	Project coordinator, European Network for NHRIs	In person
69	11 June 2018b	Senior administration, European Network for NHRIs	In person
70	11 June 2018c	Senior administration, European Network for NHRIs	In person
71	12 June 2018a	Development officer, European Network for NHRIs	In person
72	12 June 2018b	Project manager, European Network for NHRIs	In person
73	14 June 2018a	Communications officer, European Network for NHRIs	In person
74	14 June 2018b	Communications and events assistant, European Network for NHRIs	In person
75	14 June 2018c	Senior leadership, Center for Equal Opportunities and Opposition to Racism, Belgium	In person
76	20 June 2018	Human rights lawyer and head of civil society organization, Belgium	Skype
77	22 June 2018	Senior staff member, Center for Equal Opportunities and Opposition to Racism, Belgium	Skype
78	25 June 2018	Senior human rights academic, United Kingdom	In person
79	1 August 2018	Senior scholar of human rights law and former adviser to human rights commissioners, United Kingdom	In person

(*continues*)

Interview number	Interview date	Current or former position, and location of interview	Method of communication
80	5 August 2018a	Senior legal scholar and government adviser on human rights, United Kingdom	In person
81	5 August 2018b	Senior staff at international organization, formerly staff at the Equality and Human Rights Commission, United Kingdom	In person
82	23 June 2018	Senior leadership, civil society organization, Hungary	Skype
83	29 August 2019	Senior staff member, Secretariat of GANHRI, Geneva	In person
84	30 August 2019	Former human rights rapporteur, OHCHR, Geneva	In person
85	30 August 2019	Human rights rapporteur, OHCHR, Geneva	In person
86	2 September 2019	Senior administration, human rights nongovernmental organization, Budapest	Skype
87	2 September 2019	Academic and human rights lawyer, ombudsman office, Budapest	In person
88	3 September 2019	Senior lawyer and former NHRI staff, Budapest	In person
89	4 September 2019	Senior lawyer, Ombudsman Office, Budapest	In person
90	4 September 2019	Senior leadership, nongovernmental organization, Budapest	In person
91	5 September 2019	Human rights lawyer, nongovernmental organization, Budapest	In person
92	5 September 2019	Program manager, international organization country office, Budapest	In person
93	5 September 2019	Program officer, nongovernmental organization, Budapest	In person

References

Agamben, Giorgio. 1998. *Homo Sacer: Sovereign Power and Bare Life*. Stanford, CA: Stanford University Press.

Agbakwa, Shedrack C., and Obidora C. Okafor. 2002. "On Legalism, Popular Agency and 'Voices of Suffering': The Nigerian National Human Rights Commission in Context." *Human Rights Quarterly* 24, no. 3: 662–720.

Alderson, Kai. 2001. "Making Sense of State Socialization."" *Review of International Studies*, 415–33.

Amnesty International. 2021. "Czech Republic 2020." https://www.amnesty.org/en/countries /europe-and-central-asia/czech-republic/report-czech-republic/.

Asia Pacific Forum. 2020. "About Us." Asia Pacific Forum. https://www.asiapacificforum.net /about/.

Arcimowicz, Jolanta. 2002. "The Ombudsman: One of the Figures in the Drama of the Third Republic." *Polish Sociological Review* 140:427–48.

Ätverket för en svensk Människorättsinstitution. 2021. "Civil Society Network Opinion on the Proposals for a Swedish NHRI." Ätverket för en svensk Människorättsinstitution.

Bailey, Michael A., Judith Goldstein, and Barry R. Weingast. 1997. "The Institutional Roots of American Trade Policy: Politics, Coalitions, and International Trade." *World Politics* 49, no. 3: 309–38.

Bearce, David H., and Stacy Bondanella. 2007. "Intergovernmental Organizations, Socialization, and Member-State Interest Convergence." *International Organization* 61, no. 4: 703–33.

Beco, Gauthier de. 2007. "National Human Rights Institutions in Europe." *Human Rights Law Review* 7, no. 2: 331–70. doi:10.1093/hrlr/ngm004.

Bell, Christine. 2003a. *Peace Agreements and Human Rights*. Oxford, UK: Oxford University Press.

———. 2003b. *Peace Agreements and Human Rights*. Oxford, UK: Oxford University Press.

———. 2006. "Human Rights, Peace Agreements, and Conflict Resolution: Negotiating Justice in Northern Ireland." In *Human Rights and Conflict: Exploring the Links Between Rights, Law, and Peacebuilding*, edited by Julie A. Mertus and Jeffrey W. Helsing, 345–74. Washington: United States Institute of Peace Press.

Blau, Judith, and Alberto Moncada. 2007. "It Ought to Be a Crime: Criminalizing Human Rights Violations." *Sociological Forum* 22:364–71.

Börzel, Tanja A., and Thomas Risse. 2012. "When Europeanisation Meets Diffusion: Exploring New Territory." *West European Politics* 35, no. 1: 192–207.

Búrca, Gráinne de. 2003. "Beyond the Charter." *Fordham International Law Journal* 27 (April): 679–714.

Burdekin, Brian, and Jason Naum. 2007. *National Human Rights Institutions in the Asia Pacific Region*, vol. 27. Leiden, Netherlands: Martinus Nijhoff Publishers.

Burke, Peter. 1980. "The Self: Measurement Requirements from an Interactionist Perspective." *Social Psychology Quarterly* 43:18–29.

Campbell, Donald. 1958. "Common Fate, Similarity, and Other Indices of the Status of Aggregates of Persons as Social Entities." *Behavioral Science* 3:14–25.

Cardenas, Sonia. 2003. "Emerging Global Actors: The United Nations and National Human Rights Institutions." *Global Governance* 9, no. 1: 23–42.

———. 2014. *Chains of Justice: The Global Rise of State Institutions for Human Rights*. Philadelphia: University of Pennsylvania Press.

Carroll, Rory. 2019. "Landmark Case Could Overturn Northern Ireland Abortion Ban." *Guardian*, 29 January. https://www.theguardian.com/uk-news/2019/jan/29/landmark-case-could-see-ni-abortion-ban-overturned.

Carver, Richard. 2000. *Performance and Legitimacy: National Human Rights Institutions*. Versoix, Switzerland: Council on Human Rights Policy.

———. 2005. *Assessing the Effectiveness of National Human Rights Institutions*. Versoix, Switzerland: International Council of Human Rights Policy.

———. 2011. "One NHRI or Many? How Many Institutions Does It Take to Protect Human Rights? Lessons from the European Experience." *Journal of Human Rights Practice* 3, no. 1: 1–24.

Casule, Kole. 2012. "Macedonia Opposition Ejected from Parliament in Row." Reuters, 24 December. https://www.reuters.com/article/us-macedonia-protest/macedonia-opposition-ejected-from-parliament-in-row-idUSBRE8BN0EX20121224.

Checkel, Jeffrey T. 2005. "International Institutions and Socialization in Europe: Introduction and Framework." *International Organization* 59, no. 4: 801–26.

Cole, Wade M. 2012. "Human Rights as Myth and Ceremony? Reevaluating the Effectiveness of Human Rights Treaties, 1981–2007." *American Journal of Sociology* 117, no. 4: 1131–71.

Cole, Wade M., and Francisco O. Ramirez. 2013. "Conditional Decoupling: Assessing the Impact of National Human Rights Institutions, 1981–2004." *American Sociological Review* 78, no. 4: 702–25.

Commission of the European Communities. 2002a. "Regular Report on Poland's Progress towards Accession." European Commission. https://tinyurl.com/ya2bvcd8.

———. 2002b. "Regular Report on Czech Republic's Progress toward Accession." COM(2002) 700 final.

———. 2003. "Regular Report on Czech Republic's Progress toward Accession." COM(2003).

Commissioner for Fundamental Rights. 2010. "Report on the Activities of the Commissioner for Fundamental Rights and His Deputies."

———. 2012. "Report on the Activities of the Commissioner for Fundamental Rights and His Deputies."

———. 2016. "Report on the Activities of the Commissioner for Fundamental Rights and His Deputies."

———. 2017. "Report on the Activities of the Commissioner for Fundamental Rights and His Deputies."

———. 2019. "About the Office." https://www.ajbh.hu/en/web/ajbh-en/about-the-office.

Commissioner for Human Rights. 2019a. "Commssioner." https://www.rpo.gov.pl/en/content/commissioner.

———. 2019b. "What We Do." https://www.rpo.gov.pl/en/content/what-we-do.

Conant, Lisa. 2014. "Compelling Criteria? Human Rights in the European Union." *Journal of European Public Policy* 21, no. 5: 713–29. doi:10.1080/13501763.2014.897742.

Conservative Party. 2015. "The Conservative Party Manifesto 2015." https://www.conservatives.com/manifesto.

"Constitution of the Republic of Macedonia." 1991. Official Gazette of the Republic of Macedonia. http://eudo-citizenship.eu/NationalDB/docs/MAC%20Constitution%20(amended%20by%20XXX)%20eng.pdf.

———. 2003. Official Gazette of the Republic of Macedonia. http://eudo-citizenship.eu/NationalDB/docs/MAC%20Constitution%20(amended%20by%20XXX)%20eng.pdf.

Council of Europe. 1997. "Establishment of Independent National Institutions for the Promotion and Protection of Human Rights, Recommendation No R(97)14." https://rm.coe.int/16804fecf5.

———. 2019. "Human Rights Treaties." https://www.coe.int/en/web/conventions/search-on-treaties/-/conventions/treaty/results/subject/44.

Council of the European Union. 2015. "EU Action Plan on Human Rights and Democracy." Brussels: General Secretariat of the Council. https://www.consilium.europa.eu/media/30003/web_en__actionplanhumanrights.pdf.

Cox, Robert. 1987. *Production, Power, and World Order*. New York: Columbia University Press.

Crowe, Christopher, and Ellen E. Meade. 2007. "The Evolution of Central Bank Governance around the World." *Journal of Economic Perspectives* 21, no. 4: 69–90.

Crowther, Neil, and Colm O'Cinneide. 2013. "Bridging the Divide? Integrating the Functions of National Equality Bodies and National Human Rights Institutions in the European Union." AJU/40464. Nuffield Foundation.

Danish Institute for Human Rights. 2019. "Acts and Bylaws." https://www.humanrights.dk/about-us/acts-bylaws.

Diskriminerings Ombudsmannen. 2016. "Sweden's Equality Ombudsman (Diskriminerings Ombudsmannen)." http://www.do.se/.

———. 2019. "Stöd & Verktyg." https://www.do.se/stodmaterial/.

Domingo, Pilar. 2006. "Weak Courts, Rights and Legal Mobilization in Bolivia." In *Courts and Social Transformation in New Democracies: An Institutional Voice for the Poor?* edited by Roberto Gargarella, Pilar Domingo, and Theunis Roux. London: Routledge.

Doward, Jamie. 2016. "Equality Watchdog's Human Rights Fight "under Threat" after Cuts." *Guardian*, 20 November. https://tinyurl.com/zcksakf.

Doyle, Michael W. 1986. "Liberalism and World Politics." *American Political Science Review* 80, no. 4: 1151–69.

Easterly, William R. 2001. "Global Development Network Growth Database." Washington: World Bank.

EHRC. 2010. "Annex 12: Memorandum of Understanding between the Equality and Human Rights Commission, the Northern Ireland Human Rights Commission and the Scottish Human Rights Commission." https://tinyurl.com/ybmdamjm.

ENNHRI. 2014a. "Annual Report." http://ennhri.all2all.org/IMG/pdf/ennhri_annual-report-2014_a4_web.pdf.

———. 2014b. "Strategic Plan 2014–2016, Including Operational Plan 2014." European Network for National Human Rights Institutions. http://www.ennhri.org/uploads/3/1/5/7/31578217 /ennhri_strategic_plan_2014_16___op_2014.pdf.

———. 2016. "ENNHRI Statement of Support for Poland's Commissioner for Human Rights." General Assembly.

———. 2017. "The Danish Institute for Human Rights." http://www.ennhri.org/The-Danish -Institute-for-Human-Rights.

———. 2018. "What We Do." European Network for National Human Rights Institutions. http:// ennhri.org/-What-we-do-3-.

"Equality Act." 2006. https://www.legislation.gov.uk/ukpga/2006/3/contents.

EQUINET. 2019. "The Interfederal Centre for Equal Opportunities." European Network of Equality Bodies. https://equineteurope.org/author/belgium_ceoor/.

———. 2021. "Office of the Commissioner for Fundamental Rights." https://equineteurope.org /author/hungary_commissioner/.

European Commission. 2015a. "Enlargement." European Commission, Economic and Financial Affairs. http://ec.europa.eu/economy_finance/international/enlargement/index_en.htm.

———. 2015b. "European Neighbourhood Policy and Enlargement Negotiations: Strategy and Reports." http://ec.europa.eu/enlargement/countries/package/index_en.htm.

———. 2017. "Rule of Law: European Commission Acts to Defend Judicial Independence in Poland." https://europa.eu/rapid/press-release_IP-17-5367_en.htm.

———. 2019a. "European Neighbourhood Policy." https://ec.europa.eu/neighbourhood-enlarge ment/neighbourhood/overview_en.

———. 2019b. "Non-Discrimination." https://ec.europa.eu/info/aid-development-cooperation -fundamental-rights/your-rights-eu/know-your-rights/equality/non-discrimination _en.

———. 2019c. "The Cooperation and Verification Mechanism for Bulgaria and Romania." https:// ec.europa.eu/info/policies/justice-and-fundamental-rights/upholding-rule-law/rule-law /assistance-bulgaria-and-romania-under-cvm/cooperation-and-verification-mechanism -bulgaria-and-romania_en.

Eva, Cartwright. 2015. "Open Letter to the Commissioner for Fundamental Rights." 12 Septem- ber. https://refugeecrisisinhungary.wordpress.com/2015/09/12/open-letter-to-the-commis sioner-for-fundamental-rights/.

Fearon, James. 1997. "What Is Identity (as We Now Use the Word)?" Unpublished manuscript. University of Chicago.

Finkel, Evgeny. 2012. "The Authoritarian Advantage of Horizontal Accountability: Ombudsmen in Poland and Russia." *Comparative Politics* 44 (3): 291–310.

Finnemore, Martha. 1993. "International Organizations as Teachers of Norms: The United Na- tions Educational, Scientific, and Cultural Organization and Science Policy." *International Organization* 47 (04): 565–97.

———. 1996. *National Interests in International Society.* Ithaca, NY, and London: Cornell Uni- versity Press.

Finnemore, Martha, and Kathryn Sikkink. 1998. "International Norm Dynamics and Political Change." *International Organization* 52, no. 4: 887–917.

"Framework Agreement." 2001. Ohrid, Macedonia. https://www.osce.org/skopje/100622?down load=true.

Freedom House. 2016. "Freedom in the World, An Annual Study of Political Rights and Civil Liberties." Freedom House. https://freedomhouse.org/report-types/freedom-world.

"GANHRI Special Envoys." 2018. GANHRI. https://tinyurl.com/y9snfzz8.

Gilardi, Fabrizio. 2013. "Transnational Diffusion: Norms, Ideas, and Policies." In *Handbook of International Relations*, edited by Walter Carlsnaes, Thomas Risse, and Beth Simmons, 453–77. Los Angeles, London, New Delhi, Singapore, and Washington: SAGE Publications.

Gomez, James, and Robin Ramcharan. 2020. "Introduction: National Human Rights Institutions in Southeast Asia: Challenges to the Protection of Human Rights." In *National Human Rights Institutions in Southeast Asia: Challenges to the Protection of Human Rights*, edited by James Gomez and Robin Ramcharan. Singapore: Palgrave Macmillan.

Goodman, Ryan, and Derek Jinks. 2004. "How to Influence States: Socialization and International Human Rights Law." *Duke Law Journal* 54:621–703.

———. 2013. *Socializing States: Promoting Human Rights through International Law*. Oxford, UK: Oxford University Press.

Goodman, Ryan, and Thomas Innes Pegram. 2012. *Human Rights, State Compliance, and Social Change: Assessing National Human Rights Institutions*. New York: Cambridge University Press.

Government of Sweden. 2019. "Förslag till En Nationell Institution För Mänskliga Rättigheter i Sverige Skickas På Remiss." https://www.regeringen.se/pressmeddelanden/2019/02/forslag-till-en-nationell-institution-for-manskliga-rattigheter-i-sverige-skickas-pa-remiss/.

Government of the United Kingdom. 1997. "Rights Brought Home: The Human Rights Bill." Command paper no. 3782.

Grabbe, Heather. 2006. *The EU's Transformative Power: Europeanization through Conditionality in Central and Eastern Europe*. New York: Palgrave Macmillan. Houndsmills, UK: Basingstoke.

Greenhill, Brian. 2015. *Transmitting Rights: International Organizations and the Diffusion of Human Rights Practices*. Oxford, UK, and New York: Oxford University Press.

Grzymala-Busse, Anna. 2006. "Disaggregating Temporal Effects." Presented at the Annual Meeting of the American Political Science Association, Philadelphia.

Hafner-Burton, Emilie M. 2005. "Trading Human Rights." *International Organization* 59: 593–629.

———. 2009. *Forced to Be Good: Why Trade Agreements Boost Human Rights*. Ithaca, NY: Cornell University Press.

Hafner-Burton, Emilie M., and James Ron. 2009. "Seeing Double." *World Politics* 61, no. 2: 360–401.

Harvey, Colin, and Sarah Spencer. 2012. "Advancing Human Rights and Equality: Assessing the Role of Commissions in the UK and Ireland." *Fordham International Law Journal* 35:1615–89.

Human Rights Act. 1998. https://www.equalityhumanrights.com/en/human-rights/human-rights-act.

Human Rights Council. 2015. "National Report Submitted in Accordance with Paragraph 5 of the Annex to Human Rights Council Resolution 16/21, Sweden." United Nations General Assembly. https://documents-dds-ny.un.org/doc/UNDOC/GEN/G14/219/73/PDF/G14 21973.pdf?OpenElement.

Human Rights House. 2016. "Rule of Law under Threat in Poland." 29 June. http://humanright shouse.org/Articles/21739.html.

Human Rights NGOs in Macedonia. 2016. "Civic Monitoring of the Office of the Ombudsman: 'The Ombudsman: Between Its Mandate and Its Capacities.'" Skopje, Macedonia. http://

nvoinfocentar.mk/wp-content/uploads/2017/05/The-Ombudsman-%E2%80%93-Between
-its-Mandate-and-its-Capacities1.pdf.

Hungarian Helsinki Committee. 2021. "Assessment of the Activities and Independence of Hungary's Ombudsperson." https://helsinki.hu/en/assessment-of-the-activities-and-independence
-of-hungarys-ombudsperson/.

Ibhawoh, Bonny. 2019. "Human Rights and the Politics of Regime Legitimation in Africa." In *Expanding Perspectives on Human Rights in Africa*, edited by Raymond M. Izarali, Oliver Masakure, and Bonny Ibhawoh. London and New York: Routledge.

ICC. 2013. "ICC SCA General Observations as Adopted in Geneva in May 2013." https://tinyurl
.com/y9cb27gu.

ILGA Europe. 2020. "ILGA-Europe Is Alarmed by Hungarian Parliament's Moves to Abolish the National Equal Treatment Authority." https://www.ilga-europe.org/resources/news/latest-news
/ilga-europe-alarmed-hungarian-parliaments-moves-abolish-national-equal.

Johnston, Alastair Iain. 2001. "Treating International Institutions as Social Environments." *International Studies Quarterly* 45, no. 4: 487–515.

Joint Committee on Human Rights. 2021. "Legislative Scrutiny: Police, Crime, Sentencing and Courts Bill, Part 3 (Public Order)." House of Commons; House of Lords. https://publica
tions.parliament.uk/pa/jt5802/jtselect/jtrights/331/331.pdf.

Keck, Margaret E., and Kathryn Sikkink. 1998. *Activism beyond Borders: Advocacy Networks in International Politics*. Ithaca, NY: Cornell University Press.

Kelley, Judith G. 2004. *Ethnic Politics in Europe: The Power of Norms and Incentives*. Princeton, NJ: Princeton University Press.

Kim, Dongwook. 2013. "International Nongovernmental Organizations and the Global Diffusion of National Human Rights Institutions." *International Organization* 67, no. 3: 505–39.
doi:10.1017/S0020818313000131.

Kjaerum, Morten. 2003. "National Human Rights Institutions Implementing Human Rights." Copenhagen: Danish Institute for Human Rights.

Lacatus, Corina. 2016. "The Design of Human Rights Institutions at the National Level." PhD thesis, London School of Economics and Political Science.

———. 2018. "Human Rights Networks and Regulatory Stewardship: An Analysis of a Multi-Level Network of Human Rights Commissions in the United Kingdom." *British Journal of Politics and International Relations* 20, no. 4: 809–26.

———. 2019. "Explaining Institutional Strength: The Case of National Human Rights Institutions in Europe and Its Neighbourhood." *Journal of European Public Policy* 26, no. 1: 1657–77.

Lacatus, Corina, and Kathryn Nash. 2019. "Peace Agreements and the Institutionalisation of Human Rights: A Multi-Level Analysis." *International Journal of Human Rights*, November, 24, no. 6: 889–912. doi:10.1080/13642987.2019.1690467.

Landman, Todd. 2005. *Protecting Human Rights: A Comparative Study*. Washington: Georgetown University Press.

Laurens, Cerulus. 2018. "The Man Who Broke Belgium's Government." *Politico*, 12 December. https://www.politico.eu/article/theo-franckenthe-man-who-broke-belgium-government/.

"Law on the Ombudsman." 2016. https://www.refworld.org/pdfid/3fcb36dc4.pdf.

Legro, Jeffrey W., and Andrew Moravcsik. 1999. "Is Anybody Still a Realist?" *International Security* 24, no. 2: 5–55.

Lerch, Marika. 2019. "Human Rights: Legal Basis." European Parliament. https://www.europarl
.europa.eu/factsheets/en/sheet/165/human-rights.

Letowska, Ewa. 1990. "The Polish Ombudsman (the Commissioner for the Protection of Civil Rights)." *International and Comparative Law Quarterly* 39, no. 1: 206–17.

Levitsky, Steven. 2003. *Transforming Labor-Based Parties in Latin America: Argentine Peronism in Comparative Perspective*. Cambridge, UK, and New York: Cambridge University Press.

Levitsky, Steven, and María Victoria Murillo. 2009. "Variation in Institutional Strength." *Annual Review of Political Science* 12, no. 1: 115–33.

———. 2013. "Building Institutions on Weak Foundations." *Journal of Democracy* 24, no. 2: 93–107.

Linos, Katerina, and Thomas Pegram. 2014. "What Happens When Soft Law Hardens? National Human Rights Institutions and the International Human Rights System." In *Implementing Commitments*, edited by Ryan Goodman and Beth Simmons. Cambridge, UK: Cambridge University Press.

———. 2016a. "Architects of Their Own Making: National Human Rights Institutions and the United Nations." *Human Rights Quarterly* 38, no. 4: 1109–34.

———. 2016b. "The Language of Compromise in International Agreements." *International Organization* 70, no. 3: 587–621.

Linos, Katerina, and Tom Pegram. 2017. "What Works in Human Rights Institutions?" *American Journal of International Law* 111, no. 3: 628–88.

MacNab, Scott. 2015. "Holyrood 'Will Block UK Bid to Scrap Human Rights Act.'" *Scotsman*, 23 September.

Malesky, Edmund J. 2008. "Straight Ahead on Red: How Foreign Direct Investment Empowers Subnational Leaders." *Journal of Politics* 70, no. 1: 97–119.

Meyer, John W., and Brian Rowan. 1977. "Institutionalized Organizations: Formal Structure as Myth and Ceremony." *American Journal of Sociology* 83, no. 2: 340–63. doi:10.1086/226550.

Mijatović, Dunja. 2020. "Commissioner Urges Hungary's Parliament to Postpone the Vote on Draft Bills That, If Adopted, Will Have Far-Reaching Adverse Effects on Human Rights in the Country." Council of Europe, Commissioner for Human Rights. https://www.coe .int/en/web/commissioner/-/commissioner-urges-hungary-s-parliament-to-postpone-the-vote -on-draft-bills-that-if-adopted-will-have-far-reaching-adverse-effects-on-human-rights-in-.

Minister for Culture and Democracy. 2017. "The Human Rights Strategy." https://www.govern ment.se/4ab459/contentassets/08bcf332d33e40908f918f0cd29a13ae/a-strategy-for-national -efforts-with-human-rights.

Ministry of Justice. 2011. "The Fundamental Law of Hungary." http://www.kormany.hu/down load/a/68/11000/The_Fundamental_Law_of_Hungary_01072016.pdf.

Moe, Terry. 1990. "Political Institutions: The Neglected Side of the Stody." *Journal of Law, Economics and Organization* 6, no. 1: 213–53.

Moravcsik, Andrew. 1995. "Explaining International Human Rights Regimes." *European Journal of International Relations* 1, no. 2: 157–89.

———. 1997. "Taking Preferences Seriously: A Liberal Theory of International Politics." *International Organization* 51, no 4: 513–53.

———. 2000. "The Origins of Human Rights Regimes: Democrratic Delegation in Postwar Europe." *International Organization* 54, no. 2: 217–52.

Murray, Rachel. 2007a. "National Human Rights Institutions. Criteria and Factors for Assessing Their Effectiveness." *Netherlands Quarterly of Human Rights* 25, no. 2: 189–220.

———. 2007b. *The Role of National Human Rights Institutions at the International and Regional Levels*. Oxford, UK: Hart Publishing.

"'National Preventive Mechanism in the Republic of North Macedonia." 2019. http://ombuds
man.mk/en/national_preventive_mechanism/npm_in_rm.aspx.

"NATLEX, International Labour Organization." 2013. Accessed 23 September at http://www.ilo
.org/dyn/natlex/natlex_browse.home.

NIHRC. 2015. "Human Rights Inquiry in Emergency Health Care." Northern Ireland Human
Rights Commission. http://www.nihrc.org/uploads/publications/NIHRC_Emergency_Health
care_Report.pdf.

———. 2019. "Human Rights Commission's Challenge to the Law on Termination of Pregnancy
in Northern Ireland Timeline." Accessed 14 March at http://www.nihrc.org/news/detail
/timeline-nihrc-challenge-to-the-law-on-termination-of-pregnancy-in-northern.

Nohlen, Dieter, and Philip Stover. 2010. Elections in Europe: A Data Handbook. Baden-Baden,
Germany: Nomos.

"Northern Ireland Act." 1998. https://tinyurl.com/y7xxpeho.

Northern Ireland Assembly. 2014. "Official Report (Hansard), Committee for the Office of the
First Minister and Deputy First Minister." https://tinyurl.com/ycwktrr4.

OBH. 2008. "The Hungarian Ombudsman Institution (1995–2008)." Parliamentary Commissioners' Office.

OHCHR. 2010. National Human Rights Institutions History, Principles, Roles and Responsibilities.
Professional Training Series no. 4 (Rev. 1). New York and Geneva: Office of the United Nations High Commissioner for Human Rights.

———. 2016. "Principles Relating to the Status of National Institutions." http://www.ohchr.org
/EN/ProfessionalInterest/Pages/StatusOfNationalInstitutions.aspx.

Parlevliet, Michelle. 2005. "National Human Rights Institutions in Peace Agreements: Establishing National Institutions in Divided Societies." International Council on Human Rights
Policy.

Parliament of Czechia. 1999. "Act on the Public Defender of Rights no. 349/1999." https://www
.ochrance.cz/en/law-on-the-public-defender-of-rights/.

Parliament of Poland. 2010. "Act of 3rd December, 2010, on the Implementation of Some Regulations of European Union Regarding Equal Treatment." Journal of Laws 254. https://www.rpo
.gov.pl/en/content/act-3rd-december-2010-implementation-some-regulations-european
-union-regarding-equal.

Pegram, Thomas. 2010. "Diffusion across Political Systems: The Global Spread of National Human Rights Institutions." Human Rights Quarterly 32, no. 3: 729–64.

———. 2011. "Weak Institutions, Rights Claims and Pathways to Compliance: The Transformative Role of the Peruvian Human Rights Ombudsman." Oxford Development Studies 39,
no. 2: 229–51. doi:10.1080/13600818.2011.568611.

———. 2013. "The Bolivian Defensoría del Pueblo and Economic, Social and Cultural Rights." In
The Role of National Human Rights Institutions in the Promotion and Protection of Economic,
Social and Cultural Rights, edited by Gauthier De Beco, Eva Brems, and Wouter Vanden-
hole. Cambridge, UK, and Antwerp: Intersentia Press.

———. 2015. "Global Human Rights Governance and Orchestration: National Human Rights Institutions as Intermediaries." European Journal of International Relations 21, no. 3: 595–620.

———. 2017. "Regulatory Stewardship and Intermediation: Lessons from Human Rights Governance." Annals of the American Academy of Political and Social Science 670, no. 1: 225–44.

Pempel, T. J. 1998. Regime Shift: Comparative Dynamics of the Japanese Political Economy. Ithaca,
NY: Cornell University Press.

Poland Commissioner for Human Rights. 2011. "Summary of the Report on the Activity of the Commissioner for Human Rights." https://www.rpo.gov.pl/en/content/summary-report -activity-commissioner-human-rights-2017-comments-observance-human-and-civil-rights.

———. 2012. "Summary of the Report on the Activity of the Commissioner for Human Rights." https://www.rpo.gov.pl/en/content/summary-report-activity-commissioner-human-rights -2017-comments-observance-human-and-civil-rights.

———. 2016. "Summary of the Report on the Activity of the Commissioner for Human Rights." https://www.rpo.gov.pl/en/content/summary-report-activity-commissioner-human-rights -2017-comments-observance-human-and-civil-rights.

———. 2017. "Summary of the Report on the Activity of the Commissioner for Human Rights." https://www.rpo.gov.pl/en/content/summary-report-activity-commissioner-human-rights -2017-comments-observance-human-and-civil-rights.

———. 2018. "Summary of the Report on the Activity of the Commissioner for Human Rights." https://www.rpo.gov.pl/en/content/summary-report-activity-commissioner-human-rights -2017-comments-observance-human-and-civil-rights.

———. 2019. "What We Do." https://www.rpo.gov.pl/en/content/what-we-do.

Poland General Sejm. 1997. Constitution of the Republic of Poland. https://www.sejm.gov.pl /prawo/konst/angielski/kon1.htm.

Powell, Walter W., and Paul DiMaggio. 1991. *The New Institutionalism in Organizational Analysis*. Chicago: University of Chicago Press.

Public Defender of Rights. 2010. *Annual Report*. Czech Republic.

———. 2014. *Annual Report*. Czech Republic.

———. 2015. *Annual Report*. Czech Republic.

———. 2018. *Annual Report*. Czech Republic.

———. 2019a. "JUDr. Otakar Kotejl: Public Defender of Rights." https://www.ochrance.cz/en /history-of-the-institution-of-ombudsman/judr-motejl-the-first-czech-ombudsman/.

———. 2019b. "Mandate of the Public Defender of Rights." https://www.ochrance.cz/en/man date-of-the-public-defender-of-rights/.

Ra'ad, Al Hussein. 2018. "Hungary: Opinion Editorial by UN High Commissioner for Human Rights Zeid Ra'ad Al Hussein." United Nations Human Rights Office of the High Commissioner. https://www.ohchr.org/EN/NewsEvents/Pages/DisplayNews.aspx?NewsID=22765.

Raoul Wallenberg Institute. 2017. "Exploring Models for a Swedish NHRI." https://rwi.lu.se /2017/02/exploring-models-and-options-for-a-swedish-nhri/.

Reif, Linda C. 2004a. *The Ombudsman, Good Governance, and the International Human Rights System*. Vol. 79. Boston: Martinus Nijhoff.

———. 2004b. *The Ombudsman, Good Governance and the International Human Rights System*. Vol. 79. Leiden and Boston: Martinus Nijhoff Publishers.

Renshaw, Catherine. 2012. "National Human Rights Institutions and Civil Society Organisations: New Dynamics of Engagement at Domestic, Regional and International Levels." *Global Governance* 18, no. 3: 299–316.

Republic of Macedonia Ombudsman. 2015. "Annual Report." http://ombudsman.mk/upload /Godisni%20izvestai/GI-2015/GI%202015-Ang-za%20pecat.pdf.

———. 2017. "Annual Report." http://ombudsman.mk/upload/Godisni%20izvestai/GI-2015 /GI%202015-Ang-za%20pecat.pdf.

Risse, Thomas. 2000. "'Let's Argue!' Communicative Action in International Relations." *International Organization* 54, no. 1: 1–39.

Risse, Thomas, Stephen C. Ropp, and Kathryn Sikkink, eds. 1999. *The Power of Human Rights: International Norms and Domestic Change.* Cambridge, UK: Cambridge University Press. http://ebooks.cambridge.org/ref/id/CBO9780511598777.

Roberts, A. 2010. *The Quality of Democracy in Eastern Europe.* Cambridge, UK: Cambridge University Press.

Russett, Bruce. 1993. *Grasping the Democratic Peace: Principles for a Post-Cold War World.* Princeton, NJ: Princeton University Press.

Schimmelfennig, Frank. 2012. "EU External Governance and Europeanization beyond the EU." In *Oxford Handbooks in Politics & International Relations,* edited by D. Levi-Faur, 656–72. Oxford, UK: Oxford University Press.

Schimmelfennig, Frank, Stefan Engert, and Heiko Knobel, eds. 2006a. *International Socialization in Europe.* New York: Palgrave Macmillan.

———. 2006b. *International Socialization in Europe: European Organizations, Political Conditionality, and Democratic Change.* Palgrave Studies in European Union Politics. New York and Basingstoke, UK: Palgrave Macmillan.

Schimmelfennig, Frank, and Ulrich Sedelmeier. 2004. "Governance by Conditionality: EU Rule Transfer to the Candidate Countries of Central and Eastern Europe." *Journal of European Public Policy* 11, no. 4: 661–79.

Scott, Richard W., and John W. Meyer. 1994. *Institutional Environments and Organizations: Structural Organizations: Structural Complexity and Individualism.* London: SAGE.

Scottish Parliament. 2006. "Scottish Commission for Human Rights Act." http://www.legislation.gov.uk/asp/2006/16/pdfs/asp_20060016_en.pdf.

———. 2009. "Holyrood to Host Major Human Rights Conference." News Archive. http://www.parliament.scot/newsandmediacentre/25931.aspx.

Sedelmeier, Ulrich. 2009. "Post-Accession Compliance with EU Gender Equality Legislation in Post-Communist New Member States." European Integration online Papers (EIoP) no. 2, vol. 13, art. 23.

———. 2011. "Europeanisation in New Member and Candidate States." *Living Reviews in European Governance* 6, no. 1.

SHRC. 2009. "Annual Report 2008–2009." Scottish Human Rights Commission. https://tinyurl.com/yalrwhdv.

Simmons, Beth A. 2002. "Why Commit? Explaining State Acceptance of International Human Rights Obligations." http://www.is.gd/yVx92p.

———. 2009. *Mobilizing for Human Rights: International Law in Domestic Politics.* New York: Cambridge University Press.

Simmons, Beth A., Frank Dobbin, and Geoffrey Garrett. 2006. "Introduction: The International Diffusion of Liberalism." *International Organization* 60 (Fall): 781–810.

Simmons, Beth A., and Zachary Elkins. 2004. "The Globalization of Liberalization: Policy Diffusion in the International Political Economy." *American Political Science Review* 98:171–89.

Smith, Anne. 2006. "The Unique Position of National Human Rights Institutions: A Mixed Blessing." *Human Rights Quarterly* 28:904–46.

Smith, Joanne R., and Michael A Hogg. 2008. "Social Identity and Attitudes." In *Attitudes and Attitude Change,* edited by William D. Crano and Radmila Prislin, 337–60. New York and London: Taylor & Francis Group.

SNAP. 2013. "Scotland's National Action Plan for Human Rights." http://www.snaprights.info/wp-content/uploads/2016/01/SNAPpdfWeb.pdf.

Snyder, Jack. 1991. *Myths of Empire: Domestic Politics and International Ambition*. Ithaca, NY: Cornell University Press.

Spencer, Sarah. 2008. "Equality and Human Rights Commission: A Decade in the Making." *Political Quarterly* 79, no. 1: 6–17.

Stephens, Jack. 2020. "Stanislav Krecek, Zeman Ally and Former CSSD Parliamentarian, Appointed Ombudsman of the Czech Republic With Support From Far-Right." *Brno Daily*, 19 February. https://brnodaily.com/2020/02/19/news/politics/stanislav-krecek-zeman-ally -and-former-cssd-parliamentarian-appointed-ombudsman-of-the-czech-republic-with -support-from-far-right/?fbclid=IwAR1N1oqqUeM-2bLQ3zBzqgoiSc8POnT7N-b1d 0qfd_ozFhy9N_jlY0b2wQo.

Streeck, Wolfgang, and Kathleen Thelen. 2005. "Introduction: Institutional Change in Advanced Political Economies." In *Beyond Continuity: Institutional Change in Advanced Political Economies*, edited by Wolfgang Streeck and Kathleen Thelen, 1–39. Oxford, UK: Oxford University Press.

Stryker, Sheldon. 1980. *Symbolic Interactionism: A Social Structural View*. Menlo Park, CA: Benjamin/Cummings.

Subcommittee on Accreditation. 2007. "Report and Recommendations of the Subcommittee on Accreditation." Geneva. https://nhri.ohchr.org/EN/AboutUs/GANHRIAccreditation/Doc uments/2007_October%20SCA%20Report.pdf.

———. 2011. "Report and Recommendations of the Subcommittee on Accreditation." Geneva. https://nhri.ohchr.org/EN/AboutUs/GANHRIAccreditation/Documents/2007_Octo ber%20SCA%20Report.pdf.

———. 2012. "Report and Recommendations of the Subcommittee on Accreditation." Geneva. https://nhri.ohchr.org/EN/AboutUs/GANHRIAccreditation/Documents/2007_Octo ber%20SCA%20Report.pdf.

———. 2014. "Report and Recommendations of the Subcommittee on Accreditation." Geneva. https://nhri.ohchr.org/EN/AboutUs/GANHRIAccreditation/Documents/2007_Octo ber%20SCA%20Report.pdf.

———. 2018. "Report and Recommendations of the Sub-Committee on Accreditation." Geneva. https://www.ohchr.org/Documents/Countries/NHRI/GANHRI/SCA%20Report%20 May%202018-Eng.pdf.

Thelen, Kathleen Ann. 2004. *How Institutions Evolve the Political Economy of Skills in Germany, Britain, the United States, and Japan*. Cambridge, UK, and New York: Cambridge University Press.

Transparency International. 2012. "Corruption Risks in the Visegrad Countries." http://www .transparency.sk/wp-content/uploads/2012/07/visegrad_net.pdf.

Tsai, Kellee S. 2006. "Adaptive Informal Institutions and Endogenous Institutional Change in China." *World Politics* 59, no. 1: 116–41.

Tsekos, Mary Ellen. 2002. "Human Rights Institutions in Africa." *Human Rights Brief* 9, no. 2: 21–24.

Uggla, Fredrik. 2004. "The Ombudsman in Latin America." *Journal of Latin American Studies* 36, no. 3: 423–50.

UK Supreme Court. 2018. "Judgment [2018] UKSC 27." https://www.supremecourt.uk/cases /docs/uksc-2017-0131-judgment.pdf.

UN General Assembly. 1993. Resolution A/RES/48/134. http://www.un.org/documents/ga/res /48/a48r134.htm.

UNIA. 2019. "The 19 Grounds of Discrimination." https://www.unia.be/en/grounds-of-discrimi
nation/the-19-grounds-of-discrimination.

United Nations Committee against Torture. 2018. "Concluding Observations on the Sixth Periodic Report of Czechia." file:///Users/coralacatus/Downloads/G1817117.pdf.

"Universal Periodic Review: Information and Guidelines for Relevant Stakeholders' Written
Submissions." 2007. United Nations Human Rights Office of the High Commissioner. http://
www.ohchr.org/Documents/HRBodies/UPR/TechnicalGuideEN.pdf.

US Department Of State. 2017. "Hungary 2018 Human Rights Report." https://www.state.gov
/wp-content/uploads/2019/03/HUNGARY-2018-HUMAN-RIGHTS-REPORT.pdf.

Vachudová, Milada Anna. 2005. *Europe Undivided: Democracy, Leverage, and Integration after
Communism.* Oxford, UK, and New York: Oxford University Press.

Van de Walle, Nicolas. 2001. *African Economics and the Politics of Permanent Crisis, 1979–1999.*
Cambridge, UK: Cambridge University Press.

Van Evera, Stephen. 1999. "Primed for Peace." *International Security* 15 (Winter): 7–57.

Watson, Jenny. 2002. "Something for Everyone: The Impact of the Human Rights Act and the
Need for a Human Rights Commission." London: British Institute of Human Rights.

Wayland, Kurt. 2004. "Learning from Foreign Models in Latin American Policy Reform: An
Introduction." In *Learning From Foreign Models in Latin American Policy Reform*, edited by
Kurt Wayland, 1–34. Baltimore: Johns Hopkins University Press.

Wendt, Alexander. 1999. *Social Theory of International Politics.* Cambridge, UK: Cambridge University Press.

Wetzel, Amanda. 2007. "Post-Conflict National Human Rights Institutions: Emerging Models
from Northern Ireland and Bosnia and Herzegovina." *Columbia Journal of European Law*
13:427–70.

Whitehead, Laurence. 2001. *The International Dimensions of Democratization: Europe and the
Americas.* Oxford, UK: Oxford University Press.

Wiseberg, Laurie S. 2003. "The Role of Non-Governmental Organizations (NGOs) in the Protection and Enforcement of Human Rights." In *Human Rights: International Protection,
Monitoring, Enforcement*, edited by Janusz Symonides, 347–72. Burlington, VT: Ashgate.

Wolman, Andrew. 2011. "National Human Rights Institutions and the Courts in the Asia-Pacific
Region." *Asia Pacific Law Review* 19, no. 2: 237–51.

Yzer, Marco. 2012. "Reasoned Action Theory: Persuasion as Belief-Based Behavior Change." In
The Sage Handbook of Persuasion, edited by James Price Dillard and Lijiang Shen, 2nd ed.,
120–37. Thousand Oaks, CA: SAGE.

Zucker, Lynne G. 1977. "The Role of Institutionalization in Cultural Persistence." *American Sociological Review* 42:726–43.

Index

Page numbers followed by "f" or "t" refer to figures or tables respectively.

www.ingramcontent.com/pod-product-compliance
Lightning Source LLC
Chambersburg PA
CBHW032133020426
42334CB00016B/1150